The Pariahs of Yesterday

THE
PARIAHS OF
YESTERDAY

Breton Migrants in Paris

LESLIE PAGE MOCH

DUKE UNIVERSITY PRESS
Durham & London 2012

Duke University Press gratefully
acknowledges the support of Michigan
State University, which provided funds
toward the publication of this book.

Designed by Jennifer Hill.
Typeset in C&C Galliard by
Keystone Typesetting, Inc.

Library of Congress
Cataloging-in-Publication Data appear on
the last printed page of this book.

for Sarah

CONTENTS

ILLUSTRATIONS
AND TABLES

MAPS

FIGURES

TABLES

ACKNOWLEDGMENTS

I am delighted to have the chance to express my gratitude for the material and personal support I have received in preparing this book. Patient friends and colleagues have provided occasions for me to discuss Bretons in Paris and internal migration at meetings of the Social Science History Association, the Society for French Historical Studies, and the European Social Science History Conference. In addition, the International Institute of Social History, the École des Hautes Études en Sciences Sociales, the Netherlands Interdisciplinary Demographic Institute, the Institut National des Études Démographiques, and Universities in Leiden, Texas, Arizona, and Michigan have invited me to speak about aspects of this work.

The Pariahs of Yesterday began as a quite different enterprise, with support for summer research from the University of Michigan, Flint, and the study expanded during a semester's research leave from Michigan State University granted by Dean John Eadie. Generous support from the College of Arts and Letters subsequently enabled stints of summer research, and then the Department of History, chaired by Walter Hawthorne, underwrote publication costs. The Center for Russian, European and Eurasian Studies and Norman Graham kindly paid the bill for the illustrations in this volume. I am especially grateful to Peter Berg, director of the Special Collections unit of the Michigan State University Libraries, and to Randall Scott, its Comic Art Collection curator, who underwrote and encouraged my interest in Bécassine. Nathan Scherbarth and John Hennessey spent hours confirming marriage records, corroborating research, and checking details of the manuscript.

In France, Nancy Green and the Centre de Recherches Historiques at the École des Hautes Études en Sciences Sociales hosted a most happy research stay, and Jack Thomas at the Université de Toulouse–Le Mirail gave me another occasion for on-site work. This study also has an important Dutch component, because the primary occasion for uninterrupted writing came from a fellowship at the Netherlands Institute for Advanced Study under the leadership of Rector Wim Blockmans. Colleagues at NIAS like Jacqueline Bel provided a rich intellectual atmosphere and friendly support; the entire staff—especially the librarian Dindy van Maanen—created a wonderful workplace. Beyond NIAS, my Dutch colleagues Leo Lucassen, Marlou Schrover, and Jan Lucassen created a welcoming scholarly home.

The hospitality of Parisian friends made research in France a pleasure and certainly eased the pangs of being away from home. I will always be grateful to Marie-Claude Blanc-Chaléard, Yves and Véronique Charbit, Alain Faure, Antoinette Fauve-Chamoux, Annie Couëdel, Nancy Green, and Lucas Tchetgnia for their conversation and kind hospitality. I am grateful to Pierre Guillard, who was so generous with his time and knowledge of the Breton community in Paris. Conversations with Suzanne Ascoët, Guy Barbichon, Catherine Bertho-Lavenir, Françoise Cribier, and Michelle Perrot furnished me with crucial information and inspiration at key points. Françoise Douzenel generously donated photos from the collection of Pierre Douzenel for this book.

In Brittany, Marie-Noëlle Jaffrézic and Yves Le Barre offered warm hospitality and information—then sent me off to Pont-Aven, where Fernande LeNaour provided another generation's insights—all thanks to Anne-Katell Jaffrézic, who provided the link between Michigan and Brittany. Claude Fagnen and archival personnel in the Finistère and Côtes-d'Armor provided gracious and knowledgeable aid.

Once the Bretons reached the Duke University Press, Valerie Millholland and Gisela Fosado treated them with care. The manuscript benefited enormously from the anonymous readers for the press, who proffered insightful suggestions that enabled me to improve this work; my editor, Fred Kameny, shook the most irritating quirks from my prose. Closer to home, Rachel Fuchs and Nora Faires each had the patience to read the manuscript in its entirety and to offer invaluable suggestions. Even closer, Lewis Siegelbaum provided alternative sources of inspiration. The errors and omissions that remain here are entirely my own.

This book is dedicated to my daughter Sarah, who was present at the beginning of this work but has since moved on to manage her own life and work with grace, humor, and acuity.

Introducing the
Pariahs of Yesterday

Every age has its pariahs, and in 1898 the Breton was declared "the pariah of Paris." This disparaging sobriquet, most closely associated with the Paris historian Louis Chevalier,[1] spread as far as the Bretons' home, the western peninsula of Brittany. Often newcomers suffer under pariah status, assigned not by their family or their own compatriots but by members of their host culture, as do some of today's Latin Americans in the United States, North and West Africans in France, and Moroccans in the Netherlands. The status can be temporary—outcast newcomers can gain a foothold, blend with the native-born, and form vital communities of their own. It is the historians' task to investigate and understand the evolution of life at the newcomer's destination.[2] Indeed, history carries the burden of explanation because historical change is at the heart of both migration and perceptions of outsiders. This book analyzes the history of Bretons in Paris during the Third Republic (1871–1940). It will be a vehicle for investigating internal migration, the integration of national minorities, and the state's inclusionary and exclusionary policies, setting migrations to the national capital in a long-term and global context.

I seek to connect internal migration with its implications for national integration and identity in France. After reading Eugen Weber's pioneering *Peasants into Frenchmen*, the noted French migration scholar Gérard Noiriel observed nearly twenty years ago that "very few historians have been interested in the history of national assimilation"; behind this lack of interest, he observed, lies the idea that the nation is considered not a historical construct but a given, populated by "our ancestors, the Gauls."[3] Since this path-breaking observation, many scholars have addressed the exclusive nature of the citizenship philosophy forged in the Revolution and after. They have established that colonial status, race, and gender set many people apart despite longstanding claims that French citizenship, and therefore identity, are universal and nonexclusive. The legacy of Republican citizenship from the revolutionary era is an inclusive yet gendered and racialized principle that constituted the French identity as a unitary one.[4] Nonetheless, internal migration has not yet received the kind of renewed examination that it deserves as part of this larger story of French nation building; I will address this deficiency with a focus on the Breton experience in Paris.

Attention to French identity and citizenship has increased along with the study of immigrants in France, in response to a lack of immigration histories and the realities of renewed immigration after the Second World War. Scholars produced incisive and vigorous studies, beginning in the 1980s with general ones such as Yves Lequin's *La mosaïque France* and pioneering, more specialized studies like Janine Ponty's *Polonais méconnus*. Case studies such as Pierre Milza's *Voyage en Ritalie* about Italians in France and edited collections like *Toute la France: Histoire de l'immigration en France au XXᵉ siecle* followed in the 1990s. This century began with the publication of Marie-Claude Blanc-Chaléard's *Italiens dans l'est parisien*, Nancy Green's *Repenser les migrations*, and Philippe Rygiel's *Destins immigrés*, each of which investigated the immigrant experience from another angle. Books in languages other than French have included the more recent Mareike Konig's *Deutsche Handwerker, Arbeiter une Dienstmädchen in Paris* and Mary Dewhurst Lewis's *Boundaries of the Republic*. In combination with studies of contemporary immigrants, these historical studies provide a diversity and depth to the history of France and its peoples.[5]

The attention to foreign immigration has changed the discourse about the French nation—a most important consequence. Migration, in the words of Laure Teulières, "has also been discussed in terms of the concepts and models of integration in the nation-making process, acculturation, adaptation, cultural differences and multiculturalism, etc. As a result, all of these notions have shaken up the 'French model' of integration and challenged the traditional vision of France."[6] The working assumption of national histories that has operated to the detriment of understanding the rich variety of peoples within each nation is on the wane, in favor of what Dirk Hoerder, Christiane Harzig, and Adrian Schubert call "the historical practice of diversity." Hoerder writes that "the powerful simplification or master narrative of 'national identity' and 'nation-state history," in *longue durée* perspective, hides a complex interactive past, hides in particular the worlds the slaves made, the migrants built, the women created."[7] Europe has not become a nation of distinct cultures only in the past five decades; rather, European history is a long story of cultural meetings and conflicts within nation and empire.

Yet as a consequence of the emerging and very fine scholarship on international immigration, we may know more about twentieth-century Italians or Poles in the capital city than about French provincials, as the historian of Paris Alain Faure has observed.[8] Provincials made the nation, however. Over 120 years ago, in 1882, Ernest Renan gave the significant and well-known address at the Sorbonne, "What Is a Nation?," pointing out the connections between provincials and national identity. While calling the nation a soul, Renan also stated clearly that the nation is a construction rather than an organic whole. A notable and controversial figure, Renan was from the coastal Breton Côtes-d'Armor and left studies for the priesthood in Paris in 1845 to turn to philosophy. This extraordinarily pious agnostic published the widely read *Vie de Jésus* in 1863, assessing Jesus as a historical figure. Virulently attacked by the church, Renan was nonetheless selected for the Académie Française and held a chair at the Collège de France. Renan asserted that the nation of France was not formed of one dynasty, race, ethnographic group, language, or geographic unit,[9] noting that "all Gallic consciousness had perished by the second century AD, and it is only from a purely scholarly perspective that, in our own days, the individuality of the Gallic character has been retrospectively recovered."[10] He understood that the French nation had been formed from distinct ethnic and linguistic groups, but also believed that the melting pot had done its work by the 1880s: "A Frenchman," Renan wrote, "is neither a Gaul, nor a Frank, nor a Burgundian. Rather he is what has emerged out of the cauldron in which, presided over by the King of France, the most diverse elements have together been simmering."[11]

Eugen Weber agreed that the French comprised many nations, and he made the case in *Peasants into Frenchmen*, as Noiriel later did, that the state was the primary instrument of inclusion—not the "King of France," as Renan wrote, but the Third Republic. While Weber recognized long-standing traditions of temporary migration that brought peasants to new fields and cities, his emphasis was on the state: The Republic built the roads, laid out the railroads, created the primary school system, forced children to attend—and to speak French while they did—and then sent young men away from home if they were conscripted into the army.[12] Although Weber did not use the analogy of the melting pot, he wrote as if the state had the pot over a hot fire while the Third Republic was hard at work making Frenchmen out of peasants.

In response to this somewhat dichotomous view of peasants and the French, scholars have come forward to present a more nuanced picture of relations between the Third Republic and the people. James Lehning stresses the importance of the discourse about rural people by those urban, educated citizens who defined themselves as French, both to point out that this was a largely Parisian discourse and to argue that those who were peasants were also French.[13] The people of France—and certainly of the France that included Bretons, Basques, Flemish, and Provençals and would again include Alsatians and Lorrainers—did not fit easily within the dichotomy of peasant and French because they were too complex culturally, economically, and linguistically. "Frenchification," concludes the historian of the Third Republic schools Jean-François Chanet, took a more complex and twisting path than once thought.[14] Although the national project of creating a French-speaking, literate, and patriotic populace required great vigor on the part of the state, as Caroline Ford demonstrates in her study of Breton politics, *Creating the Nation in Provincial France*, a subtle two-way process did the work rather than an active and heavy-handed imposition from Paris.[15] Those provincials who left home are missing from these studies.

Scholars of migration within France have set the stage for linking issues of internal and international migration by regarding human mobility in its own terms. Since the posthumous publication of Abel Châtelain's *Migrants temporaires en France* in 1976 and Abel Poitrineau's *Remues d'hommes* seven years later, it has been clear that migration has been part of French life since the old regime. Likewise, the connections between rural migrants and city life were highlighted in the 1970s by Alain Corbin's early work *Archaïsme et modernité en Limousin* and then by Jean-Pierre Poussou's *Bordeaux et le sud-ouest* in the subsequent decade. The focus on Paris that began with Françoise Raison-Jourde's *Colonie auvergnate de Paris* in the 1970s has been both broadened and sharpened by studies of foreigners in Paris such as Blanc-Chaléard's *Italiens dans l'est parisien* and by the masterly comparative study of the French who move to Paris by Jean-Claude Farcy and Alain Faure, *La mobilité d'une généra-*

tion de français. More recently, Faure followed numerous studies of the processes that create Parisian life with a sensitive study of the housing possibilities for newcomers, *Une chambre en ville.* Each of these endeavors highlights the connections between migration and settling in Paris, opening the door to a more theoretically comprehensive view of migrants in the city that can encompass both native-born and foreigner.[16]

A TRIO OF NARRATIVES

This book signals a key element of "Frenchification" and national integration overlooked in many discussions—internal migration, and in this case the migration of Bretons to Paris, and their lives in the city. The recognition of ethnic diversity which has come from attention to foreign immigrants allows us to turn our attention to French groups such as the Bretons. As Teulières writes, "in relation to the consequences of a nationally centered historiography, there is a patent lack of studies which cover the regions of origin and the settlement areas, regardless of state frontiers."[17] This investigation of Bretons will have the advantage of addressing a distinct group in France, thereby weakening the barrier between studies of internal and international movement. If we are to understand migration as a historical as well as global phenomenon, we must discard the idea that different intellectual frameworks apply, and rather strengthen and emphasize the common intellectual frameworks, instead of separating migrants depending on whether or not they cross an international border. We should employ widely applicable theories and concepts, any of which work at the group level, attending to such phenomena as migration systems, networks, and migrants' demographic traits.

To write migration histories that include groups like the Bretons or Basques is to take up the opportunity to relate studies of internal migration to those of inclusion and exclusion from the nation, and to scrutinize the role of the state as an instrument of inclusion as well as exclusion. We must give up the widespread idea that the state is only active in matters of transnational emigration and immigration, even though when scholars turn to migration politics, they usually do so to investigate international migration.[18] Yet inclusion and exclusion work at the same time. Indeed, just as the French state was seeking to identify, regulate, and exclude foreigners with registration laws, employment restrictions, and citizenship laws between 1889 and 1899, it was taking inclusive measures as well.

Scholarship and family lore have demonstrated how children were being encouraged, if not coerced, and taught to use the national language in schools. The most acute memory in many quarters is one of loss. As Mona Ozouf writes, "The French school tried to persuade little Basques, Bretons or Catalans that the renunciation of their original identity, stamped with insurmountable inferiority, would be the price to pay for their emancipation."[19] Moreover, French-language newspapers were disseminated more than ever before, and conscripts and schoolchildren both learned loyalty and the national language.[20] This inclusion was experienced as something of a rough one but it was nonetheless a state-inspired effort. Inclusion and exclusion were two sides of the same process that produced both loyal French people and foreigners. Here the forces of inclusion and exclusion created different possibilities for Bretons than for foreigners in twentieth-century Paris.

This book investigates and explicates the view of Bretons as outsiders to French culture and society on one hand and part of the French nation on the other; it creates the opportunity to see how some characteristics and patterns of behavior of distinct internal migrant groups like the Bretons set them apart. These include use of the Celtic Breton language, extraordinarily faithful religious practice, distinctive coloring (in particular their light hair), work as unskilled laborers and domestic servants, and self-identity. At the same time, internal migrants have much in common with transnational immigrant outsiders in the ways they are treated by members of the host society. One unfortunate tendency in the last two decades, noted by many scholars, novelists, and journalists, has been to identify newcomers by their culture and religion and to see them as people who cannot be assimilated.[21] And here, historical memory is short. In *The Immigrant Threat* Leo Lucassen shows that our contemporary views of migration underestimate the suffering of newcomers in the past and overestimate that of their counterparts today.[22] We ignore or misunderstand the situation of past migrants—particularly those who move within their own nation like the Bretons, who were derided for their religion and language. This is not a new phenomenon.

Migration scholars are increasingly taking a global perspective and seeking to understand large-scale and long-term continuities and discontinuities in migration patterns. To these ends, two outstanding histories of world migration have been published in the last few years: Dirk Hoerder's *Cultures in Contact* and Patrick Manning's *Migration in World*

History.[23] The broadest works on migration depend on detailed case studies for the micro- and meso-level information that explains much about the experience of human migration. These studies are most useful when the experience of one group is situated in several broader histories, as is the experience of the Bretons—participants in the "First Empire" in North America; soldiers, nuns, settlers, and priests of the French empire in Africa; latecomers to the capital city at the peak of urbanization; and now skilled entrepreneurs in the global market for luxury dining. I will frame the Bretons who go to Paris in these global contexts.

This book joins three historical narratives, the first of which is the story of inclusion and exclusion that produces national identity, as discussed above. The second narrative relates the role of the Bretons of Paris to the long-term history of the labor force. We have understood for some years that the history of urban workers is also the history of proletarianization, since in many regions the industrialization of the city came on the heels of the deindustrialization of the countryside and the loss of property for peasant and artisan alike, making the property-less most likely to join the urban labor force.[24] Students of this narrative have traced the entry into waged labor of rural people; some have explored the key role played by domestic service in the lives of newcomers to the city, particularly women.[25] Scholars see domestic service as temporary employment—normally either a life-cycle stage or a mode of entry into urban life. It is atavistic because live-in servants who receive room and board as part of their pay are on call and dependent on their employers in ways atypical of the modern workforce. Until the 1970s domestic service was on the wane as waged labor became the norm, but with the increased entry into the labor force of married women, in combination with new waves of immigrant women, this occupation has come to be part and parcel of the twenty-first-century labor force in Europe and North America.[26] The Breton labor force in Paris during the Third Republic was varied, but in general it included domestic servants, unskilled day laborers, skilled laborers, and white-collar workers. Over time, Bretons moved into more secure waged work, marking a point in labor history that comes under our purview. In our own time the landscape is changing yet again, as employment is moving beyond the age of secure wage labor that flowered after the Second World War. As Geoff Eley points out, "Today the social relations of work are being drastically transformed in the direction of the new low-wage, semi-legal, and deregulated labour markets of a mainly service-based economy increasingly organized in complex trans-national ways." In the present, "new forms of the exploitation of labour have been accumulating around the growing prevalence of minimum-wage, dequalified and deskilled, disorganized and deregulated, semi-legal and migrant labour markets, in which workers are systemically stripped of most forms of security and organized protections."[27] In this book we meet the Bretons as they move from agricultural and small-town work toward more secure and protected occupations in the twentieth-century city, occupations albeit currently on the wane.

These Bretons also characterize a particular phase in the history of the people of Paris, the third narrative. They highlight a paradox about that history best articulated by Louis Chevalier, who depicted a city with lively and distinct regional subcultures in the mid- to late nineteenth century in *La formation de la population parisienne*. In the better-known and noto-rious *Dangerous Classes and Laboring Classes in Paris during the First Half of the Nineteenth Century*, first published in the late 1950s, he portrayed a city which devoured newcomers by reducing them to poverty, criminal degradation, and sexual misery.[28] This vision of historical Paris has been remarkably sturdy, despite the work of fine historians whose systematic research contradicts Chevalier's image of newcomers.[29] The sources em-ployed by Chevalier—such as doctors' reports and bourgeois fiction—depict Bretons in direly negative terms. Indeed Bretons come off very badly in all portrayals, including Chevalier's first book, in which, as noted earlier, they are called "the pariahs of Paris," and in Raison-Jourde's fine study of Auvergnats in Paris, in which the Bretons are set up as a contrast with the successful migrants from the Central Highlands.[30] They fare poorly even in the most fair-minded study of Parisian mortality.[31] In these depictions Bretons are the exception proving the rule that newcomers do quite well. This book is a corrective: it attends to the integration of newcomers over time, examining the image and realities of Bretons in the hierarchy of Paris over a period of some fifty years in the life of the Third Republic.

Remarkable changes in both image and reality mark this period, and the lives of Bretons changed dramatically from their days as domestics in the city and day laborers in the industrial *banlieue* of Saint-Denis. Time, as Nancy Green has pointed out, is a key element in studies of integration and assimilation; historians' and sociologists' time frames have shaped their assessment of the success of newcomers.[32] This historian's study will give Bretons a half-century of time.

Neither time nor space is a simple entity in historical studies of movement. It is very difficult to know when individual migrants arrived or how long they remained—or even whether they remained. In the past twenty years it has become apparent that historical migrations are not necessarily marked by a single move. On the contrary, fruitful records outside France and nuanced readings of French information have made it clear that people often move not just once, but many times and also back and forth between two or more destinations.[33] And the rural exodus, seen as most problematic in the interwar period and again after the Second World War, is not the historical reality that was once imagined. Paul-André Rosental has capped recent scholarship showing that the countryside is not static but alive with human mobility, and that the French did not leave rural areas en masse in response to crises.[34] The Bretons pose a special problem because they were apparently newcomers at a given time—beginning to move to Paris in large numbers only during the Third Republic—and because they were notorious for retaining country ways. In many cases this generation was the first to live in an urban area. Consequently, Bretons of these years look like quintessential "rubes" or country bumpkins, newcomers fresh from the countryside. What grain of truth there is to this—and how it may have changed—is part of this book.

Bretons in Paris also join the new global histories of migration centered in Europe. Those Bretons who, along with other French people from the provinces, joined urban life during the Third Republic and after the Second World War contributed to the growing urban population; they were part of the urbanization of the highly developed countries in Western Europe. It was these French (and other Europeans) who became the city's secure workers, shopkeepers, artisans, white-collar workers, and elites. Although this history emphasizes Bretons' initial decades in Paris, over time they took on the white-collar and skilled positions, leaving a vacuum in positions such as those of *terrassier*, construction worker, domestic servant, and hospital aide that would be filled in turn by workers from abroad. Thus the Bretons are part of the great shift from a native-born to an immigrant labor force—especially visible in unskilled and unattractive jobs—that has transformed Europe since the 1950s.

🌼

Although Bretons had come to Paris since the Middle Ages—and certainly during the Revolution, when a separate Breton deputation and a Breton Club existed in 1789—the number of Bretons was small. During the nineteenth century they were no match for compatriots from the Auvergne, Limousin, or Savoie, whose numbers grew to give Paris a picturesque and hard-working rural element. In the 1830s there were only about 11,000 Bretons in the city.[35] Mass migration to Paris came later, as I describe below, so that by 1891 nearly 69,000 men and women from Brittany lived in the city, and over 88,000 in the greater Paris that included its suburbs.[36]

Distinct landscapes coexisted in the richly varied landscape of greater Paris, and I have chosen to study two of them as sites of settlement and potential Breton community. The first is the Fourteenth Arrondissement, the area beside the Montparnasse railroad station where Bretons disembarked when they arrived; known as a Breton area, it had retained marks of Breton institutions and even now continues to do so. The second is the industrial banlieue of Saint-Denis, just north of the city limits, once called "the Manchester of France" for its heavy industry and unrelieved industrial landscape. Saint-Denis too had the reputation as a place for Breton settlement, although like the Fourteenth Arrondissement it was home to locals and newcomers from other provinces and eventually from the colonies and abroad (see map 1).

Not all Bretons in Paris—no matter when they arrived—were alike, of course. Bretons, like most newcomers, saw themselves as being from a particular town or region, from the Trégorrois in the Côtes-d'Armor or the Cornouaille in the Finistère; it was at their destination that they took on or were assigned the more general identity of Breton. I have sought to pay special attention to several points of distinction among them, the first of which is gender. In the realities of the labor force, Breton men an experience quite different from that of women, since most jobs in Paris were gender-specific. Moreover, and more visibly, the reputation and image of Breton women was distinct from that of men—each humiliating in its own way, despite the common image of the unsophisticated rural newcomer. Moreover, Breton men and women perceived and articulated their urban experience differently.

That experience also depended on where one was from, because Brittany itself has never been homogeneous. In the first years of mass migration to Paris the *département* of the Côtes-d'Armor to the north sent the most newcomers to Paris of the five départements of Brittany, giving way to migration from the Finistère to the west and the Morbihan to the south only by the 1920s. Yet the most crucial distinction among Bretons

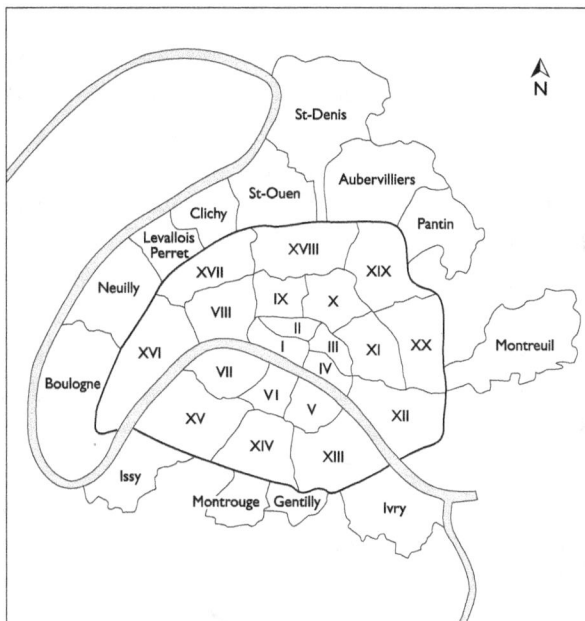

MAP 1. The Arrondissements and Suburbs of Paris

was whether they were from "Basse Bretagne" (lower Brittany, farther from Paris, where the Celtic Breton language was spoken) or "Haute Bretagne" (upper Brittany, closer to Paris, and home to the French dialect of Gallo rather than to a distinct language). The majority of Bretons who moved from the Côtes-d'Armor to Paris during the Third Republic came from the inland, western half of the department, which was Breton-speaking and Bas-Breton. The Finistère at the tip of the peninsula is altogether in lower Brittany, as is most of the Morbihan. As Marc Dutertre wisely notes, the distinction between Basse Bretagne and Haute Bretagne is one of experience, of the spoken language, that does not correspond to any administrative unit. And the definition of Haute Bretagne is purely a negative one, because it is the area where Breton is not spoken.[37]

Breton—evolved from the language of the British conquerors of the late Middle Ages—was never spoken in eastern Brittany but remained the language of western Brittany and had an especially long life in rural areas, where according to the Breton scholar Fañch Broudig the majority of the adult population was monolingual until 1914.[38] Village children learned French in the schools of the Republic.[39] Urban people learned French throughout Brittany. The departments of the Ille-et-Vilaine and the Loire-Atlantique (including many of the largest cities of Brittany, the provincial capital of Rennes, and the port cities of Nantes and Saint-Malo) make up the lion's share of upper Brittany, linguistically and culturally closer to national norms than lower Brittany.[40] Language scholars confirm earlier impressions that there are two Brittanys because the language frontier separates two peoples—the "real Bretons," with a distinct language, more rural culture and folkways, and greater isolation from the rest of the metropole, from the upper Bretons, who more closely resemble other provincial French. At the same time, they confirm that the linguistic frontier has a transient quality and that Breton continues to be spoken and understood in rural areas, in the cities of Brittany, and also in cities where Bretons gather, including Paris.[41] The distinction between upper and lower Brittany is important enough that I mention it throughout this book as I discuss the origins of Bretons in Paris (see map 2). The Bretons in greater Paris—men and women from town and country, upper and lower Brittany—have much to demonstrate about how "diversity occurs and operates."[42]

The Bretons' lives in the city and Parisians' views of Bretons—as these evolved across the history of the Third Republic—constitute my focus. One major source of information about the fortunes of newcomers is the Actes de Mariage of Bretons in Paris, because for Bretons—especially for relative newcomers in their twenties—weddings were a major Parisian event, whether or not they resulted from a Parisian courtship. The wedding records are far from a perfect source, for the many reasons discussed in the Appendix, but they reveal a good bit: they situate brides, grooms, witnesses, and parents—if still living—in a specific neighborhood of Paris, in the Paris basin, or beyond, and in the local economy. And the records give a social context to Bretons in Paris by revealing informal social ties.

For more direct reportage I have turned to the rare published family memoirs of Breton migrants to Paris: one of Yvonne Yven, who arrived in Paris in 1882 from the Finistère; the other of François Michel and Marie Lepioufle, who arrived over twenty years later from the Morbihan. Each memoir is told through the eyes of a son who gathered family documents and took care to relate a detailed story. Although the sons, like other family authors, may not reply to precisely the questions that I would ask, they wrote about their parents' work, family, and social contacts, as well as how their parents felt about their Parisian lives. These memoirs are

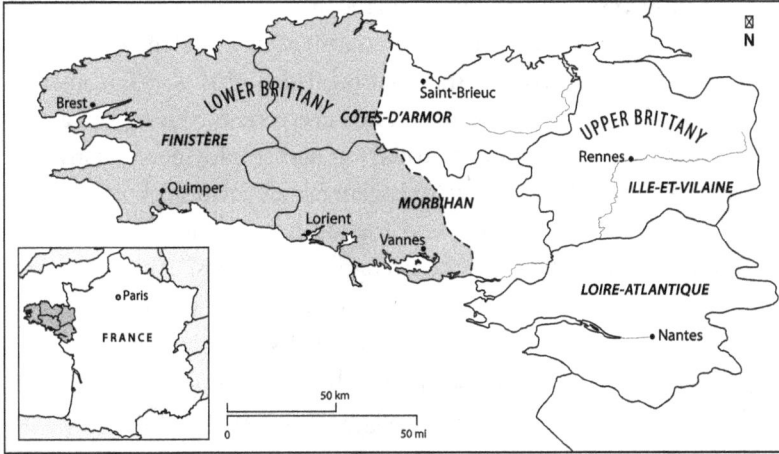

MAP 2. Brittany

colored by family feeling, and so they lack the regimented quality of a sociologist's survey, but they nonetheless provide valuable insight into the Breton experience in Paris. The memoir of Emma Girard, who came to Paris from the Côtes-d'Armor in the mid-1920s, provides a more direct expression of this experience, although like all life writings, it is an outcome of Girard's own perspective. Interviews by Françoise Cribier, Alain Faure, Catherine Omnès, and Didier Violain, as well as those by Guy Barbichon and Patrick Prado, yield the words of newcomers in response to direct questions about their experiences of migration and life in greater Paris; these allow us to hear the voices of Bretons who arrived after the Great War.[43] I am aware, as Paul-André Rosental has indicated, that the focus on the individual migrant carries the risk of reversing what he calls "the black legend" of misery and failure, transforming this legend into an equally schematic image of triumph. We will see that a core narrative of failure was often assigned to Bretons, but the individual experience visible in memoirs and marriage records can nonetheless give life to the full range of experience without whitewashing the difficulties of migrant life.[44]

The social networks of migrants provide crucial aid—aid highlighted by Charles Tilly's typology of networks, which elucidated especially the chain migration that connects origins to specific destinations where compatriots gather. Scholars understand that networks of contact are the linchpin of success for newcomers and the material from which migration systems, whether local, national, or transnational, are made. Durable networks accrue the resources that have been identified as social capital by Pierre Bourdieu. Yet as we shall see, not everyone travels to join a supportive network that can offer protection and employment. Many new arrivals lack contacts, arrive with only general information about employment, and then form contacts and friendships after arrival, relying on what Mark Granovetter calls "the strength of weak ties." Although social capital is often used to characterize what newcomers possess or can acquire, marriage records allow a more refined view that can distinguish longstanding and new relationships, neighbors and kin.[45]

Research based on these sources suggests that state policies only provide part of the explanation for the integration of newcomers. Because Bretons were French and crossed no international border at which their papers were checked, they could gain entry to Paris, but their community, networks, friendships, and employment depended on human ties and economic opportunity. In the words of Paul-André Rosental, a host of considerations "between macro and micro" were at work.[46] The state played a role, as it does today, but human and economic factors went a long way toward shaping the life of the newcomer, and in the long run lifting the label of pariah from the Breton.

CHAPTER ONE

Contexts

Although Paris is the focus of this book, it was not the sole destination of Breton émigrés. Bretons had a history of departures abroad and a shorter but important history of moving within France, which along with Brittany itself provides a crucial context for the late-nineteenth-century mass movements to Paris.

BRETONS IN THE WORLD

The people of Brittany had long moved over ocean and sea to the western and southern hemispheres. Although Bretons represented insular provincials to Parisians during the Third Republic, international contacts and emigration have marked this region since late antiquity and the early Middle Ages. Bretons from Saint-Malo and Nantes were among the medieval navigators who traded with northern Europe. The sugar and slave traders of Nantes and the coastal traders faded in the nineteenth century, but fishing remained important; men fished for cod and tuna on the high seas, for sardines off the south coast, and for local fish along the west and north coasts of Brittany, where fisherman and peasant were not entirely separate. In addition, over three-quarters of naval officers and sailors in 1890 were Breton, not counting apprentices and cabin-boys. In the words of the historian Gérard Le Bouëdec, "the sailor belongs to global society."[1] The maritime traditions of Brittany directed emigrations from France across the Atlantic in the seventeenth and eighteenth centuries. Many parts of coastal Brittany were part of a maritime culture and economy that lined the Atlantic and North Sea coasts, essential to the history of Breton mobility. These areas "belonged to an outwardly turned and mobile sector of French society" that sent men abroad.[2]

Yet the history of emigration from France is less clear or complete for the French than for other Europeans. This is partly because French emigration was neglected by historians until recently.[3] Publications since 1985 include case studies of the French in Algeria, the United States, and Canada, as well as Annick Foucrier's study of the French in California and a history of Alsatians in the United States.[4] In addition, the "administrative construction of the émigré" reveals that the French state long discouraged emigration and was somewhat hostile to those who chose to leave for the New World. It promoted and encouraged migration to Algeria, however—without great success.[5] Finally, in the old regime émigrés were understood by the French to be criminal and immoral, "a random sweeping of rogues and sluts." This reputation persisted even though only a small proportion of émigrés were criminals and France did not export prisoners on a large scale as did the British, for example.[6]

Some Bretons went to the West Indies in the seventeenth and eighteenth centuries, leaving via Nantes or Saint-Malo after having journeyed from a smaller town or village. Migration to the West Indies carried the possibility of quick fortunes, and to be "rich as a creole" was a byword for splendour in France.[7] In the century after 1632 the vast majority of emigrants departing from Nantes were headed for the Caribbean.[8] The most fortunate, like the family of Pierre Dieudonné Dessalles that left Brittany in the mid-seventeenth century, became successful sugar planters and notables while some, including Dessalles, took on a creole identity.[9] Men like Dessalles were few among Bretons, since Breton ports turned to the Atlantic more than to the Caribbean; moreover, the Haitian revolt of 1791 severely attenuated these fortunes.

In the eighteenth century northern Brittany sent many men abroad as fishermen and sailors for the merchant marine, which depended on the market for salted cod. They quickly turned to Canada, where the small French settlement on Île Royale (now Cape Breton Island) was over one-quarter Breton in 1734; these were fishermen and navigators, but also men in the building trades, commerce, and the priesthood. In the 1750s many Malouins moved into the Acadian settlement.[10] The northern Breton port of Saint-Malo was more oriented toward New France in Canada than toward the Mediterranean, unlike La Rochelle and Bordeaux to the south. Nonetheless, the number of French settlers in the eighteenth-century colonies was relatively small; in 1754 there were only 55,101 French inhabitants in the most populous colony, Canada.[11]

Leslie Choquette has demonstrated that French migration to Quebec was far different from what scholars had thought, because it was not the movement of permanent settlers who arrived from their home village. Rather the Breton migration to New France was seasonal, temporary, and often part of a series of moves from villages to port towns and on to Quebec—and then back to France. Choquette and Peter Moogk concur that during the seventeenth and eighteenth centuries the work of overseas Bretons was part of widespread French temporary and seasonal migration both within France and beyond its borders, and that the unemployed in port cities were most likely to sign on for trips to North America.[12] Bretons figured heavily among the thirty thousand or more Old Regime French migrants who went to Quebec and most of all among those who did not stay.[13] Many had already moved within Brittany, to Nantes or Saint-Malo. And these were men: *bretonnes* rarely made this trip, since the women who settled in Canada, the *filles du roi* who were sent to provide brides for French men, were recruited primarily from the Hôpital Général of Paris.[14] Recruitment and labor contracts were necessary to get the French to Canada, and even this movement was cut off by the British victory in the French and Indian War of 1754–63.

All of these migrations were, however, small in number. It was not until Bretons joined the well-known emigrants in French political history, the Royalist "émigrés" who were enemies of the government during the revolutionary period, that they departed in large numbers. Because Brittany is bound by the sea and emigration requires no border crossing, and because of the state of revolt and civil war during the Revolution, it is difficult to know the precise volume of political emigration. Nonetheless, Donald Greer's tireless research of every département of France demonstrates that Breton départements were among those that sent many émigrés abroad—the Côtes-d'Armor (over 2,500), the Finistère (2,000), Ille-et-Vilaine (2,000), the Loire-Atlantique (1,700), and the Morbihan (1,300).[15]

In the nineteenth century Bretons were attached to the mission of the church worldwide. As James Daughton has pointed out, "a century after the Revolution had inflicted a dizzying blow to Catholicism, the Third Republic boasted an apostolic system with the recourse to recruit, train, place, and support missionary work on six continents"—and Bretons were crucial to this effort.[16] The primary fundraising organization was the Oeuvre de la Propagation de la Foi, whose *Annales* gave the faithful a missionary's-eye view of the world; notably, 6,500 copies a year were published in the Breton language in the 1890s, a figure that only dipped slightly by the time of the Great War.[17] Breton priests were important among the settlers in Canada, and they were also key to France's mission in nineteenth-century Africa. Orders such as the Frères de Ploërmel "assured public instruction to Senegalese youth in contact with French colonial authorities." According to a history of the order, "State employees, the brothers were nonetheless, first and foremost, missionaries of the gospel and men of the church, with an open attitude and in dialogue with Islam, the primary religion of their students."[18] In 1836 the minister of the colonies contacted the prefect of the Morbihan, who wrote to the founder of the order, brother of the famed Catholic author Robert de Lammenais from Saint-Malo, to suggest that the order take on primary education in the colonies. Thus began the engagement of the order in the Antilles, Martinique, Guadeloupe, Guyana, St. Pierre and Miquelon, and then Senegal. Between November 1841 and 1904, 174 brothers worked in Saint-Louis and the Island of Gorée—and then other coastal towns of Dakar and Rufisque—beginning with the arrival of Brother Euthyme, a thirty-year-old Breton, and Brother Heraclien, a creole from Martinique. By April 1842 the two had 110 students.[19] Over the course of the nineteenth century the Frères de Ploërmel sent over eleven hundred priests abroad, among which Bretons were eager participants. For example, when eight teachers were called for to replace those killed by the epidemic of 1867 in Saint-Louis, four hundred Bretons volunteered.[20]

Regular orders, missionary orders, and smaller orders of every kind recruited successfully in Brittany and sent members to China, Indochina, South and North America (including the United States), the Caribbean, South Sea Islands, and Africa. Many of the Jesuits in China were from Brittany, for example, and Bretons accounted for over half the Trappists who founded a monastery in Algeria and planted the first French vines there in the 1840s. The Soeurs de Saint-Joseph de Cluny, who taught with the Frères de Ploërmel in Senegal, worked as teachers and nurses in Africa, Asia, Oceania, and the Americas. Among them was the nurse and administrator Marie Dédié, from near Brest in the Finistère, who arranged marriages for her charges in Brazzaville; described as a "valiant little Breton" and the "little mother of the Congo," Dédié was honored by the Académie Française in about 1913 and the Legion of Honor in 1927. The Filles de la Charité de Saint-Vincent de Paul sent 245 bretonnes to

Asia, Africa, and the Americas between 1850 and 1910, among them Hermine Simon-Suisse, sister of the statesman and reformer Jules Simon; born in Lorient in the Morbihan, she died in Lima, where she worked in a mental hospital between 1856 and 1880. In all an estimated twelve thousand Bretons worked abroad as missionaries for the Catholic church between 1800 and 1990. As important as these men and women were to their families, the church, and French colonial efforts, they were few in number compared with those who went to Paris.[21]

Bretons also supplied bodies to the imperial settlements in Algeria, although considerable efforts to recruit fishermen and farmers to North Africa (not simply Algeria, but also Tunisia and Morocco) did not have great success. Like the seventeen boatloads of Parisians sent to Algeria as part of the relief of the economic and political crisis of 1848, Bretons met with a hard reality that contradicted any ideas of a tropical paradise.[22] The founding of the Société Bretonne de Colonisation en Algérie by M. Auguste Roncière of the Côtes-d'Armor was among the efforts to attract Bretons. Roncière's idea was to recruit rural religious families, with the goal of implanting Catholicism in North Africa. The deputy from Saint-Brieuc, le Comte de Champagny, had the same idea when he declared in 1853 that "no emigrant can offer greater aptitude for colonization than the Breton farmer. A Breton colony would carry to the African soil the image of the fatherland and its simple and religious ways."[23] These schemes did not enjoy significant success, and perhaps for this reason, in the 1890s the state tried to lure settlers with free passage and one hundred francs per man (two hundred per household), plus ten francs a month for lodging. Bretons moved to the coastal towns of Annaba, Skikda, and Collo; in 1891 an entrepreneur in Concarneau opened a sardine cannery and curing facility in Skikda. Most successfully, just afterward the governor general opened three seaside villages within thirty-five kilometers of Algiers. Finally, after 1904 free lands were offered to poor French settlers who would live on and farm the land, and similar efforts were made to settle Breton fisherman.[24]

Emigrants saw more promise in the western hemisphere, so despite government discouragement hundreds of thousands of French departed in the nineteenth century, especially to Argentina (the destination for nearly 227,000 between 1857 and 1924), the United States (nearly 492,000 between 1820 and 1924), and Canada. Others went to Mexico.[25] The nearby sea offered an exit to adventuresome Bretons. When the handloom weavers of Brittany lost the New World market for their goods in the face of competition from Silesia, Saxony, and England and high tariffs in the early nineteenth century, one of their choices was to join the crews of whaling boats. It was by this means that Joseph Leroy from the Morbihan got to Monterey, California, in the 1830s, where he abandoned ship, along with the weaver's son Vincent Louis Saget from the Côtes-d'Armor. Bretons in early California like these two—each born near a port town—seem to have sold their labor at sea as part of a young man's way out, rather than part of a collective movement.[26] Small groups of Bretons from the Finistère set out for Montevideo, at the mouth of the Plata River in Uruguay, including a young hat maker and a sixty-four-year-old merchant with his wife and two daughters in March 1854. The same year five men in the building trades sailed for Lima. The following year a group of fifteen men in all trades, the majority in their twenties, left for Tova Island off the coast of Argentina.[27] A pharmacist and a *propriétaire* set out to do business in New York, a teacher to Boston. Destinations were scattered from New York to Patagonia for these small groups of emigrants.

This was true at least until news of the California Gold Rush reached France. Coming in 1848, at a time when the European economies were at a nineteenth-century nadir, the Gold Rush brought Europeans, men, in the main, to the West Coast of the United States, which also attracted men from China, Mexico, Latin America, Australia, and New Zealand. The French, by and large in their twenties and thirties, numbered over ten thousand. These included some three thousand out-of-work Parisian men and women transported in a shadowy lottery scheme—or at least those who survived the long journey around Cape Horn in seventeen sailing vessels.[28] By 1860, when they first appeared in the U.S. federal census, nearly 8,500 French remained in the state. A good number of Bretons came along, like the *cultivateur* Jean Le Berre from the village of Plogonnec in the Finistère, twenty-four, who declared himself an emigrant and struck out for California in 1856.[29]

Canada remained a privileged destination for Bretons into the twentieth century, offering an attractive alternative to the poverty of Brittany.[30] The islands of St.-Pierre and Miquelon, just south of Newfoundland, continued to be destinations after Argentina faded as an attraction at the end of the 1880s. The French increasingly headed west, especially to Manitoba and after 1900 to Saskatchewan.[31] The parish of Saint-Brieux was founded north of Saskatoon in Saskatchewan by Bretons in 1904, when twelve hundred seasonal fishermen and three hundred other emigrants made a forty-three-day trip from Saint-Malo to Prince Albert.[32] But as the dire warnings to prefects in correspondence from Paris indicated, life across the Atlantic was fraught with danger and the threat of failure.[33] Thus the sudden death of the pioneer Joseph Bélébuic after two years in St.-Brieux, Saskatchewan, for example, necessitated help for his widow and four young children (one born after his death), who could only survive if they returned in 1912 to Douarnenez, where the widow could open a *maison des modes* and work with her three nieces and the help of a faithful maid. Madame Bélébuic, like many Bretons, had relatives who had left for other shores; she had a brother in the colonies, a Père du St. Esprit who had officiated at her wedding in France in 1907 and was in the French colony of Gabon when she returned to France.[34] Bretons continued to come to Canada throughout the twentieth century: during the interwar period, when the United States closed its doors almost completely, Canada was where most of the 16,200 French emigrants settled.[35]

Thus Bretons, as part of an outward-looking, mobile sector of French society, participated in France's global activities—as seamen in early North Sea trade, as sailors and aspiring planters in the Caribbean, as settlers in what would become Canada's Maritime Provinces and prairies, and in Latin America and the United States, from coast to coast. Bretons were part of the civilizing missions of the French state and the Catholic church, as well as of fishing and whaling fleets, worldwide.

Many returned to Brittany, and even more aspired to return. This Breton (but not uniquely Breton) strategy of traveling the ocean rather than sticking to land may have been part of the reason why Jean-Marie Déguignet, who called himself a man of the soil in his autobiography *Mémoires d'un paysan bas breton*, could be a seafaring Breton soldier and world traveler but still think of himself as a peasant. Déguignet was born into the family of an agricultural laborer not far from Quimper in 1834 and was begging at ten and working as a shepherd at seventeen before he entered military service in the Breton port of Lorient. From there the military sent him to fight in the Crimean War, to Jerusalem (where he lost his faith), to fight against Italy in 1859 and Algeria in 1861, and then to take part in the "ignoble and criminal intervention" in Mexico; he then returned to farm in the Finistère and descend into poverty and psychiatric incarceration before his death at the age of seventy-one in 1905.[36] Yet he called himself a Breton peasant. This Breton, lauded and published to wide acclaim nearly a century after his death, is understood to have embodied regional culture despite his wide travels; he also demonstrates the capacity for multiple and ambiguous identities.

BRETONS MOVE WITHIN FRANCE

Bretons did not migrate much within France before the mid-nineteenth century, however. Unlike the famous Limousins, Auvergnats, and Savoyards, who established a presence in Paris in the eighteenth century and the early nineteenth, Bretons did not enter the history of Paris as a group, nor were they engaged in large-scale migration repertoires. Certainly there was little demand for migrant labor within Brittany as elsewhere along the Atlantic coast—and there was little temporary migration, particularly in comparison with the mountainous regions of France that sent people out annually.[37] In addition, before about 1850 the Breton customs and *mentalités* kept people at home. Brittany, especially the westernmost département of the Finistère, was "the most stay-at-home in Europe," according to its prefect. "The Breton male," Gabriel Désert intoned, "lived apart from interregional human exchange."[38] The great historian of temporary migration Abel Châtelain attributes this tendency to Breton misogyny that demands keeping the woman at home and out of sexual danger, as in Corsica, but also to women's practice of weaving and doing other necessary work at home such as caring for the farm, the children, and the elderly. However, "even *Bretonnes*," he noted, eventually came to Paris to work as domestics.[39]

As farm workers began to leave temporarily or permanently before the First World War, scholars concerned with Brittany articulated the nationwide concern with the rural exodus in a number of important writings,[40] culminating in the law dissertation of the Breton Georges Le Bail, defended in Paris in November 1913. Le Bail placed himself in the company of scholars like Emile Vandervelde, the Belgian socialist whose long political life included the presidency of the Second International in 1900, and who published *L'exode rural et le retour aux champs* in 1903.[41] Le Bail described temporary and permanent emigration from the Finistère in great detail, and did so with an explicit point of view. These words of the Breton poet Auguste Brizeux followed the dedication of the dissertation:

> Oh, I tell you, never leave
> The doorstep where you played as a child.

> Never leave the doorstep,
> Die in the house where your mother died.[42]

Brittany is in crisis, Le Bail asserted; it is in a period of adaption, of struggle between the elements from the routines of the past and those reforming and scientific elements that the present brings.[43] His presentation of the temporary and permanent emigrations and their causes are cloaked in a hope to reverse the process. The dissertation ends in a reverie that has nearly the tone of a hallucination, as Le Bail dreams that the children of Brittany will desert Paris and return to the fields. It is worth taking in: "May they return! May they take, one evening, one of those trains that leaves the Gare Montparnasse for Brittany, and when the night has passed, when the great cities are far away, as the locomotive glides lightly along the rails across the Breton countryside, when the first dawn begins, the Mother Earth will suddenly appear before their astonished eyes, still enveloped in the blue fog of spring dawn, the fertile earth, the indulgent earth, forgiving of their abandonment, offering her fecund and rich loins to the labors of their arms."[44] Le Bail, and those who shared his interests, saw the extraordinarily high fertility of Brittany as one of the virtues that separated it from the rest of France. The birth rate for France was 207 per 10,000 inhabitants in 1909, and about 270 for the Finistère at the same time. The international comparison is telling of France's unusually low birthrate and growing pronatalism; the rate was 486 in Russia, 350 in Austria, 335 in Germany, 275 in England, and 260 in Sweden. In a proposal for assistance to large families, the deputy from the Finistère M. Argeliès pointed out that had France had the birthrate of the Finistère since 1871—year of the shameful defeat at the hands of the Germans—France would have a population of 53 million rather than 39 million. Finistère, like the rest of Brittany, was seen to be gifted with "perpetual increase." If only France would follow its example.[45]

When Bretons left home before the Great War, some headed for the sea. In addition to the kinds of overseas travel and settlement described above, Bretons worked as fishermen, supplying the regional markets as well as sardine canneries on the coast. For example, by 1906–7, of the 216,642 men who made their living from the sea, over 45,500 were from the Finistère, France's westernmost département.[46] Aside from those who went to the North Atlantic for cod, this work did not take men from home, as did panning for gold in California or working in Argentina. Nonetheless, fishing was dangerous work. The navy, however, did take men away from home, and Bretons were more likely than other French-men to join the navy. Le Bail contended that nearly a quarter of naval conscripts in France, and virtually all the naval volunteers, were from the Finistère. Likewise, the young men of the Côtes-d'Armor were more likely than non-Bretons to go into the navy.[47]

The kinds of seasonal work that enlivened the fields in the nineteenth century took some Bretons abroad, especially those who lived in the northwest of the peninsula. The farming and marketing of *primeurs* (deli-cious spring vegetables such as peas, onions, potatoes, and artichokes) took Bretons from St.-Pol-de-Léon to England, as well as to the cities of Brittany and to Paris. Strawberries from Daoulas, just east of Brest, were marketed in England.[48] A very well-organized contingent from around the northwestern commune of Roscoff—some twelve hundred at the beginning of the twentieth century—packaged and sold onions along the south coast of England between July and January. This hard-working contingent of traders formed a small English-speaking and tea-drinking subculture near the tip of Brittany.[49] With the exception of pockets of people from Roscoff headed for England and agricultural workers in Jersey, however, there was little maritime emigration by the turn of the century.[50]

As elsewhere, the cities of Brittany drew upon people from the sur-rounding region—in the words of Jean-Pierre Poussou, the "demographic basin."[51] Among these was the provincial capital of Rennes. Nantes, the seaport on the Loire (Loire-Atlantique) and the sixth-largest city of France in 1851, grew to 96,000 at its peak. Brest (Finistère), at the tip of the peninsula, was the eleventh-largest city at the same time. Bretons left the countryside beginning with a crisis in the rural textile industry in the 1830s that forced them to flee the villages of the Ille-et-Vilaine and the Côtes-d'Armor for Rennes and the Loire-Atlantique, where Nantes and Saint-Nazaire offered employment.[52] Young women went to large towns such as Brest and Lorient in the Finistère, where they could find work as servants or wet nurses and make higher wages than they could closer to home.[53]

After 1850 a pair of changes began to move Bretons out of their home area en masse, a trend that transformed mobility before the outbreak of the First World War. First of all, the railroad brought Brittany into con-tact with the rest of France. Although regions with long traditions of seasonal and temporary emigration on foot and by coach, like the Auvergne, had sent people out for some two hundred years, it is clear that railroads allowed easier travel for women as well as men, in addition to returns home. For Brittany the railroad played a more fundamental role. All signs confirm the findings of a study published in 1905 that "regular emigration . . . could only begin when the modern means of communication made a breach in the longstanding isolation of the region . . . the two great arteries of emigration, temporary or permanent, were the two [railroad] lines North and South, Brest to Rennes and Brest to Nantes."[54] The line from Paris to Nantes in southeast Brittany was completed in 1851 and extended out to Lorient on the south coast eleven years later. The line to the provincial capital and central city of Rennes opened in 1857 and by 1865 connected the outermost city of Brest to Paris. The railroad was only the most visible manifestation of Brittany's opening in the nineteenth century; nonetheless Bretons understood its importance. "You are invited to attend the funeral procession for the mores, customs, language and traditions of old Brittany. . . . The ceremony will take place tomorrow, December 7, 1863, at the station, about three in the afternoon," wrote a contemporary in Quimper of the railroad's arrival.[55] And the opening would continue, as other lines crisscrossed the province in the following years, and narrow-gauge railroads connected Bretons in towns of three or four thousand with national lines by about 1907.[56] The railroad lines facilitated seasonal fieldwork by charging laborers for their trip out but bringing them home without charge.[57]

Second, the demand for seasonal agricultural labor outside Brittany increased. With the end of use of the fallow, cultivated acreage increased by a third in the Paris basin, and the scythe became the tool of choice for a labor force that now included Flemish and Breton workers, according to the national agricultural inquiry of 1866. They replaced the local workers who had deserted the fields for Parisian industries and public works. Those from the mountains stayed in the South and Southwest, where the grape harvest was most pressing, leaving the demand for harvest labor north of the Loire to the Bretons and Belgians. Indeed, "without the Bretons, it would never have been possible to get the number of working arms necessary" in some villages outside Paris. Breton agricultural workers were needed in the three départements west of Paris, especially the rich Beauce region near Chartres.[58] And Breton farm workers—whose salaries were among the lowest in France—were willing to go. Nearly all emigrants, Le Bail reported in 1913, came from the farm.[59]

By the beginning of the twentieth century Breton men were circulat-
ing throughout northwestern France. A study by Jean-Claude Farcy and
Alain Faure of the conscript class of 1880—those men born in 1860 in the
Côtes-d'Armor—reveals their itineraries. The Côtes-d'Armor, like much
of the rest of Brittany, was a primarily rural département where over two-
thirds of young men worked the land, especially those who lived inland
from the coast. More mobile than past generations, over a third of the
men in this département departed, and a quarter of those went to greater
Paris. Nonetheless, the Bretons were the least likely to live in a city of
any French group under study. Men from the poorest areas—inland parts
of the west of this department—were most likely to emigrate, and least
likely to go to a city. A marked contrast distinguished young Breton men
on the coast from those inland: coastal areas, with their rich agriculture,
maritime activities, and diversified economies, produced conscripts with
higher levels of physical health and culture, and men from the "golden
belt" on the coastline were more likely than their poorer inland compatriots to seek out an urban destination at some point in their lives.[60]

The Bretons cut a distinct figure in comparison with other provincial
men, and stood in particular contrast to two of the best-known groups of
migrants to Paris, the Limousins from the Creuse and the Auvergnats
from Cantal, each of whom had a long tradition of migration to Paris and
of working as stonemasons and in construction (the Limousins) and in
café and barkeeping (the Auvergnats).[61] Brittany had a large and fertile
population, but its people were underprivileged; Breton conscripts in the
class of 1880 were on average the shortest of any group at a time when
stunted growth signaled undernourishment. The illiteracy rate of the
men born in 1860—schooled before compulsory primary education—was
the highest in the country (34 percent), because many did not know
French.[62] The Limousins were rooted in a tradition of seasonal and temporary stays in Paris, and in their mid-forties were likely to remain in Paris
(52 percent) and more likely to return home (28 percent) than any other
group; the Auvergnats, part of a close community in the city, were most
likely to remain in Paris (66 percent) rather than return (17 percent). By
contrast, emigrant Breton men were less likely to be in Paris than either of
these (50 percent)—but strikingly more likely than Limousins or Auvergnats to be in the *banlieue, or suburbs* (8 percent), or somewhere else in
France (17 percent), and less likely to go to a city at all. Of those who left
home in adulthood, far more Limousins and Auvergnats than Bretons

touched down at some point in greater Paris. Generally speaking, Breton men did not become city people: when they reached the age of forty-five, in 1906, over three-quarters of the men under study lived in settlements of fewer than two thousand residents; this set them apart from not only Limousins and Auvergnats, but the other provincial men as well.[63] Bretons were however a bit more likely than others to travel to the colonies and abroad, most likely to take seasonal work on the British islands of Jersey and Guernsey and to join fishing sojourns to Saint-Pierre and Miquelon.[64]

Nonetheless, one-seventh of these Breton men did go to greater Paris —this in contrast with the one-quarter of the men in the class of 1880 from other areas of France.[65] What set them apart in the Parisian Basin was the tendency of Breton men to go to the banlieue of Paris, rather than to the city itself. Even when very few were in the Paris area at the age of twenty, the moment of conscription, over a third were in the banlieue— presumably with their parents, because they had moved before reaching the age of twenty. By 1906, when one-quarter of the Bretons were in greater Paris, two-thirds of these men were in the banlieue.[66] Of all the newcomers to arrive from the class of 1880 from throughout France, Bretons had the shortest stay—over a third stayed less than five years, and one-sixth stayed for less than a year.[67]

Breton men moved on to other locations in northwestern France without returning home. Among these were the men who stopped in the town of Bonnières northwest of Paris to work on a model farm, and in its grimiest industries—a distillery, a petroleum refinery, and a glue factory.[68] From Paris they went back to the Ille-et-Vilaine, a more prosperous département in upper Brittany, to Normandy, and particularly to the Seine-Maritime and its primary city of Le Havre.[69] The colony of Bretons that formed in the port city of Le Havre grew with speed during the period 1875 to 1900. Numbering ten thousand in 1891 and thirty thousand a decade later, Bretons would come to be a substantial minority of Havrais. Bretons settled especially on the Île Saint-François in the heart of the city—men from the Côtes-d'Armor displaced by the fall in New World fishing and others from the inland Finistère who worked in port construction, followed by customs clerks from the Morbihan, southern Finistère, and Saint-Malo. Bretons in Le Havre were noticed for their accents and language: they were said to "baragouine" because they used the Breton words for bread (bara) and wine (gwin). Their appearance—the wives' starched headwear, coiffes, and men's garters and stockings—also set apart the Bretons of Le Havre.[70]

Although Breton men who moved to Paris to stay at the age of twenty were as rare as "aloe in Siberia," this was not necessarily so for towns of the banlieue like Saint-Denis. Moreover, with "half the world is missing" from the analysis of male migration by Farcy and Faure, theirs is a very incomplete portrait of Breton migration, especially because the city itself was clearly a more important destination for women than for men. The census of 1901 reports that among Bretons living in the city limits there were sixty-nine men for every hundred women, and among those from the most important source of newcomers, the Côtes-d'Armor, sixty-four men for every hundred women.[71] Like nearly all cities, Paris had much to offer women, and as in most cities women outnumbered men. Bretons from the Côtes-d'Armor offer the extreme case.

BRITTANY

The past half-century of scholarship on Brittany reveals a unique and heterogeneous province marked by waves of change. The work of the noted Breton scholar Yves Le Gallo underscores the longstanding existence of "two Brittanys," in terms not only of language but also culture and traditions.[72] Although Brittany is justifiably reputed to be among the most Catholic of provinces, religious practice was less fervent in the cities and some rural areas and more so in the Léon of the northern Finistère. The faith, we shall see, was closely affiliated with the Breton language, so that the Combes Law (1905) banning the use of Breton in the church and teaching congregations was particularly controversial in Brittany.[73] Moreover, pre-Christian Celtic practices, Druidism, and Bardism were part of Breton culture for some men and women.[74] Finally, the markers of high fertility and illiteracy for which Brittany was well known also varied by area.[75] And they evolved, shaken by the changes wrought during the Third Republic. "Between the Brittany of the eighteenth century and that of the postwar period, another Brittany emerged. A Brittany that, little by little, accepted the Republican model, knew its demographic peak, saw its children emigrate. An agricultural Brittany that evolved toward small holdings and improved its yields, a coastal Brittany in the throes of change. *Bref*, a social universe constantly renewed to which Bretons adapted."[76] Thus whatever Parisians' view of Brittany and Bretons, the region was not only heterogeneous but also an arena of change over the course of this history. The historical anthropologist Martine Segalen wisely warns us against the error of assuming a changeless backdrop: "Let us not make the mistake of supposing," she writes, "an immemorial, frozen past."[77]

Nonetheless, in the words of Mona Ozouf, Brittany offers the "canonical example" of resistance to national integration.[78] Breton regionalist movements are part of its past—they have a rich and lively history in Brittany that blossomed during the Third Republic—and reach to the present. Issues of language and identity are at the heart of these movements. Seated in reactions to the centralizing forces of revolutionary Jacobinism and the triumph of the Republic after 1871, activists formed the Union Régionaliste Bretonne in 1898 to promote political decentralization and economic and cultural expansion. In the Belle Époque a less conservative Fédération Régionaliste de Bretagne broke off to leave religion off the table; the more religious Bleun-Brug (Heather Flower) was founded the following year. Regionalism flowered after the Great War and gave birth to autonomist movements such as the Union of Breton Youth, founded in 1920, which transformed itself into the Breton Autonomist Party in 1927. During the interwar period some Breton activists became more fascist in orientation and looked to Germany for confirmation, but the German occupation did not recognize the claims of Breton nationalists and showed more interest in guarding the coastline against invasion from the west; Vichy gave little satisfaction to these groups, and by the end of the war Breton nationalism was discredited for its fascist associations. After the war's end regionalism found new activism in political, economic, and cultural life beginning in the late 1960s, continuing with the Socialist government of the 1980s and expanding with the European Union.[79]

The famous regionalists of the Belle Époque and interwar period that will appear in these pages include the militant Marquis de L'Estourbeillon, the composer and singer Théodore Botrel, and a number of young activists, but they will not play a starring role. Three observations lie behind this: regionalism, especially in the beginning, was an elite affair. In the main, elites joined these organizations, especially the Union Régionaliste Bretonne, whose one thousand or so members belonged mostly to the nobility (25 percent), the priesthood (17 percent), and the liberal professions (11 percent).[80] Most of the Bretons in Paris did not enjoy elite status. Second, the politics of federalism that constitute a fundamental thread of regionalism are peripheral to this story. Like regionalism in general, federalism attacks "the centralized unitary state, for which France . . . has become the archetype" and is part of a long tradition in French politics that is bearing fruit today.[81] The Bretons in the federalist movement also acted as leaders in the Paris community, and it is from this perspective that I view them. Caroline Ford has given a thoroughgoing treatment of the political relationship between Brittany and Paris as it was played out in Brittany in *Creating the Nation in Provincial France*.[82]

Finally, the regionalism that has been highlighted by Anne-Marie Thiesse emphasizes the desires to preserve the Breton language and costume.[83] As important as these were in the context of Breton organizations, the maintenance of language and costume was not a central concern of many Bretons who had moved to Paris. On the contrary, these were a hindrance to their making their way in the city and colored how they were viewed by urbanites. As one postwar arrival quipped, "When I arrived, I didn't want to speak Breton anymore, because I really needed to learn French."[84] The representation of Breton speakers and their clothing, and of Breton culture in the International Exhibits of 1900 and 1937, was crucial, but language and costume find less emphasis in this book. Indeed, I open with a pioneering newcomer who came to Paris in 1882, more concerned with a secure livelihood than with the linguistic and sartorial marks of Breton identity.

CHAPTER TWO

A Breton Crowd in Paris

The Beginnings

Born in a *bretonnant* village by the north coast of the Finistère in 1864, Yvonne Yven knew poverty, paternal drunkenness, and family discord early on. The death of her beloved mother when she was twelve years old unleashed a chain of hardships: the displacement of the family, her father's remarriage and the consequent dispersal of her siblings, and three years of inhumane employment as the servant of two miserly dowagers. Two personal interventions rescued her from this situation. Her mother's sister brought her to the capital city of Brest, where she was less isolated and better fed, but constantly harassed where she worked in a bistro. Then a new friend—a widow in her thirties—saw that Yvonne was hired along with her, and the two traveled to Paris in 1882 as servants of a wealthy merchant family. As her son recalled, at eighteen she "packed her bag and joined the cohort of *Bretonnes* migrating toward Paris . . . to escape from the misery of the West."[1] She would stay on in the city, working as a domestic cook, and thirteen years later would marry another provincial introduced by mutual friends. In some ways Yvonne's life is emblematic of the Breton story; in others it is distinct.

This chapter places Yvonne Yven squarely in the company of the first sizable crowd of newcomers from Brittany—those who arrived before the dawn of the twentieth century. Nearly 69,000 men and women from Brittany lived in Paris in 1891 (not counting their children born there), along with 3,600 in Versailles and 3,200 in Saint-Denis—over twice the number as from Normandy, for example.[2] During this time, between 1880 and 1910, there was a fundamental change in the representation of Brittany and Bretons: they became objects of ridicule.[3] Perceived in the nineteenth century as mystical and savage, then romantic and mysterious, Brittany previously had been the subject of a select few bourgeois literary visitors. However, with the change in accessibility by rail and the flood of Bretons into Paris between 1880 and 1910, more tourists saw Brittany—at least its beaches and spas—and more Parisians saw Bretons in their city.[4] It is no coincidence that Bretons at this time came to be seen as ridiculous, simple, and uncouth.

Bretons suffered by comparison with other provincials in Paris. Most notably the Limousins, who had worked in the Parisian building trades since the eighteenth century and been an important presence throughout the nineteenth, settled in skilled Paris occupations with decades of seasonal labor, housing, and networks of contact behind them. Auvergnats, whose work as water carriers, wood sellers, and then cafetiers and hoteliers going back to the eighteenth century, integrated into the urban life that was part of their occupational profile.[5] In addition, the timing of their arrival worked against Bretons' favor: they came to Paris when the need for artisans was not expanding but rather when large-scale centralizing industry grew, in need of an army of proletarian laborers. And they were a relatively small contingent at first, one without a critical mass of established contacts to protect and promote itself.[6]

"The pariahs of Paris" was a phrase coined in 1898 by a cleric to describe Breton workers in Paris who did the jobs that no one else wanted: "he is yoked to the most unpleasant labors, sometimes even the most deleterious," said Father Rivalin to a gathering of worker associations in Brittany. It was those who wanted to protect Bretons who articulated this status of pariah.[7] Employers saw this as well, hiring them as unskilled laborers in the belief that Bretons were more rustic and less prepared than earlier provincials for the new tasks presented by city jobs.[8] Men of science—sociologists and physicians—would weigh in on the disabilities of Bretons faced with urban life, as we will see. Finally, the literati would denigrate Bretons in a way that emphasized one fact setting them apart from other newcomers: the majority of Bretons in Paris were women.

Because young women were a majority of those who went to the city of Paris, this chapter opens with the profile of a domestic servant who would become a caricature of Bretons in Paris. Yet contemporary studies gave scant attention to women or gender. I turn to the most credible source for studies of Bretons in the 1890s from the budding field of social science, Jean Lemoine.[9] His observations published in 1892 of Bretons throughout the Paris basin—systematic yet embedded in the notions of his time—take us to the industrial suburb of Saint-Denis, and then into the city and its Fourteenth Arrondissement. For both locations I compare Lemoine's observations with the marriage records of Bretons to sketch an intimate, although necessarily partial, portrait of this first important wave of Bretons in Paris.[10] This chapter therefore offers views of Bretons before 1900 as well as an understanding of the reality of family, friendship, and working life for these newcomers. It sheds light on what migration scholars see as migration systems and networks of contact. Finally, it provides a dual perspective, juxtaposing published perceptions of Bretons as the mass migrations to Paris began with the realities of their lives in the Paris basin.

DOMESTIC SERVANTS

Yvonne Yven was in good company—or at least extensive company, because country girls had been coming to work in the cities for centuries. The households of medieval and Renaissance Italy, for example, clearly included young servants.[11] Women particularly came to the city to work as domestics in the early modern period, and the scholarship of the last thirty years has deepened our understanding of the importance of the domestic servant in early modern and modern Europe.[12] With the expansion of the middle classes at the end of the nineteenth century, a domestic servant became a figure even more crucial to the workings of the urban family.[13] When Guy de Maupassant depicted the hardship caused by the loss of the family's maid of all work in his short story "The Necklace" (1884), he drew a sharp portrait of the family of a clerk, whose status depended on having a domestic to do the rough work.[14] The central irony of this situation rests in the contrast between the growing middle class—modern in that it was regular in its work hours, was salaried, and consciously limited its fertility—and its dependence on servants who had no contract, no regular work hours, and virtually no right to privacy, as abundant testimony reveals.[15] Servants did not even own their own name: many, like Yvonne Yven, were asked to shed their name for one that the employer preferred.[16] Domestics' rights depended almost exclusively on the inclinations of their employers.[17]

Nonetheless, domestic service was an attractive option for the newcomer in the city, and a huge serving class labored in Paris by the end of the nineteenth century, filled by crowds of willing newcomers.[18] Once a job for men and women, domestic service became more feminized as it increasingly called for a cook and a ladies' maid, or even a sole *bonne à tout faire*—a maid for all the household tasks—rather than a staff that included valets, chambermaids, cooks, coachmen, and scullery maids. This expansion and reconfiguration of household employment meant that four of five domestics would be women at the beginning of the twentieth century.[19]

And servants' quarters became a recognizable site in Paris, especially after Haussmannization established the "sixth floor" in new buildings and housing regulations in 1884 allowed some buildings to add another floor. With a corridor of single, unheated rooms under the eaves, lit solely by a ceiling window, glacial in winter and stifling in summer, the sixth floor often housed servants. The rooms were often unlocked and did not promise privacy, and there was no guarantee that servants had their own room at all—some slept in the kitchen or in a closet or cabinet. Nonetheless, the sixth-floor rooms quickly came to have a vivid place in the image of Parisian life for the domestic servant. They offered such poor conditions that the legislature discussed "la question du sixième," and moralists regarded them as sites of vice and promiscuity.[20]

Enter the Bretonne, part of the newest stream of newcomers from the countryside, prized for her docility, simplicity, and in some cases her religious faith. She needed not only work but also a place to live and the apparent protection of a middle-class family. By every account, service in the city was preferred to the rural alternative that many young women like Yvonne had experienced, with the outdoor work, filth, and muck of barnyard labor, to say nothing of the special humiliation of being at the bottom of a hierarchy in which everyone knew one's lowly status. As the city of Paris expanded from 1,991,000 to 2,700,000 people in the last twenty-five years of the century, Bretons came to the city, and the Breton women among them made up the freshest wave of new female domestics. They would be the last group of French women to enter this occupation in large numbers. After the Second World War domestic service passed to international immigrants, particularly Spanish, Italian, and Portuguese women. As French women entered more exalted positions in the labor force after the 1960s, they would increasingly hire domestic servants and cleaning women, like their counterparts in North America and throughout Western Europe. By the twenty-first century, domestic service would regain an important place for the middle classes and immigrants alike.[21]

Émile Zola spotted the Breton domestic and placed her at the bottom of the hierarchy in his novel *Pot Bouille*, published in 1882—the year of

Yvonne Yven's arrival in Paris. Although this nasty portrait of servants and five bourgeois families on a quiet street in the Second Arrondissement is hardly one of Zola's masterpieces, it reverberated in the Parisian understanding of master-servant relations for years to come, and painted an indelible portrait of the Breton maid Adèle, "fresh from Brittany, dull of wit and lousy."[22] The reader is introduced to Adèle when she throws rabbit guts out the window, to the disgust of all the other cooks whose kitchens share the rear courtyard. Abused by other servants and starved by her employers, she is also eyed and pinched by visitors as she serves the dinner; one nearsighted ladies' man "thought she looked pretty with her heavy Breton features and her hair the color of dirty hemp."[23] Although he calls her a "filth-bag" to a confidante, both he and a married man in the building visit Adèle's room in the night. Adèle's response to the resultant pregnancy set the standard for portraits of Breton women ignorant of sexuality: "She became besotted by fear. Within her dullard brain surged up all the crude fancies of her native village. She believed herself lost, that the gendarmes would come and carry her off if she confessed that she were pregnant."[24] Hardly knowing what she is doing, Adèle gives an agonized birth in solitude one freezing December night in her sixth-floor room. She wraps the breathing infant in old cloth and newspaper and then deposits her in a nearby passageway in the cold dawn.[25]

The bretonne Adèle's lack of hygiene, ignorance, and country ways are visible to her employers and fellow servants, but not her suffering. In Zola's novel she stands in for the person with the least protection in bourgeois Paris. Yet in portraying the cruel, hypocritical, and miserly ways of the bourgeoisie, Zola also felt free to make a point of this character's Breton origins and to draw a detailed portrait of her lack of hygiene, education, beauty, wisdom, and character, a portrait as vicious as the one he drew of her employers. The image of the Breton servant would proliferate and grow in importance in the twentieth century. Even before then, men of science—both social and medical—would take a close look at Bretons who left home for the Paris basin.

SOCIAL SCIENCE AND BRETON EMIGRANTS

By the 1890s Breton migration had attracted the attention of Jean Lemoine, who wrote in the new field of sociology and published in *La science sociale* in 1892.[26] Lemoine lays claim to a systematic investigation of Breton emigrants in the tradition of Frédéric Le Play, and has been taken at his word, understood as a careful observer by today's historians of Paris and Saint-Denis.[27] Lemoine wrote as a Breton who could gain the confidence of his interviewees. One of the many Paris dwellers who vacationed in Brittany, he saw country people boarding the train not as travelers but as emigrants headed for the factories of Paris, the market gardens of the Île-de-France, and the great farms of the fertile Beauce that lies between Brittany and Paris. The emigration phenomenon cries out for analysis, he wrote, because although Bretons had departed for centuries, into France and then to Canada, Brittany was currently "a site of intense emigration."[28]

Lemoine reported a collective migration, one that might be discussed today in terms of local practices, chain migration, or migration streams. Although the agricultural laborers on large farms are not the center of this story, they belong to the Bretons around Paris, and Lemoine saw their intense grouping—always together and ready to hurry home at the end of the season. "They're not Frenchmen," Lemoine reported, quoting those who saw them; when a Breton recalled to another French worker, "The first time I came to France . . . ," the other replied, "You're not French?," and the answer came: "Oh no . . . I'm Breton."[29] Likewise, he saw the migration to Saint-Denis as a collective one, carried out in groups by people who had barely left home before and who in many cases went to the same destinations as their compatriots: "Ask 100 Bretons in Saint-Denis, and 70 will tell you they are from [the inland bretonnant commune of] Plougonver."[30] Perhaps laborers were hired one by one, but communications among them reflect lively networks. "When we have a vacancy in the factory" a director told Lemoine, "we are always sure that one of our Bretons will have three or four compatriots to recommend."[31] He used the example of one former factory worker from the inland bretonnant commune of Bourbriac in the Côtes-d'Armor who brought his seven sisters and brothers to Saint-Denis, and after seventeen years had nineteen family members there, including children. These observations of strategic collective behavior, networks among migrants, interdependence, and a desire to return home echo in studies of emigrants to this day.

But for Lemoine these communal-minded habits reflected fundamental flaws in the Breton people rooted in disabling collective social norms. Bretons, he contended, counted on each other in times of need and were incapable of taking the initiative as individuals. Studying several groups of emigrants, he saw each as marked to a greater or lesser degree by a lack of initiative.[32] As he described Bretons' fatalist and communal-minded habits, he based many of his observations on a longstanding and widely used source, Émile Souvestre's *Derniers bretons*, first published nearly sixty years earlier, in 1835.[33] If remaining among one's own was a symptom of weakness, so was assimilation: "The Breton, once out of his primitive milieu, has an extraordinary tendency to lose himself in the new milieu in which he finds himself." Bretons take on the habits of those around them—they speak inexpert French, but insist on speaking it all the same. One explained his absence from the Breton Easter service by saying, "Oh, me—I'm going with the French"—especially important, according to Lemoine, given Breton attachment to their religious practices. The transformation that began with parents was completed with children: Lemoine reported that several children born in Saint-Denis of Breton parents had nothing Breton about them, could not speak Breton, resembled all the other children, and looked at new arrivals with the same astonishment and curiosity that they displayed when they looked at foreigners. Lemoine observed that even though the Bretons who came to Saint-Denis were uneducated, unambitious, and even insular, they had nonetheless come to a melting pot.[34] Understanding them to be fundamentally weak, he managed to be as critical of Bretons' assimilation as of their insularity.

Lemoine called for more individualism, prescribing an English counter-scenario for the young woman of Brittany who became a domestic servant. He claimed that a single institution called women to leave for Paris: the Soeurs de la Croix, who placed young women, half of them Bretons, as domestics.[35] Why domestic service? Rather than seek an explanation based in the structure of the Parisian job market, Lemoine attributed this practice to the extremely patriarchal nature of Breton society, which bred a need for protection and patronage once a woman was away from home. Breton women were so dependent, Lemoine stated, that they let friends and relatives influence their choice of Paris—indeed he knew one woman who had brought her five sisters to Paris, one after the other. And so dependent were these women that they imagined they only needed to present themselves to the Soeurs de la Croix to be taken care of. Here Lemoine drew a long contrast between the Bretonne and his imagined independent and ambitious "jeune *girl* anglaise," a young woman with a proper upbringing who would scan newspaper ads, write letters to obtain information, save money before her departure, and take any job in the short term while living in a rented room and looking for a better job and a fiancé, so that she could eventually own a shop and a home.[36] Not so the young Bretons. According to the Soeurs de la Croix at their headquarters on the rue Vaugirard, Breton women suffered terribly from homesickness, and as Lemoine learned in Saint-Denis, they remained under the influence of their family. According to Lemoine, the remedy was for the Breton to be less collectivist and more individualistic. Like the English girl, the young Bretonne should leave home, save for herself, marry wisely, and build a good future. Lemoine did not show an appreciation of the networks that scholars have come to see as a support for newcomers, nor did he understand the Parisian job market or the constraints facing women like Yvonne Yven, who nonetheless was able to marry wisely.

Lemoine judged the railroad workers who left Brittany for greater Paris—*hommes d'équipe* and *manoeuvres*—as being a cut above those who went to Saint-Denis and nearly as numerous. Although railroad workers, like them, performed manual labor, they had a stable job. For Lemoine this made all the difference, because he considered the Breton emigrant perfectly capable of saving but unable to prepare for unforeseen problems. The railroad worker, unlike the others, usually had military service and some education behind him, as well as some resources to save him from the vagaries of misfortune. When he married, the railroad worker's prestige as a state employee allowed him to attract a woman with a dowry. "You have to have lived in a little Breton town to understand the prestige enjoyed by those employed by the government," he observed.[37] Lemoine cites the example of a Breton woman in Versailles, wife of a *cheminot*, threatening to break relations with a younger sister who had married a peasant. Lemoine's understanding of Breton women is threaded through his observations of men's professions. Wives of cheminots, he observed, had usually left home in "the ambitious and pretentious desire" to move toward Paris. The railroad worker himself had given up his desire to return home, and as for the children, they had been raised entirely "à la française," encouraged to go into administrative employment and indistinguishable from other children in greater Paris.[38] In the case of these scrupulous workers, Lemoine approved of integration and assimilation.

Factory workers in Saint-Denis came in for special attention because a migration stream was established between two or three cantons of the Côtes-d'Armor and the workers of Saint-Denis—many more than the 3,218 Bretons enumerated by the census of 1891, which included neither their children born nearby nor passing workers. Lemoine considered them more developed than the agricultural workers because they had the initiative to come to Paris on their own rather than in a team, then lodged together with compatriots and worked together. They did share their vice—drink: "To be Breton is to be a drunk, it's the same thing," Lemoine wrote, then recalling the unequivocal statement by the director of a large factory in Saint-Denis: "Our Bretons? Sober as camels during the week; on Sunday, as drunk as Poles!"[39] And the "esprit de retour that marked nearly all Breton migration was keenly felt here."[40] To illustrate, Lemoine recounted his interview with an exemplary forty-three-year-old Breton in Saint-Denis, victim of tuberculosis after sixteen years of factory work and alcohol abuse, who held on to his sole pleasure—the promise of return to Plougonver.[41]

Lemoine perceived a particular form to Breton marriages and households in Saint-Denis. Men went home to marry, and if they married in Saint-Denis almost always married a Bretonne, having come to the city alone at twenty-three or twenty-four years of age. Compatriots provided lodging because, once married, Bretons took in boarders while their wives did the housekeeping. Wives did not work outside the home in Saint-Denis, Lemoine contended, since the factories were "reputed to be dangerous," but they rather made the meals and took care of the children in a rented room or small apartment.

The picture was completed by a portrait of the elite emigrants of Brittany, the exceptions who proved the rule that Bretons were neither farsighted nor sensible.[42] *Marchands de vins*, or café owners, were the first and most important case, since Lemoine observed that they were found in every Breton community large or small, be it in Saint-Denis or Versailles.[43] One did not find many café owners among Italians or Belgians: owning a café was truly a Breton specialty, he claimed. They had certain characteristics: never new arrivals, they were like the Breton in Saint-Denis, who had arrived seventeen years earlier and then gathered kin there. Lemoine believed that the collectivist Breton identity allowed café owners to succeed: their compatriots were both a source of capital, which they were more than willing to lend, and a ready-made clientele. The café owner played host to everyone; he organized dances on Saturday night, often served as a witness to weddings, cultivated friendships, and encouraged his customers' fondness for the bottle. It was especially young people, newcomers, whom the café owner attracted, and Lemoine concluded that the café owner was the patriarch of emigration, his business relying on continued contacts with other Bretons. He sent for relatives and friends to work in his business for low salaries and was a friend to all. In the language of the migration scholar, the marchand de vin was a node joining networks of newcomers and longtime residents.

Lemoine's valuable observations alert historians to the role of the café owner as a wedding witness, and more generally to the shape of the Breton community in Saint-Denis.[44] He allows the reader, from the distance of over a century, to see how emigrant Bretons were employed and how they were perceived by employing the observations of budding social science, pointedly imbued with the values of his age. These are explicitly secular values—he does not see Bretons' high fertility as part of faithful religiosity, for example, but rather as part of a trust that the community would care for children, and attributes emigration to the worldly causes of the railroad and army service, as did secular observers in the next century.[45]

The finest recent historical study of Saint-Denis around 1890 corroborates Lemoine's findings with the use of sources such as electoral lists and censuses.[46] Jean-Paul Brunet first analyzed the problems of socialism and communism, then the integration of newcomers like the Bretons at the end of the nineteenth century, using the sources and methods of social historians of the 1970s and 1980s, as well as Lemoine's work. Brunet found that 61 percent of the Breton electors worked as day laborers, with only 11 percent in metallurgy, which was so important to Saint-Denis industry, and 19 percent in various other branches of production. Brunet carefully traced the dwellings of the electors, placing them in certain neighborhoods and in scattered rented rooms. He also confirmed their rural origins, writing that certain small villages and little towns had been "bled white" by departures over a twenty-year period.[47] Indeed, the Bretons of Saint-Denis offer a specific profile.

SAINT-DENIS AND ITS BRETONS

Saint-Denis is a banlieue of Paris that reaches north from the city borders in the shape of a tree. The long trunk of the tree is an industrial district crossed with railroad yards, the top an ancient city which became an industrial center. Saint-Denis was a mix of the very old and the industrial, of massive capital investment and poverty, of open fields and environmental degradation. Heavy industry came to the town over the course of the nineteenth century. The area flooded with newcomers, especially workers, from the Île-de-France, from the north, and in the 1880s from Brittany, as well as from Belgium and Italy. More were to come from farther afield by the beginning of the twentieth century.

The plain of Saint-Denis stretched from the city limits of Paris to the historic city center. Industry began on the plain with a perfumery and producer of beauty products founded in 1827. The plain of Saint-Denis had an iron-bound future: a natural entrepôt and market location, it could receive coal and iron from the north and northeast by rail and materials from the sea via Le Havre and the Seine by ship to the canal Saint-Denis. The railroad came in 1873 with the creation of a passenger station and then a large freight station constructed between 1874 and 1878. The Société du Chemin de Fer Industriel de la Plaine Saint-Denis et d'Aubervilliers started with three lines in 1884 and was operating with twenty branch lines by 1890. Of the six freight stations supplying Paris, the one on the plain of Saint-Denis would be the largest. Connections to Paris were made by more rails: trains and tramways ran every quarter-hour from Paris to Saint-Denis beginning in 1888.[48]

Industries proliferated—many of them noxious chemical and fertilizer producers. In 1847 the Combes and Company Tannery opened, treating lamb- and goatskins. The family firm Coignet on the west side of Saint-Denis began producing glue and fertilizer in the early 1850s. Seven chemical factories opened that served the dye industry after 1860. François Dorvault, who bought the Pharmacie Centrale de France at the end of the 1860s, is the one who named Saint-Denis "the French Manchester," a label that stuck.[49] The vocation of Saint-Denis is clear from the *Enquête Industrielle* of 1872, in which large industries were simply categorized rather than listed individually. The largest industries, it reported, produced materials for rail production and steam engines. The second-largest employers produced a range of goods, from gloves, shoes, horsehair products, and mirrors to pianos. Next were the makers of candles, soap, perfume, chemical products, pharmaceutical products, and dyes. All in all large industry employed nearly 5,500 men, 900 women, and 400 child apprentices. Small producers of machine tools and dyes, laundries, and fabric processing facilities together employed several hundred workers. Only laundries fared badly, because as the report explained, they depended on the city's water, which was being soiled by industry.[50]

Metallurgy was king: six metallurgy companies were founded in the

1860s and more in the 1870s. The jeweler Charles Christofle opened an annex for manufacturing nickel in Saint-Denis in 1875 and then adopted a technique for plating with silver or gold. A whole new class wanted silverplate; this was a great success because after 1880 it sold not only to individual clients but to trains, restaurants, hotels, spas, and casinos. Christofle thrived. Luxury industries had their niche as well: Dyonisians (as the residents of Saint-Denis call themselves) produced not only perfume, beauty products, and silverplate but also pianos. In 1897 the Austrian Ignace Pleyel, composer and music publisher, founded the Pleyel piano firm, which later turned out organs and harmoniums as well. Metallurgical plants took in nickel, copper, brass, and iron, making steam generators, wire, iron grills, metal bridges, rolling stock—every kind of domestic and industrial metal product. In the 1880s the gas industry developed, a new sector of production, processing the natural gas that furnished light for Paris. By the end of the century huge gas storage tanks were sited in Saint-Denis, where the Paris electric company located in 1903; all the plants were fueled by coal brought in by boat and by railroad. Thus Saint-Denis became the largest supplier of electricity and gas to Paris and the suburbs, and local historians claim that its plain became the premier industrial zone of continental Europe.[51]

The most industrial suburb of the Paris basin, Saint-Denis was a "glutton for unskilled labor."[52] In 1891 over 55 percent of people working in Saint-Denis were industrial workers. And this was big industry—in 1900 86 percent of factory workers toiled in firms with over one hundred other people. At this time one of the large metalworking firms employed over a thousand people, and metalworkers were the largest group of industrial workers; one of the large glassworks employed eight hundred workers, Christofle about eight hundred, and Pleyel six hundred. The original beauty products company employed three hundred workers year-round; one wire and grill company employed eight hundred men and women, a dye company up to thirteen hundred, and one tannery about a thousand workers in 1900, of whom two hundred were women.[53] By 1902 Saint-Denis and the plain counted eighteen metallurgy factories, thirty-one chemical factories, and thirty-six manufacturers of paper, textiles, glass, and food.[54] Most jobs were for men; nonetheless, women did find factory employment, especially in the perfume and clothing industries. Unlike in Paris and wealthy suburbs such as Neuilly, more men than women lived in Saint-Denis.[55] This was the most populous suburb of Paris, with

51,000 people in 1891 and 60,000 in 1901. Nonetheless, there were crops of all kinds, vegetables and market gardens, because a fifth of the area was still under cultivation.[56]

Long before its industry developed, Saint-Denis was known for its distinguished history as the most ancient city in the Île-de-France, along with Paris. A second-century Gallo-Roman village, Saint-Denis thrived as a medieval market center. It became the burial place of the martyred first bishop of Paris, for whom it was named, and thereafter an important site of worship. Its extraordinary twelfth-century Gothic basilica houses the tombs of French royalty, including the elaborate tomb of Anne of Brittany and that of Louis XII. For its tombs and architecture, the basilica has long attracted visitors and continues to do so today.[57]

Saint-Denis is also known for its political history. A proletarian commune, it would become socialist and then communist during the twentieth century, a light to what many believed would be the future.[58] Its politics grew out of brutal working conditions and years of conflict well documented by historians including Brunet and Michelle Perrot. These conditions gave rise to anger, like that of the Breton Pierre Meubry, chauffeur for a chemical company, who put three bullets into his foreman after his salary was cut in 1885.[59] Workplaces in the banlieue were known for their distance from Paris and hard working conditions. "It's like Cayenne," wrote the militant smithies in Paris in 1903, using the word *bagne*, a slang term for a French penal colony.[60] Michelle Perrot is succinct: already in the 1880s, banlieues like Saint-Denis represented the "failure of urban history, and already terrifying the bourgeois."[61]

Saint-Denis was also known for its misery—for the wretched poverty and unsanitary housing endured by its inhabitants. In 1885 one journalist called it "the city of starving rats, scabrous factories, streets with greasy paving stones, dirty houses, of the muddy canal, its banks fouled by rotting carrion."[62] Two years later an inquiry on housing described this "anti-impressionist landscape" with equal distaste, and like many others emphasized the stench, quoting a worker who moaned about the ammonia that "seizes your eyes" when the odor would rise.[63] The stifling odor came not only from the factory but from the notorious housing. Lemoine was looking at worker housing, he recalled, when he was stopped by a woman who threw herself in front of the concierge to prevent his seeing her place, because she had mistaken him for the management and was lodging seven men in a room intended for three. One household that he did visit was a family of four lodged in one room. The son and daughter occupied one bed, the parents another; the wife had been bedridden with tuberculosis for two months.[64]

The "Breton colonies" cited by Brunet were crowded indeed: the census of 1891 lists twenty-two households in the building at 10, rue de la Charronnerie. These included several people who lived alone—masons, day laborers, a dressmaker—but also households like the Breton family Le Cloarec, which included the day laborer head, his wife, and four children aged five to fifteen. Of the twenty-two heads of household, sixteen worked as day laborers. Closer to the canal, the building at 10, rue des Poissonniers housed sixty households, the majority headed by day laborers, many of whom were Bretons. One household gathered five single men with Breton names ranging in age from seventeen to forty-nine and another five men from twenty-three to fifty-two, but there were also a few solitaries and many couples. For example, the day laborer Robic and his wife, who was a cook, lived with their two babies, while the household of a shoemaker and his wife outnumbered all the rest with seven children aged six to twenty-five. Some households listed a lodger as a "friend." Thus the dwelling at the rue des Poissonniers held every kind of household—single people, widows and widowers, male workers living together, young and mature families with and without boarders, and blended families like that of the hat maker, whose three eldest children bore the surname of his wife, now forty-six, while the younger children, two, four, and nine, bore his own.[65]

Where exactly did the Bretons of Saint-Denis come from, and when? By all accounts the mass migration of Bretons to the Paris basin began only in the 1880s, and the dozen Bretons who married in Saint-Denis in 1875 were hardly typical of the mass migration that would come later.[66] The men were skilled laborers for the most part, and came from other départements than the Côtes-d'Armor. They were coppersmiths, ironworkers, shoemakers, and blacksmiths. A widowed tinsmith from the town of Lorient in the Morbihan married the mother of his two children, ages five and three, herself a worker in the pearl industry; four metalworkers served as witnesses. A smith from the Ille-et-Vilaine married a dressmaker from Paris, and his two brothers—also ironworkers—stood up for him. The son of a shoemaker in Nantes, and himself a shoemaker, married the mother of their three young children who was herself a day laborer. Of the three women from the Côtes-d'Armor, one was a perfume worker, daughter of a single mother, who married a fellow perfume worker from the west the year after she had been widowed; two Breton friends from the nearby suburb of Pantin stood up for the bride. Another was a cook in Saint-Denis who married a coppersmith also from the Côtes-d'Armor; her brother-in-law, who lived in the same building as the groom, stood up for her. Marriages of compatriots like these would become very common by 1890 as the Breton community expanded.

BRETONS MARRY IN SAINT-DENIS

According to Lemoine, the Breton household in Saint-Denis was formed by a laborer who arrived in the banlieue as a single man, then found one compatriot to marry and another, a café owner, to witness the wedding.[67] The marriages of Bretons in Saint-Denis during 1890 support some of Lemoine's observations about Breton endogamous marriages, but they offer a more nuanced view of the Breton community because marriage records have a rich tale to tell. Marriage acts are valuable, because unlike conscription and electoral lists they bring women and families to center stage as brides and mothers.[68] We know that Saint-Denis was a predominantly male place, with many jobs for men, and marriage records complement this understanding with a portrait of both men and women in the Paris basin. They identify the bride and groom by place and date of birth, occupation, and residence, as well as lineage—age, occupation, and location of parents, if living. In a list of four witnesses, they identify friends, neighbors, and often relatives by occupation, age, and address. In short, marriage records locate the bride and groom in the spaces of greater Paris and in its economic and social hierarchy, enabling us to link one generation to the other. As a consequence, marriage records allow a glimpse of the degree to which migration is a break from the past, a break with the family, and a break with family occupations.[69]

The wedding experience of provincials provides a contrast with that of Parisians, and Bretons offer a special case. Maurice Garden's revelatory analysis of a thousand marriages in and around Paris in 1885, including in Saint-Denis, discerns this general pattern, yielding a context for the Breton marriages in Saint-Denis five years later.[70] Parisian weddings usually joined two young people under the age of twenty-five who both lived at home with their parents, and whose parents and family were in attendance; those of provincials joined two people several years older who lived far from home and whose parents had in many cases long since passed away. The majority of marriage partners came from the provinces and, Garden wrote, nothing proved cultural mixing more than the lack of marriages among compatriots, since fewer than one marriage in five joined people from the same département. Most grooms were older than their brides, and brides who were born in the provinces were older than Parisiennes. Finally Garden, like Lemoine before him, found that café owners served as witnesses in nearly one-fifth of the marriages. He imagined the worker wedding, normally late on Saturday morning, to be followed with a drink at the establishment of the café owner, who was not only witness but friend and neighbor. Over one-eighth of these weddings in 1885 included the legitimization of a child, usually a baby born in the preceding year or two.[71]

Breton marriages hold a distinct place: Breton brides were not only older on average by five years than Parisians, but also older than brides from any other province, marrying at about the age of twenty-eight. While 80 percent of Parisian women married before their twenty-fifth birthday, only 41 percent of Bretonnes did so.[72] Yvonne Yven, whose story opened this chapter, married at thirty-one. In addition, Breton women were much more likely than Breton men to marry in greater Paris. Although marriages generally demonstrate that Paris was a melting pot, Garden found that some Bretons offered pockets of resistance to marriage with partners from other départements—those from the Côtes-d'Armor. Fewer than a fifth of the marriages were between provincials from the same département, but among those from the Côtes-d'Armor, it was over half.

Breton weddings in Saint-Denis were on the increase in the 1880s. Father Gautier counted twenty-seven Breton marriages in the parish of Saint-Denis-de-l'Estrée by 1884, recognizing Breton names: "des Le Gal, des Le Guilloux, des Le Goff, des Le Dantec, des Lecorre, etc., et puis des Yves-Marie, des Pierre-Marie, des Marie-Anne, des Marie-Jeanne, des Marie-Yvonne."[73] Nearly fifty couples from Brittany married in Saint-Denis in the year 1890; wedding parties gathered in the imposing new city hall that dated from 1883. In comparison to all couples, and even all Breton couples in the survey taken in 1885, the Breton wedding partners of Saint-Denis in 1890 constitute a distinct group that in many ways conforms to Lemoine's impression. They were very likely to marry one another: the vast majority (two-thirds) of brides and grooms from Brittany married another Breton; likewise, two-thirds of the Bretons were from the département of the Côtes-d'Armor, which at that time furnished the most Bretons to the Paris basin.[74] Moreover, these were precisely the ones who married a fellow Breton; it was Bretons from the départements of French-speaking upper Brittany who married people from elsewhere in France (see Appendix, table 1).

Second, in this male banlieue men constituted the majority of Breton wedding partners. Moreover, as the cases below demonstrate, many of the Breton women who married in Saint-Denis made their living elsewhere in greater Paris. Neither men nor women demonstrate much education: only about two-thirds of the Breton brides and three-quarters of the Breton grooms could sign their names to the marriage act.

Finally, these brides were much younger than most Breton brides by a good five years, marrying on average at about twenty-three. And about a third of them resided with at least one parent who had also come to Saint-Denis, validating views like those of Lemoine that newcomers from Brittany tended to settle in Saint-Denis en masse.[75] In 1890 unmarried cohabitating Breton couples seemed relatively rare, since they were unlikely to live with their partner before marriage. Consensual unions in Paris, which I will discuss below, were much more common but produced few babies before marriage.[76] Breton marriage partners in Saint-Denis were therefore insular, usually marrying other Bretons. This proletarian group was minimally educated, but nonetheless resistant to the Parisian practice of consensual unions.

Witnesses to the weddings conducted in 1890 traced ties of friendship within and outside the community of Bretons. Family was often present in the Paris basin and in attendance at the ceremony—relatives counted for almost 60 percent of the identifiable witnesses in Saint-Denis, most often brothers, cousins, or uncles; neighbors counted for over 40 percent. Relatives in many cases lived very nearby or in the same building. The café owners indeed acted as friends to these Breton migrants, much more than to the average bride and groom in the citywide survey of marriages in 1885, serving as witnesses in eighteen of the forty-nine weddings of that year and sometimes serving in more than one wedding.[77] The stories of emblematic couples demonstrate common patterns of sociability, work, and migration trajectories.

Marie Guillou and François Bernard were a couple from two inland villages of the French-speaking area of the Côtes-d'Armor, and when they married each had a brother who served as a witness.[78] Other witnesses were a friend (another worker in the same building as François) and Yves Barre, the café owner who was a witness to no fewer than three Breton weddings in 1890. The groom worked as a laborer in Saint-Denis, like his father and his brother; his mother had stayed at home in the Côtes-d'Armor but had sent her consent to the marriage, as the law required. François's father and brother lived together nearby. This marriage reveals connections among Bretons across the Paris basin, since the groom, his brother, his father, and the bride's brother, Alexandre, lived close together in Saint-Denis; the bride, however, lived in a more prosperous neighborhood north of the Opéra in central Paris, where she worked as a domestic servant. The couple may have met because the two brothers were friends or workmates; they probably lived in Saint-Denis after the marriage but not necessarily—after all, Yvonne Yven, kept on as a domestic after her marriage, did not live with her husband for years.[79]

Other marriage records confirm that the Breton community, even that of unskilled laborers, stretched across Paris. Two laborer grooms twenty-six years of age, Yves Martin and Jacques Le Pierre, came from villages near one another in Brittany and lived in the same building. Both were sons of laborers. In the winter of 1890 they married Marguerite Parlouez and Marie-Louise Le Goaët, brides from two villages near their own. All four were born in Breton-speaking communes.[80] The two young women worked as nurses, not in Saint-Denis but rather in the huge psychiatric hospital called Vaucluse, south of the city near today's Orly airport and very far from Saint-Denis; Vaucluse was built on the grounds of an estate and had opened in 1869 for a thousand patients. Nursing in such French hospitals did not require prolonged education; on the contrary, it was an occupation close to that of hospital aide, one that offered steady employment along with housing and a modest salary and attracted many women from Brittany.[81] The key location for the two weddings between laborers and nurses from the Côtes-d'Armor was a building in Saint-Denis, where both grooms and their brothers resided. Witnesses lived close by, except for one cousin who worked in Paris as a concierge. The men were tied to Saint-Denis, but the brides found their work elsewhere. Their courtships could have begun at home or at Sunday outings. In any case, we cannot assume that marriage allowed the couples to live together, for the women may have continued their jobs at least until the birth of their first child.

Breton grooms mirror the Breton electors in Saint-Denis.[82] Over two-thirds of the grooms were unskilled laborers, *journaliers*. Also young, they came from the same towns and villages. Correspondingly, the com-

mune that sent the most electors to Saint-Denis also sent the most marriage partners: Plougonver, an inland commune in the Côtes-d'Armor
that was home to 2,500 people in 1891. When Lemoine wrote in 1892 that
70 percent of the Breton men in Saint-Denis were from Plougonver he
was exaggerating, but not by much.[83] This little town was the centerpiece
for the pair of weddings described above, joining a groom from the town
with people from three nearby villages; likewise, the wedding of François
and Marie described above joined people from the same canton.

Participants in many of the weddings in 1890 match the portrait of
Bretons in Saint-Denis: they were from the part of the Côtes-d'Armor in
lower Brittany, of low status, and lived in poverty. For example, prac-
tically no one was able to sign the document at the wedding of Marie
Yvonne Barenton and Auguste Le Gros,[84] day laborers on a Breton street
in Saint-Denis. Their wedding was witnessed by four friends, all of whom
lived nearby and were day laborers. Of the entire party of six, bride and
groom included, only two were literate, and they were witnesses.

To end a description of Bretons in Saint-Denis with such couples
would be to make a caricature of this community. As homogeneous as it
was, it also included others with more skills and more resources. As
Brunet wrote, emigrants from the Morbihan and Finistère had a different
profile and were more likely to be from towns.[85] For example, Jacques
Garel from Pontivy, an administrative center in the Morbihan, a café
owner and son of a property owner, married Anne Le Joly in the spring of
1890.[86] Anne was the daughter of fish sellers, born and raised in Saint-
Denis. The witnesses were two bakers, another café owner, and a skilled
laborer. Everyone could sign the document.

The burgeoning community of Bretons in Saint-Denis thus belongs to
a quite homogeneous commune in that most industrial of banlieues.
However, not all Bretons were alike, and those from the upper Breton
départements of the Ille-et-Vilaine and Loire-Atlantique tended to have
better jobs and more comfortable lives. As late as 1995 Brunet executed a
stereotypical portrait of Bretons in Saint-Denis, drawing from Lemoine:
"Unlike other immigrant groups, who seem to melt into what one could
call the 'Dionysian melting pot' without losing their personality or their
native strength, the Breton in Saint-Denis seemed uprooted, bruised by
life, tossed at the mercy of circumstance."[87] A grim and damning portrait
indeed, but one that reminds us that integration and community do not
necessarily produce stability or prosperity.[88]

The Paris basin offered other destinations as well that also had the reputation as a destination for Breton newcomers, and so I now turn to the city itself and to an area profoundly distinct from Saint-Denis: the Fourteenth Arrondissement, which borders the railroad station where Bretons debarked upon their arrival in Paris.

FOURTEENTH ARRONDISSEMENT AND ITS BRETONS

The Fourteenth Arrondissement covers a hilly plain that stretches south from central Paris, created from a slice of southern Paris and rural communes between the Boulevard Montparnasse and the fortifications surrounding Paris until after the Great War. A premier result of the will of Napoleon III and the urbanism of the Baron Haussmann, it shows all the signs of Second Empire city planning. But the Fourteenth also possesses an older history, a history of agriculture, of important institutions, and of rural communes that shaped it well into the twentieth century.

From the beginning of the seventeenth century, religious institutions were founded outside the city in what would become the Fourteenth Arrondissement. The Capucins seated their novitiate in the middle of a spacious agricultural domain early in the seventeenth century, part of which would become a hospital for victims of venereal disease. Another hospital, founded by the Prêtres de l'Oratoire, opened in the next year, followed at mid-century by a hospital called the Santé for victims of the plague, renamed Saint Anne after its founder Anne of Austria. It would also serve the insane who were well enough to work the earth. The sisters of Port-Royal founded a house which would be condemned as Jansenist by Louis XIV and serve a number of functions before it was transformed into la Maternité in 1796; it would function as a maternity hospital to the present day. Subsequently a magnificent building was constructed from which the arrondissement would take its official name: the Observatory. And a few years before the Revolution, the Abbé Cochin built a hospital for the poor; Cochin was particularly interested in the quarry workers who were subject to so many accidents, an especially grave problem because all these institutions were built from stones dug out of underground quarries in the area—quarries which left dangerous subterranean voids that occasionally collapsed.[89] Some underground quarries were filled upon implementation of the great Parisian health measure of the end of the old regime: the emptying of the cemeteries and the creation of the catacombs, where lie the bones of generations of Parisians. The final old regime structure that shaped the Fourteenth was the Farmers-General Wall of 1787. Although it had no military value, this wall promoted development just inside its parameters, which ran south of and parallel to the boulevard Montparnasse; in the opinion of the historian René Cottard, this development marked the beginning of neighborhood life.[90]

With the Revolution came the founding of the communes of Vaugirard and Montrouge and the repression of religious institutions that became hospitals and asylums, although nursing religious orders remained to care for the sick, the pregnant, and foundlings.[91] A firm foundation had been laid for hospitals and other institutions in what would become the Fourteenth Arrondissement. This complex space would be cut off from the south by the massive fortifications built to encircle Paris in the 1840s. These were ten meters high, and stretched to an enormous vacant area two hundred meters across, effectively creating a formidable divide between the city and suburbs to the south. The barrier of the fortifications meant that when Paris was enlarged it would extend from the Farmers-General Wall out to the fortifications, and indeed this is exactly what occurred in 1860.

The new Fourteenth Arrondissement founded in 1860 was home to some fifty thousand people, most of whom lived away from the fortifications and closer to the boulevards, which had long been part of Paris. These were rentiers, workers, and members of the petty bourgeoisie, along with horticulturalists, market gardeners, and millers. Like many parts of Paris, the Fourteenth became a construction site for new urban works during the Second Empire, works that would open wide new streets, plant trees on boulevards and avenues, and create a system of water and sewers. One of the great creations was the enormous green zone of the Parc Montsouris, nearly forty acres of plantings, lawns, ponds, and a great reservoir. Old buildings were renovated; a new and spacious Saint Anne asylum was finished in 1867, as was the prison on the site of Santé Hospital that would also bear the name Santé, and a new façade for the foundling hospital. New bourgeois apartment buildings distinguished the avenues and boulevards, and in neighborhoods like the Plaisance little houses appeared, many occupied by worker newcomers who helped to construct the Universal exposition of 1867 on the Champ de Mars.[92] They had arrived by the Chemin de Fer de l'Ouest (Western Railroad Line), which served Normandy and Brittany and whose rails bordered the arrondissement and ended at the Gare Montparnasse. Among those who debarked in 1868 was the engineer Fulgence Bienvenüe (thirteenth child of a notary in Uzel, a French-speaking village in the Côtes-d'Armor), the father of the Paris Métro. This arrondissement, in short, was one of the privileged fields of urban development during the Second Empire, and one where institutional life would clearly continue to be important. By 1870 seventy thousand people lived in the Fourteenth Arrondissement: in the Plaisance (40 percent), the central neighborhood called the Petit Montrouge (30 percent), Montparnasse, consisting of the neighborhoods along the most central boulevards (23 percent), and the neighborhood of La Santé, which reached out to the Parc Montsouris (7 percent).[93]

Like most peripheral areas of the city, the Fourteenth Arrondissement was a heterogeneous space that included residents of all kinds by the late nineteenth century. Professionals and members of the bourgeoisie lived on the boulevards, their servants and underlings in the same buildings (but up under the eaves), with shopkeepers and café owners doing business on the ground floor. The densely populated Plaisance near the busy Montparnasse railroad station and the railroad tracks housed thousands of workers. Beyond the boulevards of Petit Montrouge, apartment buildings gave way to villas and little houses, interspersed with farms and gardens. The fortifications and the so-called zone beyond provided sites on the periphery for marginal people. Contemporary observers and Atget's photographs show us caravans of gypsies, communities of rag pickers, and a host of shady and not so shady characters found throughout the city's periphery, including the famous delinquents labeled Apaches.[94] This was also an area for market gardeners, and as family photographs and postcards attest, it was a great site for Sunday outings, walks, and picnics.[95] Émile Zola wrote that these illustrated Parisians' "immoderate taste for the countryside" and had people reduced to "going several kilometers on foot to go see the countryside from the top of the fortifications."[96] Such walks out of Paris to the countryside at the end of the rue Vercingétorix be were part of the pleasant memories of the quartier.[97]

Leisure was hardly limited to the outskirts: there was also plenty to do in the densely populated urban zone of the Fourteenth Arrondissement. The celebration of the first Bastille Day holiday in 1880 included fireworks at the Observatoire and a huge street dance at the Impasse du Maine—celebrations that would become more widespread in the years before the Great War. Notably, the rue de la Gaîté near Montparnasse became famous for entertainment. The Montparnasse Theater opened in 1819, followed by other theaters and music halls like the popular Gaîté Montparnasse and eventually by casinos and cinemas, so the rue de la Gaîté deserved its reputation as a party street. This was also a quartier known for its prostitutes on both boulevards and sidestreets.[98] More closely bound to Parisian night life than Saint-Denis, the Fourteenth had a lot to offer.

Worker life developed especially in the Plaisance neighborhood, where the lodging trade developed, especially the trade in *garnis*: furnished rooms above a bar run by the proprietor, who was usually a café owner. To reach one's room or apartment one had to pass through the bar, with its attendant demands and temptations.[99] Industries expanded, bringing on new workers, many of whom were hired to work at the Gare Montparnasse or by the Compagnie de l'Ouest on the railroad. Some employers especially needed skilled workers, like the precision optics shop of Jules Charpentier that opened in 1878, the post office print shop, and the chocolatier Salavin, but the asphalt company that opened about 1880 and the workshops of the clothing manufacturer La Belle Jardinière hired men and women with less training.[100] Nonetheless, in contrast to Saint-Denis, for the most part this was not big industry. Indeed, in the *Enquête Industrielle* of 1872 the Plaisance neighborhood was declared to have no large industry whatsoever. The largest industries in the arrondissement were a water piping company in the Montparnasse quarter with 250 workers, a cotton mill employing 130 women and 25 men, the Sceaux railroad, which employed about 120 men, and the company that made clothing for the gendarmerie, employing about 120 men and women.[101] Machine industries, carpentry shops, and tanners employed 50 to 60 men, and the production of shoes, locks, hats, clothing, buttons, and carriages employed several hundred men and women in small workshops throughout the arrondissement.[102] The population of the Fourteenth Arrondissement dropped with the Franco-Prussian war and the Commune, but then came back to 92,000 by 1881.[103]

The Fourteenth has had the reputation of a home to Bretons, and the Montparnasse railroad station brought people directly from the countryside beginning in 1852 and connected with the westernmost city of Brest in 1865. Memorialists of the Fourteenth Arrondissement write that "if it were a province, the Fourteenth Arrondissement would wear sabots and a round hat. Just as Auvergnats took over the Bastille, Bretons conquered Montparnasse. For the same reasons that explorers first settled in their landing port before going any further, Bretons set down their suitcases near station where they got off the train. At the end of the iron umbilical cord which tied them to their home country."[104] This reputation is well deserved, for the Fourteenth Arrondissement, particularly around the Gare Montparnasse, has long been dotted with Breton cafés, hotels, crêperies, and other gathering places. Census and marriage records bear out a concentration of Bretons in Paris, but not exclusively in the Fourteenth. As Alain Faure has written, Paris has no real ghettos; its economy has been varied, vast, and strong enough to employ Bretons and other newcomers all over the city and in the banlieues.[105] By 1875 Bretons had begun to come to the Fourteenth, some as distinguished as the engineer Fulgence Bienvenüe, but others as workers, many of whom were women.

We see some of these Bretons—a mere thirty-four of them, twenty of them women—in marriage records in 1875.[106] What is most striking about these marriages is that in the majority of cases they joined a Breton bride with a groom who had been born somewhere else in France; these were marriages of women who were not going to return home. Most of the Bretonnes married men who had reasonably good jobs as housepainters, policemen, clerks, bus conductors, and railroad workers (only two married unskilled workers).[107] Among these was the glove maker Victorine Bouget, from the Breton capital city of Rennes, who married a typographer from Alsace late in the year, and the dressmaker Héloïse Bruère, from a town in the Côtes-d'Armor, who married a housepainter from Paris in the spring.[108] At Héloïse's wedding only her husband's relatives and workmates stood up for the couple, but Victorine had family at her wedding; her mother was present and her cousin, a locksmith, served as a witness. This was probably a case of family migration that had brought parents to the city with children in tow. A few of the newcomers were as fortunate as Victorine, because they had family in Paris and so were able to live with their parents and to hold the kind of skilled jobs normally preserved for Parisians.[109] A few Breton women who came to Paris with their families were able to enter a marriage "sans profession," with no job at all; only two of the Breton brides were domestic servants, and one worked as a cook.[110] This is a bit surprising, because domestic service was primarily a job for the unmarried women, often newcomers, and especially because later on Breton women would become famous for their presence in domestic service.

Likewise, the Breton grooms had skilled or white-collar jobs, as carpenters, brush makers, bronze workers, machine operators, transportation workers, and clerks. Georges Tabour's work was typical: he was a machine operator from Nantes who married an umbrella worker from the central Highlands in January. His father, also a machine operator, and mother lived nearby, in the Sixth Arrondissement, and they attended the wedding along with his brother, a wood carver. The bride's brother, an umbrella merchant, and her cousin, an architect, stood up for her.[111] Like their brides, Breton grooms reflected the heterogeneity of the Fourteenth Arrondissement, which offered employment to people in commerce, production, and services. Over half the brides and grooms were from upper Brittany, the départements where Rennes and Nantes were located and in which the Gallo patois rather than the Celtic Breton language was spoken. Many of the thirty-four Bretons came from cities (five from Rennes alone) and other towns rather than from the countryside. Only about 15 percent were from the Côtes-d'Armor, which would send so many Bretons to Paris later. The Bretons who married in the Fourteenth Arrondissement in 1875 were relatively skilled and urban, and came from parts of Brittany that were the most fully integrated into the life of the nation. Like the brides and grooms from Brittany who married in Saint-Denis in the same year, they hardly fit the image of the unskilled newcomer or country bumpkin.

Fifteen years later, in 1890, the Fourteenth Arrondissement was a fast growing neighborhood of over 100,000, on its way to 142,000 people by the turn of the century.[112] The census tells us that the largest employers were clothing and toilette manufacturers, with over 13,000 women and 2,500 men workers. The building trades employed over 6,000 men; metallurgy, 2,500 men. But over 2,500 men and 3,000 women worked in a wide range of industries that "related to science, the letters, and arts;" including paper production, printing, binding, the making of print characters, and the publication of books, music, newspapers, and journals, as well as the theater, concerts, and the production of musical instruments and chemistry equipment. In the transportation sector nearly 1,400 men worked with horses (as coachmen and stable hands, and in carriage rentals), some 16,000 of which were required by the system of coaches, tramways, and omnibuses; another 700 worked with the railroad. Postal workers numbered 600. Rentiers and propriétaires made up most of the 4,500 people listed in the "liberal professions" in the census, and they were served by over 1,500 domestics, the vast majority of whom were women. In addition, over 550 cooks worked in the arrondissement, along with 2,600 laundry and pressing workers, most of them women. Finally, there were 750 hospital workers in the arrondissement, two-thirds of whom were women. And 300 people worked the land. The Fourteenth Arrondissement offered an enormous variety of employment to rich and poor alike; it offered industrial work to men, but it was also an arrondissement that employed an enormous number of women in the needle trades and in domestic service, those classic areas of female employment, as well as in the new secular occupations of nurse and hospital attendant.[113]

More heterogeneous than Saint-Denis, the Fourteenth Arrondissement was nonetheless marked by the railroad and the Gare Montparnasse. The novelist Georges Duhamel left a precious memoir of growing up by the railroad lines in the Plaisance neighborhood in the 1890s as part of his novel *La chronique des Pasquier*. His childhood home was on the fifth floor: "The staircase climbed, climbed across family upon family superimposed like geological layers. You could hear a mandolin here, a yippy little dog there, on the right the consumptive who breathed with such difficulty. And the fat lady with the eternal song 'I love you, do you understand that word?' . . . and the tap . . . tap . . . from the apartment of the monsieur who works at home on incomprehensible things. And everywhere, sewing machines and the patter of children in the hallways and the voices of men and women who talk about and quarrel about family affairs. All of that so clear to the acute and distracted ear of the little boy."[114] This neighborhood, since demolished and rebuilt in urban renewal projects of the 1960s, was at the mercy of the railroad. When the trains came, "like a torrent of furious energies," they beat the side of the buildings.[115] With each passing train the entire building trembled, beginning in the cellar and working up each story. Bottles knocked against the wall of the kitchen, and fine powder rained on the balconies; the odor of coal came in with gusts of winds, "the smell of the trains."[116] The view from the windows of Duhamel's childhood home was one of incoherent city rooftops—little houses in some areas, apartment buildings in others —marked by a partial view of the Eiffel Tower. Little hotels, stables, public baths, and a wash house marked his street. To Duhamel as a child, the most obvious sign of order and wit from this view was the railroad yards and workshops, roundhouses, and semaphores.[117]

BRETONS MARRY IN THE
FOURTEENTH ARRONDISSEMENT

By 1890 the marriages of the Fourteenth Arrondissement were celebrated in considerably more beautiful surroundings than the apartments bordering the railroad tracks: in the town hall, enlarged and renewed in the late 1880s. Three frescoes decorated the walls of the marriage room, evoking the most beautiful locations in the arrondissement: the first, called the engagement, depicted a couple in the Parc Montsouris; the second, the wedding dinner on a restaurant terrace; the third, a family at ease, outdoors on the fortifications.[118] Who were the people from Brittany who entered this room to marry in 1890, where did they fit into the society of the Fourteenth Arrondissement, and how did they fit with the citywide survey of marriages in 1885?

The nearly one hundred Bretons who resided and married in the Fourteenth are a distinct group, quite different from the Bretons who married in Saint-Denis and from those in the citywide survey. They reflect the late-century surge of migration from the Côtes-d'Armor, since about half are from that département and another quarter are from the upper Breton départements of Ille-et-Vilaine and the Loire-Atlantique. Continuing the trend set by the few Breton marriages in 1875, a clear majority are women (61 percent), so that they are a much more female group than the Bretons in Saint-Denis or the Bretons surveyed by Garden, reflecting perhaps the youth of newcomers and work available for women in the Fourteenth. The pattern of intermarriage is very different as well: it seems that these are the newcomers whom Garden was describing when he wrote that "coming to Paris is really a complete change of existence: young men and women don't come to Paris to find themselves among natives of their home region, but to try a new adventure, to make their life as Parisians and not as transplanted provincials."[119] About a quarter married another Breton, but the clear majority of marriages joined a Bretonne with a man who had been born elsewhere. As in Saint-Denis, those who did marry another Breton were most likely from the Côtes-d'Armor. And these brides were much older than the Bretonnes in Saint-Denis; those who married for the first time did so at about twenty-seven years of age rather than at twenty-three—perhaps because they had been living and working in the Paris basin longer than the women in Saint-Denis and had come on their own, rather than with parents.[120] Everyone was able to sign the marriage record (see Appendix, table 2).

About half the Bretons of the Fourteenth Arrondissement reported the same address as their spouse at the time of the wedding, and so it is likely—but not certain—that they were living in a consensual union.[121] Although such an arrangement was common in Paris, no record reveals exactly how common. According to partial records almost a third of some groups lived in stable consensual unions, but in the working-class neighborhood of Belleville, for example, only one in six or seven marriages regularized a consensual union. Bretons in the Fourteenth were much more likely than those in Saint-Denis to be living with their partner than with a parent when they married. Although antibourgeois ideology sanctioned state marriage during the Third Republic, poverty is likely to provide more of an explanation than ideology.[122] Consensual unions have been firmly tied to poverty and a lack of social resources on the part of the woman and man.

Also in contrast to those in Saint-Denis, many Bretons—a quarter of them—had borne or fathered a child before their wedding. This is a high proportion as well, in contrast with only about 15 percent of marriages serving to legitimize a child in Garden's citywide survey of a thousand marriages in 1885, from which he concluded that consensual unions were an important social phenomenon, and that marriage after a child's birth provided another significant pattern.[123] Consensual unions and births to single mothers were common in Paris, but births out of wedlock were a rarity in Brittany, so shared addresses and children born before the wedding indicate that many Bretons adopted the courtship and cohabitation practices of the Parisian working class. The status of working-class women—especially newcomers without brothers or fathers in town to enforce a marriage promise—clearly made them more vulnerable to bearing children while they were single.[124] Indeed the high proportion of Bretons with children born while they were single testifies to their social vulnerability, as well as to poverty and the difficulty of gathering all the requisite documents for marriage, such as birth certificates, notarized documents attesting to the consent of parents, and death certificates of deceased parents; Yvonne Yven undertook this considerable task after she and Jean Chabot agreed to marry.[125] Yet poor women and men did marry, and among most who legitimized a child at their wedding, it seems that the groom was the father of a baby recently born in Paris.[126]

Neighbors played a large role in these weddings. Of the witnesses who could be identified, most dwelt in the same building as the bride or groom—about 15 percent of the witnesses all told. Only about 10 percent were related to the bride or groom, and the town hall of the Fourteenth Arrondissement did not specify the relationship between the relative and the marriage partner that year: overall, parents, siblings, and other relatives were less likely to be present than in Saint-Denis.[127]

The stories told by *actes de mariage* are worth recounting, for they tell us a good deal about the origins and trajectories of Bretons in Paris. In 1890 these marriages fell into three distinct groups: those which joined a Breton woman with a man born elsewhere, those which joined a Breton groom with a woman born elsewhere, and the marriages of two Bretons. Couples in every group were likely to have a child. Brief exemplary stories from each group of Breton marriage partners convey lived histories; I emphasize those of the Breton bride with a groom from another province because this pattern predominates.

The occupations and friendships of the bride and groom suggest that the weddings were embedded in a web of urban relationships and that the bride and groom looked to a future in Paris. Most seem to have resulted from a courtship in Paris. This is true for the women who married men born elsewhere, the majority of brides in the Fourteenth Arrondissement who married men in skilled and secure occupations. Yvonne Le Corre, a housewife, lived with her railroad worker husband François near the station in the Plaisance neighborhood when they married in January 1890, at the same time legitimizing their son Pierre, who had been born two years earlier. Yvonne was twenty-seven; her husband was thirty and from western France, where his widowed mother worked as a day laborer. Yvonne's mother and her father, a shoemaker in her Bretonnant village in the Côtes-d'Armor, sent proof of their consent to the marriage, as law required. Who witnessed this wedding? Three men in the same building, and the café owner from around the corner.[128] This wedding was a neighborhood affair, rooted in a crowded building near the railroad tracks. Like many couples in Paris, Yvonne and François had probably been living together for some time.

Marie Lesigne was a typical Breton bride in the spring of 1890, a cook from the bretonnant area of the Côtes-d'Armor. Marie married a policeman from northern France who lived in the same building as she—an avenue apartment building—and an assortment of men in the neighborhood witnessed the wedding. She and the groom were both twenty-eight years of age, and neither had a relative at the wedding; Marie's parents worked the land and sent proof of their consent.[129] The origins of these relationships are ultimately mysterious, but that of Marie may well have originated in the avenue apartment building, in the neighborhood where she shopped for food, or at a street dance or other public gathering.[130] In any case both Yvonne and Marie were likely to remain in Paris, where their husbands had a history of secure work.

The grooms from Brittany in the Fourteenth Arrondissement who did not marry women from their home area worked at a skilled trade. And like the Breton brides, they married later, in their thirties and forties. Among these was Jean Scolan, from the port town of Lorient in the Morbihan, a baker in Paris who at the age of thirty-nine married Zoë, a twenty-two-year-old florist from the Ardèche who lived and worked with her mother in the same building as Jean on one of the boulevards of the Fourteenth Arrondissement. Jean's widowed mother was a rentière in his hometown who sent her permission for the union; although Zoë's father had disappeared years ago, her mother attended. Two bakers stood up for Jean; a neighbor and a fellow migrant stood up for Zoë.[131] It seems that Jean's future looked bright for a man in his forties; his vocation and his comrades at the wedding suggest that it would be a future cradled not by the Breton community but rather by his comrades in the workplace.

The Breton couples who married in the Fourteenth Arrondissement probably met in Paris. When Jeanne Dupuis, a twenty-one-year-old type-setter from the Ille-et-Vilaine in upper Brittany, married Yves Le Roux, a twenty-four-year-old railroad worker from a town in the Côtes-d'Armor, she was living with her mother in the rue Daguerre, and Yves was in the same building. Yves's parents were property owners at home, and Jeanne's widowed mother was a day laborer. The witnesses to this wedding were three men who lived in the same building: a day laborer, a chauffeur, and a property owner; the other witness was a coachman who lived across the street.[132] The couple had started their lives in Breton villages but had good urban jobs and an urban future. Like most of the Bretons who married in the Fourteenth Arrondissement that year, they had relatively few close connections to family, and seemed to be on the threshold of a shared urban life. These were newcomers in the melting pot that was Paris, deserters from provincial life and new citizens of the capital city.

BRETON WOMEN IN PARIS
AS THE TWENTIETH CENTURY APPROACHES

The 1890s saw a surge in the number of Bretons in Paris basin—especially those from the Côtes-d'Armor, who increased their numbers from nearly 26,000 in 1891 to over 30,000 five years later and 36,000 at the turn of the century. At the beginning of the decade the Côtes-d'Armor was in twenty-first place among the départements that sent people to greater Paris, but by the turn of the century it ranked tenth, and 59 of every 1,000 people in the Côtes-d'Armor lived in the Paris basin.[133] The lack of work in Brittany provided a push and the possibilities of Paris the pull. It is no wonder that Lemoine wrote of some villages being "bled white" by emigration. Women especially left Brittany for Paris. The abbé Gautier ascribes the large number of Bretons in central Paris in 1896 to the presence of Breton women who worked in bourgeois homes as domestics.

Although the poorer men and women of Brittany were both subject to exploitation in Paris, but of course only women were at risk of pregnancy. This was especially true for migrant women, who were the most financially and socially vulnerable in this relatively new and very female migration stream. As George Alter has shown, these women did not have fathers or brothers in town to enforce a marriage when pregnancy occurred. They were the women who did not live with their parents but on their own in a rented room or garni, like most couturières in the city.[134] They had little leverage in the marriage market and were more likely than other women to live in consensual unions.[135] The domestic servant was perhaps even more sexually vulnerable, often housed in an unlocked room on the sixth floor, apart from both her employer's family and her compatriots in an unsupervised and unprotected setting. There are many stories like that of the domestic who complained to the family of the adolescent son who had come to her room at night to have sex with her, a narrative greeted with laughter by the family. The social relations of nineteenth-century Paris meant that middle-class men expected to have unfettered access to working women—especially those close to hand. Indeed, over a third of the women in the maternity hospital for the poor were domestic servants in the 1890s. The "poor and pregnant in Paris," as Rachel Fuchs has called the women who needed aid in the nineteenth century, numbered in the thousands.[136]

The Fourteenth Arrondissement was home to the venerable institution of La Maternité, the primary free public hospital in the Paris basin, at the edge of the arrondissement on the boulevard Port-Royal. An estimated 200,000 women delivered babies there between 1830 and 1900, an average of 2,000 to 4,000 per year.[137] Because women preferred the services of a midwife, only the poor delivered in this hospital, and an invaluable portrait of these women can be drawn from the hospital records.[138] For the most part the women were between the ages of twenty and twenty-seven, with an average age of twenty-four for single mothers, and in the 1890s 72 percent of women who gave birth in La Maternité were single. Between 1870 and 1900 46 percent of the single mothers who delivered in La Maternité worked as domestic servants, and about 14 percent worked as seamstresses; others were day laborers, laundresses, linen menders, and cooks.[139] Most important in this context, the mothers in La Maternité were overwhelmingly migrants to Paris, born outside the Paris basin (75 percent of the married women who gave birth in La Maternité in the 1890s, and 82 percent of single women, had been born outside the Seine). Yet the vast majority had become pregnant while living in Paris.[140]

Moreover, just as there was a surge of Bretons to Paris in the 1890s, so there was also a surge of Bretons to La Maternité in the same period. The Côtes-d'Armor, which until then had provided under 3 percent of the patients to La Maternité, now sent the highest percentage of single women to the hospital of twenty-one regions—one out of seven. Between 1890 and 1900 they came especially from the Côtes-d'Armor (see map 3).[141] And although over half the single mothers in La Maternité worked as domestic servants, nearly all the Breton mothers were domestics. The sudden appearance of Bretonnes in La Maternité is particularly striking, because other areas that gave birth to women in La Maternité, like the Nord and Alsace, had higher rates of illegitimacy in those home areas, whereas illegitimacy rates in Brittany itself were low throughout the nineteenth century.[142] The presence of Breton women in La Maternité signals not only the importance of women among Bretons in Paris but their acute social vulnerability.

Neither consensual unions nor bearing a child out of wedlock precluded marriage for women, including Breton women. The Breton brides in 1890s certainly show this. Many lived with their husband before marriage, sometimes for years. For example, when the postman Charles Taupin and the day laborer Marie Garel married in March they did so at

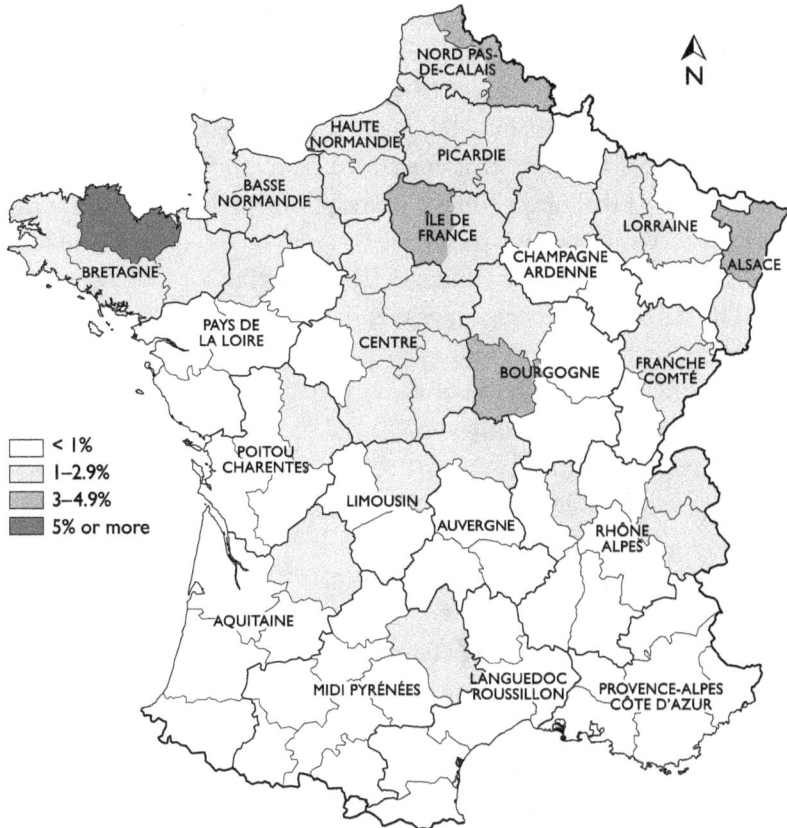

MAP 3. Percentage of single mothers in La Maternité accounted for by each region, 1890–1900. Daniel Courgeau, "Three Centuries of Spatial Mobility in France," UNESCO Reports and Papers in the Social Sciences, 51 (1982), 53; Archives de l'Assistance Publique, l'Hôpital Port Royal, Registres des Entrées, 1890, 1895, 1900.

home, because Charles was on his deathbed at the young age of thirty-seven. They took the occasion to legitimize their daughter, born four years earlier, and their son, born the previous year, both in the Fourteenth Arrondissement. Charles was born in a French-speaking hamlet in the Morbihan, Marie in a hamlet in the Ille-et-Vilaine.[143] Marie was not among the most highly skilled or highly paid of Breton emigrants.

Breton women were also part of the traffic in wet nurses (*nourrices*), foundlings, and mother's milk that linked women in Paris and other cities to the women in the French countryside before the First World War. Families from the Côtes-d'Armor took in abandoned children from the hospice in Saint-Brieuc for a fee, just as rural families in many parts of

France took in abandoned children.[144] Women from the Côtes-d'Armor and the Morbihan, along with women from other rural areas of France, served as wet nurses in the city.[145] Recently delivered women left their own newborns in Brittany while they went to serve as nourrices for Parisian babies, a practice that appalled the Breton Father Bourhy. He claimed in 1894 that nearly half the women from his parish of Hénon left for Paris as wet nurses, and then stayed on for two or three years to take care of the children they had nursed. Their appetite for gain was nourished by the 800 to 900 francs per year that they earned in Paris, and so, he claimed, the women wanted a new pregnancy right away so that they could leave again, encouraged by the eager recruiters who hired women with newborn babies. Bourhy emphasized the disastrous consequences of high mortality in his parish in 1894, when parish records recorded thirty deaths of children under the age of two (at a time when the mean number of births was seventy-two), and laid the blame on neglectful, departed mothers. According to Bourhy this disaster was not only demographic but social. Having left the laundry and cooking to the man of the house, returning women would be appalled at their situation back home after living in considerably more luxurious circumstances.[146]

Today these conditions are understood quite differently as part of the "traffic in misery" linking migration, wet nursing, and deserted children.[147] This traffic centered in the Morvan in Burgundy, which received hundreds of foundlings from Paris and furnished 302 wet nurses to elite families in the capital during the spring of 1901.[148] Nonetheless, the Breton départements of the Côtes-d'Armor and the Morbihan were also engaged in this traffic—the Côtes-d'Armor furnished 165 wet nurses to Paris and 188 to the département of the Seine in 1901; for the Morbihan these figures were 95 and 111. Together the two furnished almost 11 percent of all wet nurses to Paris and the Seine.[149] Yet this traffic was almost invisible to Parisians.

Much more visible to Parisians, and reputedly more Breton, was the nightlife behind the Boulevard Montparnasse and the railroad station, in the Plaisance neighborhood of the Fourteenth Arrondissement, understood as a party neighborhood and the place to find Breton streetwalkers. We can learn something of the *vie du quartier* from the hastily scrawled police blotters. They report the essence of various incidents, along with the careful identification of the characters involved, especially the accused.[150] This impressionistic view from the Plaisance quarter in the mid-1890s reveals most importantly that Bretons played a very small role in disrupting the neighborhood: only 4 percent of some 1,650 neighborhood disputes and scandals mention a Breton. As several scholars have shown, it was Parisians rather than newcomers who committed most of the crimes of Paris.[151] Nonetheless, those Bretons who appeared at the police station had a particular profile.

It was women who earned the attention of the police in the majority of cases. One-third of all the Bretons in question either were prostitutes or were brought in for clandestine prostitution (soliciting), petty theft, complicity in minor crimes, or disorderly conduct.[152] The obstreperous Jeanne Rebillart, from a northern village in the inland Côtes-d'Armor, must have been best known to the officers, for she was brought in five times during 1896 for soliciting, as well as for simply throwing a bowl of water out her window and then two days later for public drunkenness.[153] This last was usually a male crime, as was abusing the police in a drunken state: men in the prime of life would call the police *vaches, sales cons, fainéants, and voleurs*, then often recognize their error when they sobered up. But name calling was not the property of men alone: the Breton presence at the police station started one night in early January when a twenty-five-year-old dressmaker from the Ille-et-Vilaine, in her cups, angrily delineated her opinion of the police.[154]

These nighttime scenes illuminate the toll exacted by urban misfortune. When Yvonne Saliou, thirty-seven, a widowed laundress with two children from an inland village in Côtes-d'Armor, was brought in on one February night, arrested for clandestine prostitution, it was the third time she had been arrested, and the second time that month. Drinking played a role, hospitalizing a thirty-three-year-old from a town in Ille-et-Vilaine for alcoholism during the summer and a melancholy twenty-one-year-old carpenter from an estuary port in the Côtes-d'Armor in the fall who had turned on his sister in an alcoholic rage. Poverty was endemic, certainly felt by the two women day laborers in their forties from the Côtes-d'Armor, one single, the other a widow, who were brought in during one week in January because they were out of work and in a state of complete indigence. Yet this is only a partial picture: other Bretons in the police blotters merely lifted groceries from a store, caroused with their spouse, or argued with a coachman over a fare or with a neighbor over a fallen flowerpot.[155]

The records and writings of the 1890s suggest that Bretons had a rocky beginning in Paris. But neither the Bretons nor Paris offers a picture that is homogeneous, or entirely congruent with contemporary opinion. Literature, social commentary, memoirs, historical scholarship, and marriage records each contribute to a complex of images and realities. They show that those who traveled to Saint-Denis were largely unskilled men from the villages and small inland towns of the Côtes-d'Armor who suffered in slum housing. Connected to family and compatriots, Bretons lived in a viable although poor community. Marriage records give life to the stereotype of rural origins and illiteracy—and for the men they are consistent with the hard-won findings of Farcy and Faure about the rural origins and scant educational level of the pioneering men who left the Côtes-d'Armor in the 1880s.[156] On the other hand, marriages demonstrate that women's experience was distinct: marriage came unusually early in the lives of the women of Saint-Denis. Moreover, many Saint-Denis brides worked at a distance from their sweethearts, whether as servants in the city or as what would today be called hospital aides, demonstrating that the Breton community, or Breton networks, occupied a wide arena early on, even before associational life or a Paris press for Bretons had much of a start. But the frequent references to the job of day laborer on actes de mariage indicate hardship on the job and perhaps disregard for accuracy, or lack of interest in it, on the part of municipal clerks. Lemoine's portrait of Saint-Denis Bretons offers a clue to such attitudes.

A greater variety of work was available in Paris, where the Bretons of the Fourteenth Arrondissement cut a very different figure from those in Saint-Denis. Many men and women found work in the service sector, the men often in transportation, and both men and women were apparently successful in the search for an urban future. Yet records suggest that Bretons in the city suffered from considerable economic and social vulnerability, and that they did so less cradled by relatives and compatriots than their counterparts were in Saint-Denis. If marriage records give life to a stereotype here, it is that of the Breton servant who bears a child out of wedlock or otherwise cannot control her sexual life and its outcomes— perhaps a patient at La Maternité, and fodder for the literature of Zola. On the other hand, the brides of the Fourteenth Arrondissement are notably older and long gone from home. They are of an age and experience less like Zola's hapless Breton servant perhaps than the determined "jeune *girl* anglaise" that Lemoine held out as a model for Breton girls in the city.

Finally, both in Saint-Denis and in the Fourteenth Arrondissement there were skilled Bretons among the unskilled. In addition, a community of notables from Brittany such as the philosopher and scholar Ernest Renan, who died in Paris in 1892, and Jules Simon, statesman and reformer who died in Paris four years later, were ignored by the social commentary of the day. Bretons at every level of society like Yvonne Yven managed to marry and form families, in some cases despite considerable previous hardship and dislocation. This pattern complicates literary evidence and the writings of social observers as well as the horrified reports of church personnel, who emphasized the pariah status of Bretons in Paris that stemmed from their lack of education and resources. Experts and observers from Lemoine to Zola, perhaps as well as the administrators of the Maternité hospital for indigent women, saw Bretons as country bumpkins ill suited to city life. Historical scholarship bears out the grain of truth in this stereotype, and shows that most Bretons, like newcomers to Paris and other west European cities today, began their careers in Paris in the least desirable occupations while they lived in crowded and unhealthy quarters. Nonetheless, there were also those who remained and carved out satisfactory lives in the capital despite the tainted lenses through which they were often viewed.

Their persistence came at a price usually overlooked today. Yvonne Yven's twenty-five years of servitude demonstrate the ambiguities and difficulties of this kind of work. At the beck and call of her employers, Yven was unable to experience the conjugal life that others could achieve. After only a few hours' break for her wedding in 1895, Yven lived separately from her husband—also a domestic—because neither employer would allow cohabitation. "Why do you want to marry?" asked her employer. If you are absent at night and "we are sick, who will go to the doctor?" asked her husband's employer. This situation could not have been unique, since over 30 percent of female domestics in Paris were married by the beginning of the twentieth century. Moreover, the couple could not live with their son, so he was raised by the gardener's family at her employer's summer house in Barbizon, southeast of Paris. Their son reports: "It was out of the question that my mother raise me, she didn't have time to take care of me, and the employers would not tolerate servants' children."[157] It was not until their son was ten years old that the couple left the constraints of servant life for the concierge lodge in the city. The heavy emotional toll exacted by their separation is evocative of and forecasts findings on the transnational family of today.[158] Parents lived separately from their spouse, and children apart from one or both parents. This "deterritorialized" family, to use Arjun Appadurai's phrase, contributes to the current global labor force, but it also makes very real sacrifices of intimate relations between spouses and between parent and child.[159]

Yet Paris offered a chance—a chance that many Bretons were able to grasp. As we will see, at the dawn of the twentieth century booksellers, the medical profession, and the church would focus their gaze on the Bretons of Paris.

CHAPTER THREE

The Turn of the Century
A Belle Époque?

Marie Lepioufle was born in an inland village of the Morbi-han in 1890, the fourth of six children whose father worked as an agricultural laborer. Without warning, Marie was taken out of school and away from home at the age of eleven to work as a farm servant at a nearby château. She suffered spiteful treatment at the hands of other servants, but lasted a year working in the barnyard, caring for chickens and cows, and cleaning out the henhouse. This would be the first of several year-long jobs close to home that followed the path of her older sister. By 1905 the sisters lived on the eastern outskirts of Paris, not far from their aunt; they worked as store helpers while their aunt hosted them on Sundays, advised them, and opened savings accounts for them. Against her aunt's advice that she avoid such a disreputable milieu, Marie followed her sister into the Salpêtrière Public Assistance Hospital in 1909. There she found hard work as an aide but also made friends with whom she discovered Paris on her days off. At her sister's wedding in 1910 she met a male hospital employee, François Michel, who had been born in another French-speaking village near her own in 1882. Younger son of a peasant, François had found life at home difficult when he returned from army service to the family land farmed by his authoritarian father and his older, married brother. He had joined his second brother in Paris, where they both worked in the Pitié Hospital. Starting as an aide, he left unskilled work behind him and trained to become a nurse by 1909, although he preferred to work with horses and carry out the many transport needs of the hospital.

The wedding of Marie and François in February 1911 took place near their hospitals in the Thirteenth Arrondissement, with siblings from near and far in attendance. They celebrated at a nearby inn and then, for the benefit of their Breton guests, visited the Eiffel Tower and the great Ferris wheel that was a vestige of the Universal Exposition of 1900. They would spend their lives in service to the public hospital system.[1] How do Marie and François fit into the community of Bretons in Paris in the years before the First World War? How did they conform to and contradict the image that Parisians had of Bretons at this time? In the year of their marriage the number of Bretons had reached over 109,000 in Paris (well above the 87,000 of the turn of the century and the 68,000 of 1891) and nearly 160,000 in greater Paris. This surge of Bretons in Paris made them a notable and well-documented presence in city and banlieue.[2]

By the turn of the century Bretons had the worst sort of reputation among newcomers in Paris. In the space of a few years they were the subject of newspaper articles, dissertations, a constellation of church organizations, a well-known salacious novel, and a sociological study. The idea that Bretons should stay away from Paris was embedded in a core narrative—a narrative of ruin and even death—that informs many of the writings by doctors, clerics, novelists, journalists, and academics, writings that were used almost invariably to illustrate how unsuited were Bretons to city life and warning them off attempts to settle in Paris.[3] The poverty of Bretons was studied from every angle, and that of Bretons in the countryside was scrutinized from faraway Paris. In 1902 the weekly *Illustration* ran a series of articles called "La misère bretonne" that graphically detailed the wretched conditions of Breton sardine fishermen and cannery workers, representing them as the most miserable of all the French.[4] The questions that were posed about Bretons were remarkably uniform (except in the case of the novel mentioned above), and nearly always included a pair of inquiries: Why did Bretons leave home? And how can they be dissuaded from doing so?

When Parisians thought of Breton women they thought first of domestic servants—those ubiquitous workers in the Parisian home who labored behind the doors of families of every status, from clerical workers to the grand bourgeoisie. Breton women made a mark in this area, numbering more than twelve thousand at the turn of the century and anticipating the Spanish and other foreign domestics who would follow.[5] Their cartoon manifestation, Bécassine, made her appearance in 1905. Before that, a more sexual character, in keeping with a second image of Breton womanhood, appeared as Célestine in Octave Mirbeau's *Diary of a Chambermaid*. Distinct and striking images of Breton men and women thus became part of Parisian life in the Belle Époque.

These images both corroborate and contradict portraits of Bretons from Parisian censuses and marriage records, but it remains clear that there were no shortages of ideas about Bretons in Belle Époque Paris. Their importance is reflected not only in adult and children's fiction but in the concerns of the religious and medical establishments. Objects of religious fervor and butts of ridicule, the Breton community in Paris grew into an articulate community with regionalist interests, all the while blending, at least in part, into Parisian society. This heterogeneous community included the wealthy and the poor, the educated and the illiterate, and men and women of Saint-Denis and the Fourteenth Arrondissement, whose experiences varied widely.

CÉLESTINE AND BÉCASSINE: BRETON MAIDS IN THE PARISIAN IMAGINATION

In July 1900 Célestine R. made her appearance between the covers of what would become Octave Mirbeau's best selling novel, *Journal d'une femme de chambre*.[6] This long-term hit, and its salacious reputation, would overshadow Mirbeau's considerable body of literary and journalistic work, perhaps to the author's detriment. In any case, his sensual heroine was not simply a chambermaid but a servant in Paris who had worked "from the Bois de Boulogne to the Bastille, from the Observatory to Montmartre, from Ternes to Gobelins, everywhere."[7] Souvenirs of her placements in Parisian bourgeois families, written while she was in a provincial post, constitute the stuff of the novel. And Célestine was a Bretonne.

Célestine permits the reader to look through the keyhole, into the life of a chambermaid with blonde hair and deep blue eyes whose story of sexual sensibilities falls into a long history of fantasy literature. Yet the novel also allows a lucid and critical look at bourgeois morals and reveals odious bourgeois traits: hypocrisy, materialism, and cruelty, with a focus on the sexual exploitation of the serving class. Célestine makes the case that "domestics learn vice from their masters."[8] She is able to avoid one master who sleeps with every servant (only because she is in bed with his son) and another who impregnates every one (only because she is partnered with the gardener).[9] Like Émile Zola, Mirbeau intended to expose bourgeois vice, and like Zola he was perceived as a "vulgar naturalist" when the book was published.[10] Mirbeau successfully portrays ugly exploitation, and the best-known film adaptation of *The Diary of a Chambermaid*, directed by Luis Buñuel in 1964, is able to do the same.[11] But it is not only the bourgeoisie that is corrupt: there is a certain moral baseness in Célestine, who appears at first to be a sort of sexual Candide but by the end of the novel is clearly possessed by an appetite for sexual pleasure.

Mirbeau places the roots of Célestine's "depravity" not in the circumstances of the domestic or the exploitation of the bourgeoisie but in specifics of her childhood in the Finistère at the tip of Brittany—her fisherman father's gruesome death at sea, her mother's consequent alcoholism followed by the rapid departure of her older siblings, then her mother's constant cruelty and whoring. Left to her own devices, Célestine has her sexual initiation at the age of twelve on a bed of seaweed with a smelly foreman from the sardine cannery, with the prize of an orange. Mirbeau presents her background only in the fifth chapter of the novel, when Célestine learns of her mother's death and recalls her childhood; she has no one with whom to share this news, since her sister has long since gone off and probably works in a bordello at Concarneau, and her brother is in the navy somewhere—perhaps China.[12] This is Mirbeau's depiction of the Breton family. The dénouement of the novel shows a certain political baseness on the heroine's part, one that was eliminated entirely from the films made from the novel: Célestine escapes domestic service by marrying the gardener Joseph and serves as a hostess in Cherbourg at the café he has purchased, named to attract military personnel; tarted up and alluring, she presides behind the counter while her brutal, anti-Semitic husband—a suspected murderer, rapist, and thief—rails against Dreyfus, who has just arrived in France for his second trial.[13]

Although Célestine herself has become an attractive and polished chambermaid by the time she relates her story, Mirbeau also provides a devastating portrait of unpolished aspiring servants from Brittany at the employment agencies of Paris, inspiring the same questions that occurred to concerned men of the church: "Why did she leave her native soil? What folly, what drama, what storm wind pushed out to run aground in this groaning human sea?" Saddened by the sight of a country girl in her telltale Breton coiffe, Célestine comments that "she was ugly with that definitive ugliness that excludes all pity and makes men cruel because really she is an offense to them." The Bretonne's thick, beautiful hair—a resplendent red—aggravated rather than attenuated her ugliness, rendering it irreparable. And that is not all: her every movement was awkward.[14] Brought to Paris by an employer who had vacationed in Brittany, she had left her first job in Paris after sexual advances were made to her. The butt of her family's cruelty, she could not go home again. "I would rather die!" she exclaimed.[15] In a long interview with an old crone, painful even to read, this young woman was declared too ugly, and then too smelly, to hire—and then was begrudged a job at one-third her asking wage.[16] Another aspirant, Jeanne Le Godec, was greeted with derision: "You're a Breton then? . . . oh! I don't like Bretons . . . they're stubborn and dirty." This opened a protracted and nasty interview that thoroughly demoralized the widow Le Godec and left her still unemployed.[17] Thus in one chapter Mirbeau portrayed face to face the most unfortunate domestic aspirants and the most arrogant of employers, all under the imperturbable eyes of a profit-minded mistress of the employment agency. In the end both Breton servants depicted in this popular novel—the sensuous and polished chambermaid and the brutish and distasteful maid-of-all-work—were fair game for novelist and employer alike. Mirbeau had it both ways, taking swipes at the bourgeoisie and denigrating the Bretonnes as well.

Another Breton maid came on the Parisian scene in 1905, one who would outsell Célestine, reach a broader audience, inspire more affection, and ultimately become a much more controversial figure and cultural icon: the cartoon character Bécassine. Her illustrated stories covered a page of the popular girls' magazine *La Semaine de Suzette* beginning with its first issue in 1905. By the end of 1914 ninety-seven stories had appeared in the magazine; hardcover comic books complemented and summarized the year's stories almost annually from 1913 to 1939. The Bécassine volumes, unlike those featuring the character Astérix after the Second World War, for example, find their roots and inspiration not in American comics or transatlantic life but in the experience of the French and the Parisian middle classes (see figure 1).[18]

Bécassine was depicted as a blockhead—a blundering goodhearted girl with no sense. In her employer's words: "That Bécassine! No brain, but so much heart!"[19] Bécassine's first appearance, titled "Bécassine's Error," reportedly came from the editor in chief Madame Jacqueline Rivière, who related the story of a blunder made by her own Breton maid which was then illustrated by an in-house artist on the eve of the initial appearance of the magazine. This first tale set the tone for Bécassine stories: her employer, Madame la Marquise de Grand-Air, asked her young Breton maid to watch for the delivery of lobsters (*homards*) to make sure

1. Bécassine's Début, by J. P. Pinchon, from *L'enfance de Bécassine*
© Henri Gautier, 1913, cover.

they were bright red and fresh; not knowing what *homards* were, Bécassine asked her employer to inspect the new arrivals she had put in the kitchen—they were red, but perhaps not fresh. These new arrivals were not the lobsters, but the guest colonel and his three young sous-lieutenants, all in red jackets. Bécassine's ignorance proved to have great comedic value.[20]

She certainly enjoyed great commercial success. Joseph Porphyre Pinchon, who provided expert illustrations, was himself an artist who drew for reviews and newspapers, submitted paintings to the salon of 1894, and was the artistic director of the Paris Opera in 1910–14. Maurice

Langereau wrote the stories under the epigrammic pen name of Caumery; he was a nephew of the publisher Henri Gautier, who possessed remarkable marketing acumen. Gautier encouraged the custom of giving Bécassine volumes to children at the end of the year by publishing each volume at that time.[21] Gautier distributed 100,000 free copies of the premier magazine issue and sent a beautiful blonde doll to each of the initial one-year subscribers, who numbered 20,000.[22] Bécassine herself was trademarked in 1910, and a doll about 7½ inches tall, in a green costume and Breton coiffe, was soon for sale. Dolls were not the only prewar product: a prize-winning toy called the "dish breaker" had a tiny Bécassine (about 5 inches tall) drop the pile of dishes she carried.[23]

Dropping dishes was typical of this character, whose ineptitude was apparent from the time of her birth. In a village where it was believed that a long nose denoted intelligence, Bécassine had only a little button nose, and her given very Breton name, Annick Labornez, was a play on the word for dull-witted. When her father found out that the milk she adored (purchased from another peasant family) was that of an ass, her father exclaimed, "A little one with no nose, and fed by an ass. She's going to be an idiot for sure!"[24] And Bécassine did pull off some idiotic stunts, such as trying to make whipped cream using a whip. But Caumery also created an extraordinarily sweet character in Bécassine, one whose goodness shone from her earliest days. When prizes were awarded at the end of the school year, Bécassine was awarded the prize for "good character." And when a visiting dignitary offered 10 francs to the student who would declare herself the least intelligent in school, Bécassine rose and held out her hand. "Give me the 10 francs *m'sieu*. It's well known that I am the stupidest!" She then declared that she would give the 10 francs to a poor widow whose husband had been lost at sea the previous week. There was not a dry eye in the house.[25] This dull-witted but sweet girl would become the faithful servant of the Marquise de Grand-Air, benefactress to the village and resident of Saint-Germain-des-Prés in Paris.

In Bécassine's prewar tales for elite girls, class distinctions were strong to a fault, and peasants and village life were clearly inferior to life in Paris. Only a few village people were somewhat distinguished: Bécassine's beloved Uncle, for example, served as mayor and former groom of the Marquis de Grand-Air. The rest were ignorant peasants in villages where animals and people lived and played together. There was no greater honor for a village girl like Bécassine than to serve the marquise; as her uncle recounted, "You see this girl who looks like she'll be nothing—she has entered into the service of Madame la Marquise. . . . I always knew she would have a brilliant career before her."[26]

It is certain that the fictional comic character had a great career; it would flower during and after the Great War, but it would inflict a great deal of pain on Bretons in Paris. The name Bécassine comes from *bécasse*, which denotes a shorebird or snipe but also came to mean a stupid woman and worse. Parisians gave the name of Bécassine to women from Brittany (and Bécassin to the men), who came to be regarded as uniformly stupid, so much so that the *Dictionnaire de patrimoine breton* declared Bécassine to be "silly, naïve, ignorant and clumsy, faithful maid of all work, is the archetype of the backward Breton woman."[27] Perhaps the most effective defender of Bretons against this image, and against the realities of suffering and isolation, worked through the church.

A CHAMPION OF BRETONS:
FRANÇOIS CADIC AND LA PAROISSE BRETONNE

So engaged was the cleric François Cadic by Bretons' situation that in 1897 he founded the Breton parish, which would last until his death in the 1920s. Cadic was the youngest of ten children born of a peasant family in 1864 in the Breton-speaking Morbihan. Ordained shortly before he had come to Paris to finish his training as a historian, Cadic had taken a post at the Catholic University of Paris when the plight of Bretons in Paris persuaded him to form a parish and take up tasks which included fundraising for charitable enterprises, operating a clothing bank and an employment agency, holding meetings for Breton men and women, and publishing a monthly journal.[28] Cadic was an energetic organizer and writer whose *Contes et légendes de la Bretagne* continues to be published and marketed today.[29] Other church organizations devoted themselves to the aid of Bretons, as we will see below, but the Breton parish was the most visible and efficacious.

The monthly *Paroisse bretonne de Paris* began to appear in 1899, providing a bully pulpit for Cadic and to us, a view into the world of the faithful social Catholic that was of premier importance in France, especially to the Breton community. The masthead announced two clear messages. The first, "Evit Doué a gar vro. Pour Dieu et le pays," used the Celtic Breton language translated into French in an otherwise French-language publication; this testified to Breton and Catholic loyalty together as one, in Cadic's words, "brotherhood in the shadow of the parish bell." The second offered a more complex message, "the Breton Parish is the enemy of emigration. It only cares for Bretons already established in Paris."[30] Like Cadic, the organization and journal deplored departures from Brittany, yet were devoted to helping compatriots in need of aid.

Cadic himself wrote some telling lead editorials, beginning with one discussing the identity of the new organization.[31] "Brotherhood in the shadow of the parish bell" meant to Cadic that the "instrument of discord," politics, would be strictly forbidden in the review, yet the organization was of a very particular political stripe. "Here there are only Bretons," Cadic wrote, "disposed neither to Jews, nor Protestants, nor Freemasons. Sons of French soil, issued from old Celtic stock, we aspire to remain untainted by foreign alloys more than other provincials. That is to say we reject all heterogeneous elements."[32] Within this exclusively French Breton and Catholic context, Cadic put forward two goals—to provide a place for Bretons, and to be practical. To the first end, news from home, history, legends, and even songs would be published in the review. Second, the charitable works of the *Paroisse* would help poor compatriots, establish links among middle-class Bretons, and give wealthy Bretons a way to help the less fortunate. Cadic explicitly recognized that the Bretons in Paris included the wealthy, the middle class, and the poor.

A variety of leaders reported on the meetings and fundraising events in the *Paroisse bretonne*; others contributed poetry and stories, and still others wrote what would become the local news pieces. Brittany was a source of pride as well as of sorrow: Charles Vincent, editor of the *Gazette de France*, referred to two themes of Breton writing when he claimed that "*no other province of France* has furnished an equal quantity of great men to all ranks of society," and moreover that the Bretons' "grace, vigorous of spirit and body, rich in heart and energy, more fertile than any other, is currently the only one capable of repopulating and regenerating France."[33] Breton patriots would constantly refer to their great men and their high fertility as points of pride throughout the Third Republic. The famed "barde national" of Brittany, the songwriter, poet, and performer Théodore Botrel, furnished some poetry. His "Breton Wolves" recounted the history of the province in six stanzas, relating how they "bared teeth" at the Roman invader, the Norman hordes, the invading English, the revolutionary enemies of throne and church, and the Prussian invader, and now, after thirty years of quiet, were ready to avenge once again.[34] The less complex poems by less famous compatriots served as warnings under titles such as "Stay at Home" and "In Danger."[35]

Good news and bad news from home appeared, with ecclesiastical news taking the lead, including appointments of curés and higher posts. Occasionally there were reports of the opening of religious schools: "in [the diocese of Saint-Brieuc] eight new free Christian schools (two for boys, six for girls) opened in 1898, 4 in 1899, which brings to 208 the number of the schools in the Department; they counted 27,815 students in 1898, making 3,773 more than in 1897," thus demonstrating the enthusiasm for non-secular education during the Third Republic for which Brittany was well known.[36] Announcements of appointments such as those of notaries and judges appeared. The bad news, with comments of sympathy at misfortunes and disapproval of crime, came in the form of miscellaneous items listed by commune: house fires, murders, thefts, and injurious accidents. Ordinary Bretons like Honoré Guitton furnished almost all the news. Guitton was coming home from the fair in Broome with his wife, son, and two neighbors when suddenly his horse bolted on a bridge and threw itself against the railings; the two neighbors were thrown into the river and got out unwounded; Guitton fell to the road and was killed; his wife broke two legs; "the son is safe and sound." Other tragedies provoked less sympathy from this Anglophobe and anti-Protestant publication, as with the death of an Englishman at the oyster capital of Concale who had won his bet with friends that he could eat four dozen oysters for lunch but had not lasted the next day.[37]

Cadic saved his real fire for his essays on the situation of Bretons in Paris. An opening essay on the causes of emigration made the fundamental point that Brittany could not support its children, but at the same time Cadic, like other men of the cloth, deplored the "terrible plague" of depopulation and held up Brittany as a region that did not abdicate its duty but rather maintained its fertility. Nonetheless, he cited a paucity of resources for too many people as the first cause of emigration. To this he added a more recent cause: the importation of grain from the United States, Russia, and Canada was undermining the peasantry: "The bread that we eat in Paris is foreign bread." Third, emigration was among the "traditions de race" in Brittany, for Bretons had gone to sea and explored since the time of Jacques Cartier of Saint-Malo. With the Revolution this stopped, since in this version of French history the Revolution brought on a period in which "the young people stayed home. It was a question of defending their priests." Brittany was thus a historical land of potential adventurers, waiting for their next opportunity. The newspapers with word of high urban wages and the railroad provided the way.

Cadic described in loving detail the life of young men before the age of military service—a description worth noting for its images and idyllic understanding of Breton life. Between the ages of ten and twelve, he writes, the boy faithfully follows catechism lessons and perhaps even school taught by the priest (not the secular teacher). He may pick up some notions of the French language that swim around in his head among Breton expressions, "but no matter! To live and die well, a baccalaureate is unnecessary; and then, there are so many Bretons saints [in heaven] who never spoke French!" From eight to fourteen, Cadic continues, the boy's occupation is to watch the sheep in the meadow. "Ah! The good life!" he wrote, extolling the beauties of the dawn, birdsong, and the meadows. From fourteen to twenty comes the apprenticeship for fieldwork, no less joyous, with harvests spent working alongside compatriots, attending village wedding celebrations, and especially taking part in the *pardons*, at which one might have the honor of carrying the statue of a saint in a Breton penitential procession.[38] After this hymn of praise to rural youth, life in the army is described as an exile that introduces young men to a life away from home, combining damaging discoveries and the luxury of high salaries, white bread, and meat.

The reasons why young women leave home get short shrift: Cadic writes only that "as for the girls, the reason is altogether different." He then observes that it is the fashion for Parisians to vacation in Brittany, and then to bring a maid back to the city, and so the naïve women go along. It is orphans who should go, Cadic suggested, once they are convent-trained: "It seems that the religious houses themselves could take on the task of developing their orphans as a prize for export."[39]

Cadic put himself in the shoes of the newcomers, sensitively imagining their experience as newcomers who lose their faith. The initial step was the first Mass in Paris, where the church and its elegant parishioners provided a grand contrast to the simple and modest village church. The organ and its majestic voice had nothing in common with the liturgical chants of the Breton church. Could the newcomers talk to a priest? Even if they could approach someone so distinguished, they did not dare, lest he not understand their Breton. The standard Parisian Mass was an intimidating first step away from religious practice.[40]

And the interview at the *bureau de placement* was even more demoralizing, Cadic wrote, a theme also followed by Mirbeau in *The Diary of a Chambermaid*. Waiting in line, being interviewed by a stranger who seemed to catalogue the applicant's qualities and inadequacies as if she were a slave on the market in ancient Rome, having her timidity and ignorance of French bring her intelligence into question—all of this was profoundly intimidating. The next step was the street—sleeping on benches, competing with dogs for crusts of bread, and risking arrest. Those able to find a place as a domestic often had the "ill fortune" of finding work for "Jews, Freemasons, or perhaps Protestants." Employers who tolerated religious practice often left barely enough time for Mass, and others derided their servants' faith; the Protestant pastor "leapt at the chance to get Breton servants to Temple." Employers offered no spiritual advice, nor did they attend to the "shameful promiscuity of the sixth floor": a contrast with the good Breton farmers who would go to Mass together with their servants. The circumstances of domestic work therefore marked the second step "away from God."[41]

With the search for a more secure life with a spouse and a family came the final departure from faith. The desires of Bretons being modest, they sought work with the railroad or gas companies. This, though, brought the kind of constant labor that destroys dreams, and even worse were the excavating, laboring, and factory jobs. This is why Bretons were regarded as "the pariahs. For them, the gross jobs, the heavy loads, and the extra duties. Their beliefs are the object of public mockery. . . . Riveted to the earth by the labor of a slave, their eyes no longer have the strength to lift toward God." Alcoholism and moral deprivation on the "vacant lots in Saint-Denis" meant that after fifteen years in the factory, the Breton worker was finished at forty, dead in the hospital, and buried in the common grave of the banlieue. What a contrast with the calm of the Breton cemetery, where the deceased sleep under a granite slab and the eyes of God, side by side with those he knew in life.[42] The nasty end and tragic death found echoes throughout the writings on Bretons in Paris.

As for what had been done for Bretons in Paris before the *Paroisse bretonne*, Cadic was forthright, dramatic, and sarcastic: "nothing, or almost nothing."[43] Turning to the solid accomplishment of the employment agency under the charge of the Soeurs de la Croix—in principle a service for all young women, but in fact one offered especially for Bretons—the chaplain and sisters themselves came from Brittany for the most part. They fed, housed, and placed domestics for the fee of one franc per day. Figures attest to the need for such an institution, since six hundred young women had come to the bureau in the past year. With scorn, Cadic attacked the charitable effectiveness of the Sociétés Provinciales, which were multiplying at the turn of the century. His opening salvo was directed at Ernst Renan, apostate writer and founder of *Le dîner celtique*, "born with rays of eloquence, it was extinguished without a sound. May the earth rest lightly upon it."[44] Leftist organizations came in for special ire, branded as relics of 1793 for their "Dreyfusardism," masonry, anticlericalism, and cosmpolitanism. Ineffectiveness came in for the worst: "the Catholic chapel, the *Blancs*, Medieval style . . . there everything was old, old people, old ideas, old methods—a real Cluny museum." This group announced that it would repatriate Bretons, but in five years the association sent home only twenty-five Bretons, at a time when fourteen hundred a year arrived in Paris.

Other tasks were more urgent, Cadic observed. First, one must fight the socialists, competitors for the Breton soul. Socialist journals had recently published a call to Bretons, understanding both their powerful numbers (some 150,000) and the importance of what was called the "Breton question" of the day. Lest the enemy harness the energy and proverbial stubbornness of the Breton, Cadic enunciated a call to action: "repatriate the unhappy, place the workers, evangelize the ignorant, organize Breton parishes."[45] As for the Breton parish, it could not hope to send Bretons home, especially because "workers constitute the noblest portion of our Breton colony."[46] Centralization was an affair for elites, Cadic wrote, but *le peuple* are set in their provinces, be they Auvergnats, Gascons, Savoyards, or Bretons. Bretons are people of a clan, in Paris or anywhere else far from home—and the parish is like the clan. Like French Canadians whose morale had been saved by French priests while working in New England, Bretons in Paris could be saved the same way, "resolving the Breton question." And so Cadic made an appeal to the Breton-speaking priests of Brittany to work in Paris: "if only . . . 10 would come to Paris, but 10 active, intelligent men resolved to succeed." "To work, Breton priests, it is time!"[47]

The Breton parish had hardly a "brilliant beginning" with a February Mass in 1897 attended by twenty people. But from this modest beginning, by the fall of 1899, the parish boasted six hundred active members out of about twelve hundred inscribed. Cadic attributed his success to the ways he went to the people, and to the excellent location, at Notre Dame des

Champs on the boulevard Montparnasse, not far from the station where Bretons disembarked, in a reputedly Breton neighborhood for wealthy and poor alike. The time of the Mass was changed to Sunday afternoons so that domestics and workers could attend. A process of admission was established: one had to be introduced by another Breton, employed, and either born or married to a Breton. The greatest need, and success, was in the placement of domestics. Begun as a society for workers, the parish had become a "Breton society" in the fullest sense of the word.[48]

Cadic catalogued the services of the parish for its members of all classes. First, because Bretons, unlike Auvergnats and Normans, were poor at saving (here Cadic was in agreement with the popular press), there was a société d'épargne, founded in December 1897. Every worker was given a savings book and encouraged to save 1 to 10 francs per month. By the fall of 1899 four hundred members were subscribed; the women were more assiduous savers than the men, and the poorest workers, domestics, had put aside over 1,500 francs.[49] In addition to encouraging savings, the parish arranged discounts with physicians and pharmacies. Wealthy women were the force behind the clothing bank, a *vestiaire*, also created in the fall of 1897. A consumer's cooperative gave a slight reduction at bakers, butchers, grocers, and a department store. Members paid to belong and reap these benefits, but fees were in proportion to income—from 10 centimes a year for women domestics to 20 francs for patronesses and *"personnes fortunes."* Benefits also accrued to the wealthy, who were granted the same product discounts and had their choice of servants at the employment agency, and to producers, who had an outlet for Breton products. Finally, at the end of 1899 the parish was about to establish a caisse de capitation so that those with a little money could increase their capital.[50] Cadic's concern was a united community of the faithful, regardless of their economic station. Consequently, he reminded the wealthy time and time again that they were brothers in Christ of the poor. "In the name of Jesus Christ, children of Brittany, let us love one another!" he exhorted.[51] "Have pity on the poor," he wrote, "you who are privileged: pity, masters for your servants; pity, employers for your workers."[52]

Cadic gave a good deal of thought to the emigration of Bretons from their home territories—not only why Bretons departed, but where they should go. As a realist, he rejected repatriation as a solution, seeing that at the close of the nineteenth century about 100,000 Bretons were in Paris, 32,000 in Normandy, 22,000 in Anjou, and 21,000 in the Paris basin département of Seine-et-Oise.[53] Cadic loathed, however, the idea of Bretons spending their "endurance, sturdiness, energies and male virtues" beyond the borders of France, where they were sought by emigration agents from Canada, Brazil, and Argentina. The greatest scourge was emigration to the Channel Islands, where Bretons from the Côtes-d'Armor and Ille-et-Vilaine worked by the thousands at vegetable harvests, and to as far north as Edinburgh, where they sold their fresh vegetables. "And who benefits from this force lost to the mother country? The national enemy, the Englishman, and with him Protestantism . . . religion of hypocrites, Tartuffes, and pretenders." Brittany being a province that produces an abundance of people, this abundance should be kept for the French. Let the English, Germans, and Italians take to the road by the millions to America and Australia, he reasoned: France doesn't have too many people and can use its own. Cadic suggested two kinds of destinations: those within France ravaged by depopulation (like the Beauce or the Perche, where birthrates were low) or by bad doctrines, like the Saône-et-Loire in Burgundy, where "workers prefer to talk politics than to use their tools." If Bretons did not remain within France, there were the sunlit alternatives of French colonies: Tunisia, Madagascar, and the grassy highlands of Guinea in West Africa, called Fouta Djallon. In such places the earth would respond to the least efforts of cultivation. Finally, with a priest and parish, Bretons would thrive, "they would found a solid race, rooted to the soil, strong as the rocks of Brittany."[54] Here, in a few paragraphs, Cadic expressed his eagerness to help his compatriots, his anti-English animus, his anti-Protestantism, his belief in the power of the church, and his faith in the colonial project.

François Cadic wrote out of genuine caring for the poor Bretons in Paris; his concern extended to their bodies, wracked by hunger, alcohol, and disease. He was not alone in pointing to tuberculosis, about which he warned: "Watch out! Paris is the city that kills."[55] For those concerned with Bretons' health, tuberculosis took center stage. François Cadic did not stint on dramatic prose when he took up the topic of "an illness, more terrible than the plague, more frightening than cholera, attacks the marrow, exhausts the blood and devours lungs . . . this illness rages particularly among Bretons: it is *tuberculosis.*" The nurse passes, sees that the patient is no longer breathing, and coldly calls the gravedigger. "Look at the name: usually it's a Breton." Citing the work of the doctor Léon Renault, an associate of the Breton parish, Cadic offered shocking mortality statistics for four hospitals in Paris in 1899: 25 Bretons among the 143 tubercular deaths at Cochin (the public assistance hospital for the poor in the Fourteenth Arrondissement), 33 among the 179 at La Charité, 30 among the 107 at Laënnec (also in the Fourteenth), and 43 among the 143 at the Necker (in the Fifteenth).[56] Cadic himself succumbed to tuberculosis in 1929.

MEDICAL SCIENCE AND BRETON HEALTH

Interest in tuberculosis was especially intense in the early years of the twentieth century, when more than thirty-five books on tuberculosis were published each year. France had a higher death rate from tuberculosis than England or Germany, and although tuberculosis mortality had been on the decline in the last decade of the nineteenth century, the decline was slow.[57] David Barnes acutely summarizes the "successive truths" about tuberculosis: in the 1820s it was consumption, or *phthisis*, viewed as an inscrutable, random killer; in the 1830s it began to be seen as socially discriminating, haunting certain professions and poor neighborhoods; beginning in the 1840s consumptive women were seen as highly sensitive and redeemed by their suffering; and as the Third Republic became established, the disease was understood to be possibly contagious. By around 1900 "tuberculosis was a national scourge, highly contagious, lurking around every corner and symptomatic of moral decay."[58] Turn-of-the-century reports targeted slum housing and immoderation in drink as the sanitary and moral roots of tuberculosis, along with practices such as spitting.[59] These foci were part of a larger concern with low birthrates, moral decay, and dangers represented by the working classes, and "tuberculosis allowed all these diverse and threatening themes to be assembled into a single coherent package."[60]

Newcomers to urban life were regarded as especially crucial to this "single coherent package," since by leaving home they were particularly likely to lower the birthrate, cast aside their virtues, drink too much, and live in slums, where they were vulnerable to the poverty that bred tuberculosis. And no one was more likely to turn from a healthy rural dweller to a dissolute and sickly city dweller than the Breton, whose poverty was legendary. In Le Havre, the tuberculosis capital of France, according to Barnes, Bretons were at the top of the list of consumptives, reported in 1868, and Breton tuberculosis was the topic of more than one medical dissertation.[61] That by Georges Bourgeois in 1904 linking the rural exodus to tuberculosis saw Breton migrants as especially vulnerable, because they were characterized by "poor hygiene, alcoholism, and lack of moral resistance."[62]

The physician Arsène-Guillaume Trégoat wrote in the spirit of the times with his thesis *L'immigration bretonne à Paris: Son importance, ses causes, ses conséquences intéressantes au point de vue médical, de quelques moyens propres à la diminuer* (1900). Like Jean Lemoine, who had written about Bretons in the previous decade, Trégoat opened with a recollection of vacations in Brittany, and like Lemoine he claimed a Breton identity; in this case, he was also a medical student and so doubly interested in writing his thesis on peasant departures for cities, especially Paris. In the little spots in the Côtes-d'Armor, he began, where everyone knows everything about everyone else, hardly a week goes by when you don't hear "Guillaume or Yves Marie so-and-so just left for Paris."[63] The few who do return, he continues, usually do so on doctor's orders—pale, thin, and in search of better air for their health, which was compromised in the big city. Some do better, of course, returning for a *pardon* or a vacation, former peasants and farm boys now spruced up and proud of their bourgeois clothes, and leaving again with a brother, sister, or neighbor in tow.[64]

As a physician and a Breton who remained in contact with his home territories, Trégoat demands our attention. He opens his thesis with thanks to his thesis director, doctors, librarian, and the chaplain of four Breton parishes in Paris. In assessing the causes of emigration, he points to military service, for taking young men from home and exposing them to other ways of life, but he rejects notions of easy money and distaste for agriculture; rather, he emphasizes the poor soil of Brittany and Brittany's extraordinarily high birthrate, which produced families so large that they were difficult to support.[65] In his negative view of high birthrates, the doctor differs from the cleric. He also departs from Léon Renault's findings of alarmingly high mortality from tuberculosis in Breton hospitals in 1899 by adding findings presented to the Medical Society of Hospitals in January 1900; he showed that immigrants and Bretons did have very high mortality, but also that the very highest mortality was in hospitals in Breton neighborhoods.[66] There was an urban geography to immigration and tubercular mortality in Paris.

A core narrative, an archetypal tale of decline and death, has a strong presence in Trégoat's thesis; in this narrative migration to Paris is followed by decline, physical and moral disintegration, even death. Contagion rather than inherited weakness is responsible for tuberculosis, and Paris itself is at fault, since the vast majority of victims are newcomers, most of whom have healthy elders. Trégoat would agree with Cadic that Paris is the city that kills. Indeed, migration from countryside to city is one of the "two fundamental dangers" behind tuberculosis. The second is alcohol: according to a report to the Medical Society of Hospitals in 1899, 88 percent of tuberculars abused alcohol.[67] And, Trégoat reasoned, "When he leaves Brittany, the Breton, however, is not an alcoholic. He likes to drink, it's true; he has a very strong penchant to get drunk, that's incontestable; and too often, market evenings or in the weighty circumstances of the draft lottery . . . you see him shouting and making a ruckus, being in a state of great intoxication in this period of excitement; but that only happens on occasion and the rest of the time he doesn't drink. In Paris, he becomes a chronic drunk and here again we have seen it's often tuberculosis that ends the story."[68] In the end Trégoat goes to a physician in the Côtes-d'Armor, whose stories relate the deadly combination of backbreaking urban work, poverty, and a lack of moral fiber. The first is the story of Jean H., *valet de chambre* in Paris for five years after his military service, who was sick for three months before he returned home; from a healthy family, he was dead within two months. The second story is that of Marie H., a single mother who went to Paris to work as a wet nurse and then stayed on with her employers as a cook after her term as a nurse had finished; four years later she was back in Brittany at her sister's home, where her health only went downhill. Marie is the only woman mentioned in this thesis and not a drinker, but as a single mother she was, Trégoat implies, on the slippery slope of moral degradation even before she left Brittany.[69] Trégoat concludes that tuberculosis is likely to be contracted in Paris, either because these Bretons were particularly exposed to the disease or because they were weakened by their urban ways.[70]

BRETON RELIGION:
A FAITH TO PROMOTE, TO RIDICULE, TO PROTECT

What could protect the Bretons in Paris? The abbé Cadic and Catholic conservatives would advise adherence to Christian standards. To the Société La Bretagne, founded in 1884, faith was the answer, particularly if accompanied by virtue. Like the Breton parish, the Société embraced a paternal concern for the poor Bretons of Paris, yet it had a less social orientation than the abbé Cadic, and its leadership was drawn from the conservative Breton nobility. At the turn of the century the count de Chateaubriand served as president and the baron de Kertanguy as treasurer; the vice-presidents were the count Albert de Mun and the count Alain de Guébriant, and the baroness de Kertanguy and countesses de Quelen and de Kermaingant provided leadership as well.[71] The society journal came to advertise a genealogical and nobility researcher on the back page, a M. Le Dault, who could provide historical documents on Breton families.[72]

The vulnerable faith of the poor Breton in Paris was the focus of the Société. The loss of faith was something of a puzzle, reflected the abbé Guillevic, head of the school in the inland bretonnant Morbinnais village of Priziac, particularly because Bretons were justly known worldwide "for their capacity to undertake the harshest of tasks; they are good workers, good soldiers, good sailors; they confront fire on the field of battle without fear and gladly face storms at sea; they back down neither to fatigue, nor illness, nor death. But when it comes to religion, when God is in question, their soul, their eternity, then they are afraid, they tremble and hide; a joke disconcerts them, teasing makes them blush and . . . they abandon the cause of God."[73] The occasion for Guillevic's speech was the annual *pardon*—the Breton religious ritual procession—in celebration of the mother of the Virgin Mary at the Church of Sainte-Anne-de-la-Maison-Blanche in the Thirteenth Arrondissement.[74] Not unusual, such occasions were faithfully reported in the society's monthly publication, *Bretoned Paris*. For example, it featured in a special issue the pilgrimage in March 1908 of Parisian Bretons to the Basilica of Sacré-Coeur in Montmartre, presided over by the archbishop of Rennes, himself a Breton, where over eight thousand attendees sang Breton hymns.[75] One heard from leading members of the society: the following summer, a report of M. de Estourbeillon's discourse exalting Joan of Arc and her love for Bretons was followed by an article by the Vicomtesse de Pitry on the virtues of Joan of Arc—who began by noting her modesty and remarked on "the contrast between Joan of Arc and most women today."[76]

Virtue was a key to the Société La Bretagne. The journal extolled the virtues of Bretons like the boy of seventeen who walked from Quimperlé in the Morbihan to Paris to seek work; the trip took four weeks and cost the boy his only 20 francs, and he never missed a Sunday Mass en route.[77] Bretons needed to help each other, the association's placement bureau urged—but it added that one could only recommend the right kind of Breton for jobs, because if a drunk were hired the reputation of Bretons would be ruined. "On the contrary, if only good ones are recommended, the quality of being a Breton will become synonymous with an excellent employee, the Office will prosper, and businessmen and industrialists will use it more and more; that is the goal that each Breton in Paris should seek to attain."[78] The same was true in the employment office for domestic servants, where "it is necessary to be very circumspect and well-informed, because obviously you cannot push charity to the point of recommending persons who are not recommendable."[79]

A clear virtue of the Bretons was their high fertility, a point of pride in the *Bretoned Paris* in this age when French social policy was so concerned with depopulation.[80] One article published in 1909 on the population since 1906 included detailed birth and death data along with the argument that France owed its good health to Brittany: without Brittany, France would have 6,722 more deaths than births every year, but as it was, France gained 24,997 people. Brittany, in short, saves France. "We will only know the [exact number of emigrations] in 1911, with the next census. But in the meanwhile . . . let us confirm, and rejoice in confirming that Celtic blood is not thinning out, because it gives in Brittany alone an increase of 13,864 and we are not talking about Bretons who are born of Celtic blood in the other Breton cities: Paris and the Seine, Le Havre, Angers, le Mans, etc." The author of this article denigrated lazy people from other regions, who no longer had children and left for Paris, turning their work over to foreigners.[81]

Aid provided by the society was meant to help people stay on the right path: it included an employment bureau for women in domestic service, another for men in search of work, a clothing bank, and meetings for Bretons in Paris. There was the Association of Saint Anne for domestic servants, and monthly Sunday services for Bretons in several parishes throughout the city.[82] Six nuns carried out home visitations in these parishes, which were enumerated in the society publication, along with baptisms, first communions, repatriations and placement of children, and visits to families and the ill. Visits were expanded to Saint-Denis in the fall of 1905, where all Bretons reportedly got to know Sister Anne, because she was celebrated there in July 1913 in a Breton program with singing, a speech, and a raffle.[83] In the meanwhile Saint-Denis was an area of real concern, because it was poor and had a strong socialist impulse—so Breton services there in the crypt of Saint-Denis-de-l'Estrée were reported with special interest.[84]

The Société La Bretagne was virulently opposed to departures from Brittany, and it had its own analysis of emigration. A series of articles in 1909 did not blame the experience of military service for emigration as many others had done, particularly because over half the compatriots who went to Paris were women. Rather, the Capitaine de Courcy, secretary of the Société and author of the articles on Breton population, laid the blame at the feet of primary education—or rather primary educators: "Because they wear a *redingote* and a melon hat, imagining themselves be a superior race to country people, they cram a hodgepodge of summaries into the heads of their unfortunate pupils . . . persuading them that their ancestors were nothing but dunces, their parents are imbeciles." These were the urban, anticlerical teachers, but even the good ones, the *instituteurs libres*, were obligated by the curriculum to impose a crushing program on the students, neglecting the perspective of life in the fields.[85] A second article blamed large industries, "especially in the factories around Paris with their fictive bait of large salaries." It was rural industry which must be resuscitated with electrification: this would put small machines in the home that could employ not only the father but also the wife and daughter.[86]

The advice to readers, to priests in Brittany, to nuns: when you hear about young men or women who want to go to Paris, have them contact us and do not hesitate to ask for advice—we will never refuse. But we will suggest that they remain *au pays*. Women's emigration was a particular danger, because it had been on the increase for the last twenty years. "Women, especially girls, are devoured by that sickness that is the need to change place and it persists during immigration."[87] "How many, among the hundreds of Bretons who arrive each year, so kind and so good," de Courcy had asked years earlier, "do we find in the hospital or wandering the streets of the big city with no resources, the city which is, for girls left on their own, what the sea is for sailors: the great devourer of human lives!"[88] The solution was to stay at home, to stay in the fields, and remain devout.

Yet faithful Catholicism was hardly a given in turn-of-the-century Paris; religion was controversial, as separation of church and state was debated. Satirical journals such as *L'assiette au beurre*, published from 1901 to 1912, had a field day with the abuses of the church. Designed for artists, intellectuals, and members of the liberal and intellectual bourgeoisie, it had a circulation of 25,000 to 40,000 copies per weekly issue, reaching many more readers than Breton publications of any stripe.[89] With a focus on "current social problems," it kept alcoholism as a "a permanent theme," yet critiques of the church and advocacy of the separation of church and state were central, particularly until 1905. The journal was best known for its subversive and destructive humor, and the bitterness—if not nastiness—of its illustrations, *L'assiette au beurre* chose as its target "Bretagne—le people noir" for an issue in October 1903, the sole issue devoted to one province of France.[90] The anticlerical essayist and poet Laurent Tailhade provided a two-page text and some captions for thirteen illustrations by Evilio Torent (see figure 2).[91]

The main target of the issue was Breton Catholicism, the "Christian fetishism" that had marked Brittany and Bretons with "their filth, their piousness, their taste for the Eucharist and strong liquors, the stink of their huts, their aversion to baths. . . ." The author opens his detailed attack on the clergy by calling the congregations "swarming vermin . . . that make us blush to be classed in the same species." Alcohol and the church both come under fire, and in the end the focus turns to Bretons themselves: "sad little groups, irresponsible victims of the priest and of alcohol!" A series of insults follows: "There are no better Christians than this Breton trash; none is more refractory to civilization. Idolatrous, miserly, sloppy, sneaky, alcoholic and patriotic, the american hypocrite doesn't eat, he feeds; he doesn't drink, he gets drunk; he doesn't wash, he greases himself; he doesn't reason, he prays, and carried away by prayer, he falls into the deepest abject state. He is the Negro of France." The author holds out hope in the end that "the dawn is breaking" in Brittany and that the Brittany of Renan and Lammenais will reject the evil shadow of its present Christianity.[92] The illustrations depict a Brittany of sexual and religious hypocrites, alcoholics, and stink, and clergy who are "insolent black crows." Envy is the "very Christian saint"; sleeping alone is torture; the sailor tells his wife "try to be faithful"; God is the "last lover of naughty old women"; cider is confused with holy water; and the priest finds a husband for the mother of his child.[93]

The more mainstream press had also featured Breton religion the year before, when *L'Illustration*—an important weekly that gave great atten-

2. *L'Assiette au Beurre*, "La Bretagne," October 1903.
Special Collections Library, University of Michigan.

tion to royal families, colonial affairs, and reflections of high society—published long articles about parishes in revolt against the series of laws that secularized French public education.[94] During its long life from 1840 to 1940 *L'Illustration* did not use satirical drawings but rather realistic drawings, engravings, and photographs for articles on life in Paris, in France, and throughout the world.[95] The Law of Associations, passed in 1901, demanded that teaching congregations seek authorization from Parliament or face dissolution, and banned members of unauthorized orders from the classroom. By the end of July 1902 the unauthorized schools run by male religious orders were closed without incident—but the Bretons of the Finistère mounted great collective and even armed resistance to the closing of schools run by a valued Breton female order, the Filles du Saint-Esprit.[96] This resistance made the Paris press: it was the object of three running issues of *L'Illustration* in August 1902.

The Breton correspondent Rémy Saint-Maurice (who had published a series of articles about Breton poverty earlier in the year) reported that the region of the Léon in the northwestern Finistère was alive with rumors of violence at the beginning of August; he was advised to stay away, lest he be shot before he reached his destination of Ploudaniel. This commune was known to be one of the Catholic bastions in the Léon area of the rural Finistère. In the town of Landerneau, where Saint-Maurice wrote, a woman in her sixties predicted that the decrees would be carried out, and then showed Saint-Maurice the revolver in her shopping bag with which she promised to shoot the first man who crossed the threshold of the congregation. In front of the building women of the people, the bourgeoisie, and the aristocracy were stationed on benches, doing needlework while they guarded access to the convent and awaited the troops.[97] The next week Saint-Maurice's story was accompanied by six photographs, and related the "Execution of the Decrees in Brittany." On 7 August troops were heard arriving in Landerneau at 2:00 a.m., and by 3:00 a.m. peasant coiffes and Breton hats were already in the main square, the crowd blocking the way of the troops and shouting, "Vive les soeurs!" The government deputy read the decree of the law in front of the convent door once the troops had cleared the way, and then read it again to the mother superior once entry had been gained. The mother superior called the sisters, who came out of their cells weeping, knelt, received a blessing from her in front of the troops, and left—taken into the homes of their supporters. Illustrations included a full-page drawing of the mother superior blessing the sisters before their dispersal, with officers standing along the wall, and another drawing of the sisters and their protectors in the town square. Saint-Maurice also reported on the village of Crozon, to the west, and included illustrations from Crozon and Ploudaniel, where barricades had been mounted.[98]

A final story in *L'Illustration* recounted what the author called a "typical expulsion," summarizing the closures in Ploudaniel, Saint-Méen, and Folgoët, as well as other locations in the region: announcements from lookouts posted in the belfry, summations at the doors of the convent, cries in response, the demolition of the door, followed by the meeting inside with the mother superior, the rector of the parish, and the deputy or senator—and at the end, the moving exit of the sisters, "saluted as respectfully by their expellers as by their defenders." There were battles, Saint-Maurice noted, but fortunately no blood; some rocks were thrown, but the principal arms were the Bretons' buckets of dirty water and garbage thrown at the troops. A sympathetic reflection closed the story: "It's finished for the present, these expulsions of the sisters for which the broader public does not understand the necessity. No more than it can understand the tactic of the congregations that ceded with good grace here and resisted there, without this difference having been explained. The decision goes to the court of the Conseil d'État. When it will have made a judgment perhaps we will know what really is the law and legality in this deplorable conflict."[99] The mainstream Parisian press was amazed but not distressed by Bretons' show of support for the church. This expensive illustrated publication, whose subsequent issue featured a cover illustration of a baron's "Mass at 2700 Meters" in the Pyrenees, purported to be as puzzled by state actions as by Breton sensibilities, however unusual those Breton sensibilities may have been.[100]

Early cinema also targeted Brittany, creating exotic and dramatic tales for the Parisian audience. Between 1908 and 1914 film studios like Pathé and the Gaumont turned out documentaries and stories featuring Brittany more than other regions. Filmed in studios of Vincennes, in the Bois de Boulogne, in southern France, or on the beaches of Dieppe in Normandy, these films related romantic and exotic tales. Eric Le Roy comments on the condescension embodied in these films: "Everyone dies at sea, women only pray to forget their sorrow, illness, alcohol and idleness ravage families and poverty reigns everywhere. But thanks to faith and God happiness makes its appearance and the miserable are aided."[101] These simple, benighted folks that Parisians saw on screen were not those they saw in the city. The core Parisian images of Bretons were neither the suffering screen actors nor religious folk in revolt but rather the ubiquitous workers.

BRETONS IN PARIS DURING THE BELLE ÉPOQUE

At the turn of the century Paris had a place for millions of workers in its rich and varied economy, an economy in which the banlieue was increasingly important. The city and banlieue were known for their industry and artisanal production, yet a growth of service work also marked the period between the turn of the century and the outbreak of the First World War. More men and women labored in domestic service and transportation services in this increasingly polished capital city.[102] Although working conditions were harsh, and in many cases miserable, the broad range of occupations gave a place for every kind of worker, from the rag picker who lived in the *zone* on the outskirts of the city to the merchant in the luxurious apartments of First Arrondissement. Parisians were everywhere in this economy, but they certainly had a place of privilege in skilled artisanal work. Many newcomers had their regional specialties: the census testifies to the predominance of the Auvergnats as barkeeps and restaurateurs, and of the famous masons from the Creuse in the building trades.[103]

Bretons too had a particular place in this labor force, but it was not among the skilled laborers or property owners. Most striking was the place of Breton women in domestic service—the single most important service occupation, providing a place for nearly 100,000 women in the city proper in 1901 and in 1911 (and another 150,000 on the outskirts).[104] Although fewer than 5 percent of the city's people were from Brittany, Breton women were between one-eighth and one-sixth of the domestic servants and cooks in Paris and the Seine in the years before the First World War; half the Breton working women labored as domestic servants or cleaning women. By 1911 over fourteen thousand Breton domestics labored in the city, and nearly six thousand more were cooks like Yvonne Yven, whose story opened chapter 2. They were so important to this ubiquitous occupation that the *bonne bretonne* became a character whose real existence provided the grain of truth on which this stereotype thrived. Eighteen years after the publication of Zola's *Pot Bouille*, as we have seen, the Breton maid was portrayed as an exploited but salacious sexual being in Octave Mirbeau's *Diary of a Chambermaid* (1900), and as the lovable fool in the long-lived cartoon for girls, *Bécassine*. Breton men worked as domestics as well, but in much smaller numbers, and they made up a much smaller proportion of male domestics.[105] It was the Bécassine, like Yvonne Yven, who was most noticeable in Paris.

The needle trades were an important domain for women in Paris, but Bretons were barely visible in it, because the *couturière* lived in her own quarters, and so was usually not a single newcomer to the city but a woman who could rent her own place or live with her family. The Breton women who made up most of those in the needle trades were part of the longest-lived and best-established migration streams: those from Gallo-speaking upper Brittany. They came from the Ille-et-Vilaine, home to the capital city of Rennes, and from the Loire-Atlantique, home to the city of Nantes. These were the women who were able to make living arrangements through the contacts they had established in the city or by living with their family. Of the Breton women laboring in Paris, 25 percent worked in the needle trades, half of these as couturières. Nonetheless, all the Breton couturières together—3,300 in 1901 and 4,701 in 1911—were only about 8 percent of the women in Paris who sewed for a living.[106]

The most pointed specialty for Breton women, albeit a rare one, was hospital work—the occupation of Marie Lepioufle, whose story opened this chapter. This was hardly easy work—scrubbing floors, emptying bed-pans, cleaning patients—and many people like Marie's aunt felt that the hospitals were disreputable places where men and women mixed freely. Some parents approved of hospital employment, however, thinking that their daughters would be safe because hospitals offered lodging and in many cases work with nuns. Before the war hospital nurses were regarded as being much like maids, with a patina of hygienic principles—"Bécassine in the hospital," in the words of the historian Yvonne Knibiehler.[107] Even in a study of his compatriots, the abbé Gautier remarked that among the numerous *infirmiers* and *infirmières* listed in the medical professions, most had no formal medical training.[108] Nonetheless, they were thick on the ground: in 1901 over a fifth of female medical professionals were from Brittany—nearly fourteen hundred women in the Seine, and over eleven hundred in Paris.[109]

As the chaplain of the Breton parish in Versailles remarked, Breton men did not have the same reputation for rectitude and modesty that served many Breton women, so the men had more trouble getting jobs, and many became day laborers working at the worst jobs—shoveling earth, cleaning septic tanks and sewers, sweeping the streets, and clearing garbage.[110] When figures for 1911 for day laborers were published, Breton men numbered 4,500 in the Department of the Seine (about 9 percent of the total) and nearly 1,900 in the city (about 8 percent of the total). Breton women figured prominently among *journalières*, in about the same proportions.[111] *Journalier* was an occupational category that was nearly twice as important in the banlieue than in the city, which confirms Lenard Berlanstein's observation that it was important to the factories of the banlieue; there the work of hauling, stocking, and piling was assigned to journaliers, who were hired by the job. This was irregular, debilitating, and often dangerous work.[112]

If Breton men had a specialty, it was transportation rather than manufacturing: the largest single group enumerated was in the employ of the railroads at the turn of the century—over 3,500 in the Seine, and over 1,850 in Paris itself.[113] To work for a *chemin de fer* was to have a secure and desirable job: in the opinion of the chaplain cited above, employees were "considered like bourgeois Bretons."[114] A decade later over one-eighth of railroad workers in the Seine and in Paris were from Brittany—5,050 in the Seine, and nearly 2,800 in Paris.[115]

The Chemin de Fer Métropolitain employed a wide range of men while the Métro was under construction; workers built 80 kilometers of track and 155 stations in Paris between 1898 and 1910, to say nothing of tunnels, viaducts, and bridges. About 15 percent of this pioneer generation of workers who were hired before the Great War came from Brittany.[116] Most were from rural areas, but the company needed employees at all levels of skill and training. One employee, the son of a storekeeper in Rennes, was a navy veteran and graduate of the École des Mécaniciens in Brest who was hired on in 1898 and rose to become a depot chief by 1905. Another, the son of illiterate peasants, arrived about 1900 and worked successively as a groom, a coachman, a machinist, and finally the driver of a gas-engine bus during the Great War.[117] Not only was there a great range of workers, but the work itself also evolved. Elise Feller, the historian of this generation, observes that "the depots that had immense stables, with the sounds and warmth of horses night and day, with the odors of hay and manure, so familiar to young rurals, were transformed or even rebuilt to accommodate the cold electric motors of the trams, and later the multitude of thundering busses." Men like the groom who became a coachman and then a machinist "passed brutally from a world that still worked at the horse's pace to an electrified and mechanized universe [and] must have shown an astonishing capacity for adaption and skill acquisition."[118]

The world of Paris transport was in evolution. And although hardly bourgeois, carters, coachmen, delivery men, and the drivers of coaches for hire had an important place in the Paris economy and were even more important among Breton men, who numbered over 3,300 in the Department of the Seine (accounting for about 10 percent of the total) and nearly 2,700 in the city itself (about 7 percent of the total), and whose numbers increased during the subsequent decade.[119] François Michel, a son of the Breton countryside whose story opened this chapter, was one of these men; he passed the nursing exams but preferred to do carting work for the hospitals, which allowed him to work with horses.[120]

FOURTEENTH ARRONDISSEMENT

Bretons worked everywhere in the city. Was there a Breton Paris by 1900? "Of course there is a Breton Paris that is, there are neighborhoods where their presence, often dictated by workplace, is more important than elsewhere," Alain Faure writes. Yet these were hardly enclaves: in 1911 the census counted 108,000 Bretons, of whom 13,600 were in the Sixth and Fourteenth Arrondissements—12.6 percent of the total. Bretons also gathered in the Thirteenth, Batignolles, and Montmartre, but there was no massive grouping. And although there were over 8,000 Bretons in the Fourteenth Arrondissement by 1911, half of whom lived in the crowded Plaisance neighborhood, people born in Brittany accounted for only 6 percent of the Plaisance and just over 5 percent of the Fourteenth.[121]

Their presence was even more scanty on the police blotters of 1910, although the lively nightlife of the Plaisance left its mark. Drunk and disorderly, yes, but Bretons also appeared for emergency hospitalization, work disputes, and loss of papers. They were written up as both perpetrators and victims of theft. Women no longer dominated those who had the attention of the police, but they held their own among the drunken and disorderly and those who had to be hospitalized. Everyone arrested for vagrancy or clandestine prostitution was a woman, and women's situations reflected the pitfalls of urban life, as shown by the experience of two childless widows: one, fifty-four years old, was arrested for vagrancy and asked for repatriation after four months in Paris without work; the other was picked up at 1:30 in the morning while sleeping out by the fortifications.[122] Things were much the same at the Montparnasse police station, except that men had an exclusive hold on arrests for drunkenness. There Marcel Gestin, a baker's assistant from a village in the French-speaking Morbihan, first drew the attention of the police in February just before 4:00 in the morning, when he called the police a *"bande de vaches"* (and those were his most polite words). Two months later he was back, this time for beating up a male nurse in a bar.[123] Despite the Breton reputation for docility, they doled out their share of abuse to police, particularly when they were in their cups. They certainly were not eager for police supervision; indeed, a combination of pride and shame was probably behind the behavior of Jeanne Perrier, twenty-two, from a small and remote village in the outer Finistère. Three times arrested for clandestine prostitution, once in the Plaisance neighborhood and twice in Montparnasse, she steadfastly refused to name her parents—in this she was unique.[124]

The Gare Montparnasse was on the front lines in Paris, and so the neighborhood saw newcomers fresh from the bretonnant countryside, like the farmer Louis Cochard, forty-six; Cochard came in to report that he had met two men on the station platform who followed him to a urinal on a nearby boulevard and lifted his wallet, containing 90 francs and his round-trip ticket.[125] This bumpkin must have caused some amusement: his situation was quite that unlike that of most marginal families illuminated by the police blotters, such as that of a woman laborer, fifty-five, who had come to Paris from a village in the central Côtes-d'Armor the month before, first staying with her son in Versailles and then with her daughter, a nurse in the Fourteenth, before being taken off to the psychiatric hospital Sainte-Anne.[126] Other incidents appear—violence between spouses, a father fighting removal of his children to the office of public assistance, a wet nurse seeking assurance that her baby at home, unexpectedly being bottle-fed, was being cared for properly. But for the most part in these neighborhoods, it was a lively nightlife and drinking that did the most to keep the police station occupied.[127]

BRETONS MARRY IN PARIS

As pointedly as Bretons were set apart in the eyes of men of science, the cloth, medicine, and the pen, were they cut off from others when they married? Was the Paris of 1910 a melting pot, or was it a place for colonies of provincials? And how about Bretons? How had it changed since 1890 for those who married? Alain Faure argues that Paris was a melting pot, even more so in 1910 than it had been twenty-five years before. From his study of over five thousand marriages in 1910–11, Faure writes that "what can be clearly confirmed is that endogamy is a myth. The norm is mixing." All the debate that remains is about the limits and contours of intermarriage.[128] Garden had found that about 20 percent of all provincials married someone from their home department in 1885; Faure found that only about 15 percent married someone from their home department in 1910–11, and only about 25 percent married someone from their home region. But like Garden, Faure also contends that Bretons had stronger endogamy than was the norm.[129] The Bretons of Saint-Denis and of the Fourteenth Arrondissement demonstrate that marriage patterns could have very different contours even within one group of provincials.

In the Belle Époque the Bretons of the Fourteenth Arrondissement continued to marry "out"; of the 197 marriages in 1910, three-quarters joined Bretons with a partner born outside their home region. As with the provincials in Faure's study of the Eleventh Arrondissement, only about a quarter of marriages involved regional compatriots. Moreover, nearly a third of Bretons in the Fourteenth married a Parisian.[130] But the migration stream had changed: more marriage partners from the Finistère and Morbihan joined those from the Côtes-d'Armor, as the proportion from the French-speaking upper Breton departments stayed about the same. The 160 Bretonnes and 89 Bretons in the Fourteenth were distinct from each other, because the men, as in 1890, were likely to marry another Breton and the women were likely to "marry out."[131] And these were older brides—older than Marie Lepioufle, the Breton nurse who married at about twenty-one. The brides of the Fourteenth married, on average, when they were nearly twenty-six (see Appendix, table 2).[132]

Like many men and women in working-class Paris, and like Bretons who had married twenty years before in the Fourteenth Arrondissement, many of those brides and grooms had lived together in consensual unions, since half of them lived at the same address before their wedding—a few more than twenty years earlier. Some of these unions produced babies, but fewer than before in 1890, when a quarter of all marriages were also the occasion to legitimize a child. In 1910 this was true of only about 15 percent of marriages. It may be that Bretons were less likely to have children before they married because they were becoming more prosperous, and Breton women were becoming more protected by better earnings and more effective networks. Yet still, only a few lived with their mother or father.[133]

Most Breton brides who married in the Fourteenth Arrondissement married a man from outside Brittany, and these brides earned their living as cooks or needle workers, like the Mouraud sisters from the Bretonnant town of Guingamp in the Côtes-d'Armor. Their parents had died by

March 1910, when the eldest, Victorine, married a mechanic from the Yonne in Burgundy, son of rentiers. Victorine, a thirty-two-year-old cook, lived on the broad rue d'Alésia, just around the corner from the groom, who was five years her junior. All four witnesses seem to have been secured by Victorine: two lived in her building, a government white-collar worker and a rentier (either of whom could have been her employer); the other two lived closer to the center of town in the same building, a widow lady shopkeeper and Victorine's sister, a dressmaker named Marie, twenty-two.[134] Marie too married a mechanic—a Parisian two years her senior who lived across town in the Twentieth Arrondissement with his parents, a mechanic and a laundress. The groom supplied two witnesses: his sister, herself a dressmaker, and a typographer friend who also lived at his address in the Twentieth; Marie's brother-in-law, now an electrician, and a library employee stood up for her. Victorine probably met her husband in the neighborhood, and perhaps Marie met her husband through her future brother-in-law—we will never know, although it is safe to conclude that these were Parisian courtships. By all appearances, at any rate, the Mouraud sisters, like most Breton brides, had bright and secure futures in Paris with skilled-laborer husbands and, in Marie's case, a family of in-laws.[135]

Many of the men who married fellow Bretons worked in delivery, in carting, or as horse grooms, and as many worked for the railroad as well.[136] Their brides were less likely to work in the needle trades, and more likely to be domestic servants or cooks than those who married non-Bretons. Typically, Auguste Blonsard, a coachman, seemed to choose a life of work with horses in transportation services. In May 1910 he married Anne Fiquet, from a village near his inland birthplace, also in the Morbihan in upper Brittany; the two were born one year apart, and both lived at number 27 in the crowded rue Vandamme near the Gare Montparnasse, where Anne was a cook. Their parents—village farmers in Auguste's case, a widowed housekeeper in Anne's—communicated their permission for the wedding but did not attend. Auguste's coachman brother Henri, who lived in the same building, served as a witness along with a neighboring coachman. Two horse grooms who lived in the same building across town also served as witnesses. Like François Michel and Marie Lepioufle, this couple could well have met in Paris, but even if they did, their solidarity could also have been rooted in their shared home area.[137] The story recounted above of François Michel and Marie Lepioufle, each of whom came to Paris at the urging of a sibling, does suggest connections among brothers and sisters like Auguste and Henri Blonsard, or Victorine and Marie Mouraud; indeed many siblings were apparent in the remarkable subgroup of Breton brides and grooms who worked as nurses.

Eighteen Breton nurses, male and female, married in the Fourteenth Arrondissement in 1910. Some married other nurses, others married fellow Bretons, and still others married provincials or Parisians. Many worked for the Assistance Publique, in the St. Vincent de Paul foundling asylum and children's hospital, or at the Maternité in the Fourteenth, but they also staffed other hospitals and some lived independently. Almost all were women, and most came from the Côtes-d'Armor. Philomène Le Borgne lived at the St. Vincent de Paul hospital when she married her fellow nurse Dominique Burneau, from the Haute-Saône in eastern France. Philomène was twenty-nine, the groom thirty-four, and both were from agricultural families with two living parents, Philomène's in their village near the sea in upper Brittany. Three nurses witnessed the wedding, including Philomène's sister and a male nurse who lived and worked at the same hospital; another male nurse lived nearby.[138] What set nurses apart are their ties with their fellow nurses and their siblings, as revealed by wedding witnesses; because many nurses lived in the hospital, they had a sort of workplace solidarity that was rare among other groups of Bretons at this time. The presence of siblings, but not parents, at their weddings signals that nursing—like work with the Métro and the railroad—was a significant entry occupation for the generation that moved to Paris.[139] And like many Bretons in Paris, these came from agricultural families. The trajectory of their lives constituted a true break from that of their parents.

Those Breton men who married women from the provinces or from Paris seem to have been relatively well placed in the Parisian economy. Many had white-collar work, others had skilled jobs, and fewer would be in delivery and transportation. Their brides were often themselves clerks, seamstresses, or cooks. Jules Daniel, twenty-eight, was among these: a Breton man with a secure job, a postal worker from an inland village in the French-speaking Côtes-d'Armor, son of a day laborer. In the spring of 1910 he married a Parisian dressmaker who lived in the same house as he— a young painter's daughter, seventeen, who resided with her parents. The bride had two relatives at the wedding, and (judging from their surnames) two fellow Bretons stood up for Jules Daniel.[140] Like Marie Mouraud he had moved from a Breton village to secure work in the capital, married into a Paris family, and was unlikely to return to the Côtes-d'Armor.

SAINT-DENIS

The Breton community in Saint-Denis reached its peak before the Great War. As the city's population grew from nearly 61,000 to over 71,000 between 1901 and 1911, Bretons became 10.9 percent of the electorate of Saint-Denis. At least among adult males, Bretons were twice as important to Saint-Denis as they were to the Fourteenth Arrondissement.[141] Many of them lived in the crowded and unsanitary houses like those on the rue des Poissonniers. Twenty-three households lived at number 59, for example, over a third of them supported by people who worked at the Combes tannery down the street at number 50—a couple of tanners, a carter, and day laborers. A dozen of the households were Breton, with characteristic Breton names such as Le Goff, Legoray, and Lezoray. A few of the children in the building were born in Saint-Denis. Other adults were from northern France, Lyon, the East, and in two cases Paris.[142] Dwellings like this provided the context for life, if not the melting pot, for the proletariat of Saint-Denis.

People lived in close proximity and knew the details of each other's lives, and although they may have hesitated to interfere when there was violence between adults (and indeed, did not do so), they came forward when children were abused.[143] In one such case on the police blotter, the concierge living below the tanner from central Brittany, thirty-six, reported on his abuse of his widowed lover's three-year-old; another woman in the building also testified, and a third opined that the abuser "is a brute and the child should be taken from [the abuser's] mistress who is lazy, of weak character, incapable of intervening between her child and her lover." The third report observed that "all neighbors are unanimous in declaring that [the widow] is unworthy of exercising maternal care over her child"; "she merits no pity whatsoever."[144] Blended families were equally dangerous to children: a case of incest reported by a neighbor on the rue Poissonniers uncovered years of abuse, involved seven other witnesses in the same building, and earned a sentence of nine years in prison for the perpetrator, a thrice-widowed worker, fifty-three, who had come to Saint-Denis from an inland bretonnant village of the Côtes-d'Armor at least twenty-five years earlier.[145] There was little privacy to be had under such circumstances; the walls were thin, and people talked.

Police blotters usually concerned public behavior, giving some clues about the neighborhood life and relations between the police and residents. Those of Saint-Denis show that although Bretons were a significant presence, they less often came to the attention of the police.[146] And when they did, their appearance often reflected the misfortunes of the poor. Breton vagrants who had been picked up on the north side outnumbered any other group—ranging in age from fifteen to fifty-nine, some out of work and homeless, some taking shelter in the gypsum quarry in Villateneuse to the north. For Bretons theft was most often a matter of food—asparagus, cabbage and other vegetables, milk, and in one case coal; perpetrators included fifteen-year-old boys. Women rarely came on the record, except in cases of sudden death or emergency hospital entry.

Drink played its role—in hospital admissions, bar fights, and explanations for every kind of misbehavior: the only Breton prostitute in all the records would have gone unnoticed had she not broken up a bar and 50 francs worth of liquor bottles on one February night in 1900.[147] Nightlife produced street fights and bar fights, so bar keeping had its risks. Under these circumstances Lucie Le Coguiec, a twenty-three-year-old café owner from a town in central upper Brittany, seemed to be both courageous and popular; twice written up for staying open too late in the summer of 1905, she had plenty of customers until a violent quarrel broke out that included her cousin and friends late on the night of 3 September. Mademoiselle Le Coguiec suffered serious cuts, risking permanent damage to her right arm; the police took in the Jutard brothers despite their protestations of innocence and forgetfulness. The elder, Frederic, had been born in a town in the lower Breton Côtes-d'Armor twenty-eight years earlier, just before his parents moved to Saint-Denis, where his father had died and he lived with his mother on the rue de Charronnerie.[148] A drinker and a fighter, he seems to have provided the stereotype of a Breton to the people around him: in June he had been in a street fight with eight men when he left a bar after midnight; in July he was accused of having threatened a railroad worker, who called him "Breton" and implied that he knew something about goods stolen from the railroad station.[149]

Disorder was the concern, and to this end the police reported on public meetings, like that of the Revolutionary Socialist Union in March 1900; they cruised through the crowd of eight hundred strikers at the Combes tannery in December 1905 and told onlookers to move along. Three young Breton workers, part of a group that had gathered to prevent scabs from entering, were brought in for possession of an illegal knife after a dustup with three officers.[150] But there were also more minor affairs, men taken in for swimming in the canal and for riding a bicycle on the sidewalk.[151] The actions of the police sometimes seemed like harassment and those arrested did not always go quietly, like one drunken laborer, whose wife and three children remained in their home village in lower Brittany, who called the officer a *sale vache vieux cochon*, a not unusual string of epithets.[152]

But as Alain Faure notes, the banlieue was also a utopia—or at least it had that possibility for workers who were attracted to this city on the edge of greater Paris.[153] Faure draws on the work of the Bonneff brothers, who in 1913 recounted a story of a Breton newcomer that is worth attending to for the texture that it gives to the urban experience. A chemical firm recruited young Jean-Marie Le Louël from central Brittany along with seven compatriots and provided simple lodgings—iron beds in a long room decorated only by a table and a mirror scratched with messages from former lodgers. The next morning at 5:00 the men were awakened for work. But this life was hard on Jean-Marie—although his work was tiring, what crushed him was the bad air, the houses, the pavement, and the gray sky. On Sundays he didn't go fishing with his compatriots but walked; he walked as fast as he could and far as he could but could never get away from the walls, the houses, the streets and the automobiles. One evening, by chance, he met Michel, a former foreman, who had seen homesick Bretons before. Michel remarked on the obvious misery of Jean-Marie, to whom he later suggested outdoor work: "I'm going to tell you, young man, to be closed up is worth nothing. That'll kill you—if I were you I would work the earth." Overhearing the conversation, a nearby worker remarked that a company was hiring for an earthworks nearby. Hearing about this, neighbors scoured their basements and their sheds and found six pickaxes and four shovels. Michel chose the best ones and offered them to Jean-Marie. The two spent the evening polishing the rusty old tools, after which Jean-Marie resigned from the factory and was hired as a laborer in nearby Courneuve. Thus the Breton became a ditch digger—and a much happier worker.[154] The Bonneff brothers meant this to be a story of solidarity and some may have read it as the story of a country bumpkin, but it can also be read as a story of integration into the urban labor force, and the entry of another newcomer into urban life, thanks to the strength of weak ties—connections made outside Jean-Marie's customary circle.[155]

Most Bretons were invisible to both novelists and the authorities, and one of the rare times that they came into official view was on the occasion of a wedding. At the city hall of Saint-Denis they offered a profile distinct from that of other wedding partners in the Paris basin, and from that of the Bretons in the Fourteenth Arrondissement. Like those who married in 1890, those who married in 1910—a hundred Bretonnes and ninety-four Bretons—were much more likely to marry another Breton than their compatriots had been in either general study of earlier weddings: over half the marriages joined one Breton with another.[156] And although a few of those who married out married a Parisian, as in the Fourteenth Arrondissement, marriages with Dyonisians were very common: like the Bretons in the Fourteenth, they married locals as well as fellow provincials.[157] Yet the migration stream between Brittany and Saint-Denis had changed over the past twenty years, since the majority of those from the Côtes-d'Armor was not as lopsided as before. Those from the lower Breton departments of the Finistère and Morbihan were on the increase. And now Breton brides were on the increase as well, so Breton women accounted for most marriage partners in Saint-Denis by a slim margin. Saint-Denis was drawing a greater variety of Bretons than twenty years before, and the gender-specific marriage pattern of the urbane Fourteenth Arrondissement began to hold in this industrial suburb: men married compatriots and women sought a partner from the outside (see Appendix, table 1).

Breton women in Saint-Denis married young compared with those in the Fourteenth Arrondissement, at a median age of twenty-two.[158] Very few lived with their parents, but nearly half lived at the same address as their partner before marriage. The housing in Saint-Denis partly accounts for this, because there were many buildings that were so-called Breton colonies, with many households in the same building.[159] Nonetheless, there had been an increase since twenty years previously, when only about a third of women lived at the same address as their partner, although housing had been similar in Saint-Denis. Consensual unions were clearly on the increase among Bretons there, since about one marriage in seven was the occasion to legitimize a child, a great change from twenty years previously.

The Breton women in Saint-Denis fell into two primary groups: those who married a fellow Breton, and those who married another provincial or a local. Many of them worked as domestic servants and cooks (30 percent), as housekeepers who did not claim work outside their home (30 percent), and as day laborers (22 percent).[160] Those women who married a fellow Breton were most likely to be housekeepers (34 percent) or day laborers (21 percent). In most cases their work kept them close to home. The significant group of needle workers in the Fourteenth Arrondissement is missing from Saint-Denis, and there is only one woman hospital employee—the ward supervisor Marie Briand, from a French-speaking village in the northern Côtes-d'Armor, who married a hospital gardener from Normandy; witnesses to the ceremony included the hospital director, a medical doctor, and the bride's sister, a nurse in Paris. Here again siblings worked as nurses across the Paris basin.[161]

The Saint-Denis trajectories are distinct from those of women who married in the Fourteenth Arrondissement because the brides were younger and less skilled, and because both bride and groom appeared to be more connected with their families. Although many parents remained at home, there is abundant evidence of family connections. Louise Thomas and Jean Baptiste Le Peltier represent many a Breton couple: having worked as a cook in Saint-Denis, Louise had taken a job a bit north in Montmorency by the time of her marriage to a bricklayer's helper from near her hometown in the French-speaking area of the Côtes d'Armor; the bride was twenty-two, the groom twenty-four, and both were from agricultural families. The bride's older sister, twenty-five, also a cook in the Paris basin, and her soldier cousin were there for the occasion. The groom's brother and brother-in-law who lived in Saint-Denis (which suggests that the groom also had a sister in Saint-Denis) stood up for him. Although the older generation was not present, members of the younger generation were there in support of one another.[162]

Most Breton grooms in Saint-Denis, like François Le Goff, were day laborers or unskilled workers, and this was even more likely to be true of those Bretons who married a fellow Breton, about a fifth of whom also worked in the transportation sector as chauffeurs or railroad employees.[163] Breton men had a place in Saint-Denis's industrial and transportation vocation, but it remained a rather modest place that included only a few skilled masons, carpenters, and metalworkers. Only among the Breton men who married women from outside Brittany did a few have white-collar or commercial work.

FAMILY AND FRIENDS

Wedding witnesses reveal a good bit about the lives of couples in Saint-Denis and the Fourteenth Arrondissement—and how they were different from one another. The records from 1910 are richer than those from 1890, because the acte de mariage noted the family relationships between the witness and bride or groom, and because women were allowed to serve as witnesses after 1900.[164] Both changes allow a more complete view of relationships among Bretons and those who witnessed their weddings in 1910; family relationships are the easiest to document (see Appendix, table 3).

Which family members came to the weddings? Most often members of the same generation—brothers and sisters, then cousins, brothers-in-law, and sisters-in-law. Most of the Breton couples who married in the Fourteenth Arrondissement had at least one relative in attendance, most often a sibling of the bride or groom—and in a few cases, more than one. Family members were even more likely to be present at weddings in Saint-Denis. Over four-fifths of five Breton couples had at least one relative in attendance, most often a sibling, and sometimes two, like the cook sister of Louise Thomas and the worker brother of Jean Baptiste Le Peltier. Over half the Breton grooms who married out, and nearly half the Breton brides, had a relative present. In some cases the parents were also in Saint-Denis—widowed and aged parents who followed their children or Bretons who had brought their families to the city when their children were younger. One-fifth of Breton brides had at least one parent living in Saint-Denis. Yet generally wedding records testify to a real and considerable break between generations in this age of urbanization, because the vast majority of Breton parents, if alive, remained at home—and normally in rural locations.

Yet when the witnesses themselves are counted—four per marriage—very few were kin. What about other solidarities—those of work and class? Like Parisian wedding witnesses from four to six decades earlier studied by Roger Gould, those of 1910 reflect only minimal workplace and class solidarities.[165] Auguste Blonsard, whose witnesses included two fellow coachmen and two horse grooms from across town, was a rarity. Only laborers and housekeepers often had witnesses with the same occupation, but because their occupational labels were vague, one cannot infer shared workplace. Nurses are the exception, particularly in the Fourteenth Arrondissement, where over half the nurses' weddings were witnessed by another nurse.

Yet clearly Bretons in Paris and in Saint-Denis knew their neighbors. The vast majority of the weddings in the Fourteenth Arrondissement included a witness not simply from the Fourteenth but from the immediate *quartier*, and nearly half the Breton marriages in 1910 included a witness living in the same building as the bride or groom (46 percent). Like the witnesses for Victorine Mouraud and her husband, many lived on the next street and around the corner, if not in the same house. The same sort of neighborhood network is visible in Saint-Denis, where virtually every wedding included a witness living in the city, and most witnesses lived there. Witnesses in Saint-Denis were much less likely to be repeat witnesses—hangers-on at the town hall—and much more likely to be people who were passed in the street and stairwell, and heard through the walls. Outsiders—from greater Paris or farther away—were often relatives, like the aunt of a bride from a French-speaking village in the Morbihan who came to Saint-Denis for the wedding from the wealthy suburb of Neuilly, where she worked as a cook.[166]

Wedding witnesses of Bretons in the year 1910 reveal a world in which both men and women called on relatives at their weddings, and both enlisted female witnesses. Men and women were roughly equal in having kin witness their wedding; the striking difference is not between men and women, but between the industrial suburb of Saint-Denis and a heterogeneous Fourteenth Arrondissement. Female friends—the married housewife in the quartier, shopkeeper, or concierge—stood up for bride and groom alike. Here again the most important difference is between the two areas of greater Paris: women witnesses were most important when the bride was Breton in Paris and most neglected when the groom was a Breton in Saint-Denis. This may suggest that Breton men in Saint-Denis were more dismissive in their attitudes toward women or that they simply had more male friends. Yet generally the evidence, rather than highlighting gender differences, suggests how interconnected, not how separate, were the social lives of men and women. The records also enable us to catch a glimpse of the older sister or aunt who helped the newcomer.[167] Without these historical records we would never know that an orphan bride (who would otherwise only appear as a statistic among the unwed mothers in Paris from a Bretonnant village of the Côtes-d'Armor) had an uncle, sister, and brother-in-law in Saint-Denis to lend familial support, or that an aunt (who worked as a cook in Neuilly) had sponsored a mother-less woman.[168]

THE BRETON COMMUNITY IN THE BELLE ÉPOQUE

By the close of the Belle Époque a large and heterogeneous Breton community of over 160,000 lived in greater Paris.[169] Like migrant communities everywhere, the Bretons were visible partly through their voluntary associations. As José Moya has pointed out, the migration process itself is the wellspring of organizations, because it "tends to intensify and sharpen collective identities based on national, ethnic, or quasi-ethnic constructs."[170] In addition, the political opportunity structure in France facilitated and encouraged the formation of clubs, legalizing mutual aid societies in 1898 and enabling the passage in 1901 of the Law of Associations, which applied to general nonprofit voluntary associations, including sports clubs.[171]

Some cultural organizations gathered intellectuals, such as La Pomme, which joined artistic and literary Bretons and Normans. Others were sure to include a banquet, like the earliest and most famous of them, the Dîner Celtique, held in such contempt by François Cadic because it had been founded by the famed apostate intellectual Ernst Renan in 1879.[172] For those who could pay the piper, Breton banquets had a bright future. Léon Durocher, an influential Druid, had been instrumental in founding the Association des Bretons de Paris in 1894. Regional amicales grew and by 1912 included the Children of the Loire-Inférieure, the Children of the Côtes-du-Nord (1910) and the Finistériens (1911). Founded by a lawyer and doctor, these groups had the same kind of members as the professional societies that also took root, such as the Amicale des Médecins de Bretagne.[173] Among the many other mutualist and helping organizations intent on alleviating the painful situation of Bretons were the Union Bretonne and the Prévoyance Bretonne.[174] By the time of the Great War, Bretons had founded cultural, professional, charitable, and sports organizations, albeit primarily for their middle-class numbers. Although social concern focused on the poor, this community had a significant middle-class and professional component. Its entrepreneurial café owners underwrote gathering places that are reflected in wedding records and neighborhood life. Helping organizations like the Breton Parish and the Société la Bretagne relied on the good offices of the very elite, the insights of their doctors and lawyers, and the charitable aid of volunteers.

Breton artists and writers contributed to Parisian culture as well as to regional associations. Some focused on Celtic culture, like Durocher, who was responsible for the Breton village at the Universal Exposition of 1900. The result was a true Celtic paradise, a cartoon Brittany with an inn named after Duchess Anne, dark wheat crêpes for sale, Breton men in traditional dress, waitresses in local costumes serving pitchers of cider, and regional instruments playing all the while. And this "typical Breton town" was complete with prehistoric megaliths, a dolmen and a menhir, on the Champ de Mars.[175] This display reflected the influence of Bretons in Paris with an interest in Celtic culture.

Middle-class Bretons shared the concerns with newcomers that François Cadic had expressed at the opening of the century, and indeed the activities of the Breton parish had broadened since its founding. From 1906 it included the Oeuvre des Gares, an organization that welcomed and protected young people getting off the train; like similar organizations elsewhere whose great fear was white slavery, it paid special attention to young women, but it also attended to seasonal workers passing through Paris. Two years later the Oeuvre des Gares sponsored a shelter for young Breton women in Paris called l'Abri Sainte-Anne, not far from the Gare Montparnasse. Bretons were part of the larger effort to protect and aid poor women.[176]

In addition, other secular and religious venues now offered support, especially in the aftermath of the laws closing unauthorized Catholic schools enacted in 1902.[177] The protection of young women, and efforts to keep them at home, took on larger proportions. The secretary general of the Oeuvre des Gares wrote to the prefect of the Côtes-d'Armor in May 1912, offering statistics and urging him to act—since in the four years from 1908 to 1911 the organization had helped nearly 18,000 French women, among whom there were nearly 8,000 domestics—626 of whom came from the Côtes-d'Armor. "We do not need to tell you the dangers to which these unhappy girls are exposed, generally uncertain of a placement, inexperienced, and too confiding: unfortunately, they too often finish by falling into prostitution after a little while." The secretary general urged the prefect to inform parents that although wages were higher for girls in Paris than in the village, unemployment and all sorts of dangers awaited. Suggesting that mayors and schoolteachers make a systematic campaign to dissuade young women from undertaking a rural exodus, the Oeuvre des Gares offered to contribute to the costs of the campaign. The next month a public poster appeared over the prefect's name, quoting the letter and his statistics and argument.[178]

And despite the Breton reputation for faithful Catholicism, anticlericalism had its place, most vividly demonstrated in the lively weekly journal *Le breton de Paris: Grand journal hebdomadaire pour Paris et la Bretagne*. This lively journal lasted less than a year in 1899, but it resembles other Breton journals in many ways: aphorisms, exhortations to Bretons, news from home, railroad schedules for the return, and Breton-language features were commonplace. Nonetheless, the political anticlericalism of *Le breton de Paris* made it unique among Breton publications in Paris: A Breton-language poem was a translation of the *Marseillaise*; long features followed the return of Dreyfus for his trial in Rennes; secular schoolteachers were exhorted to spread the Republican spirit; and the columnist Amoric urged the Bretons of Paris to spread the light of Republicanism at home, because "the Bretons of Paris are numerous . . . over 125,000, a veritable army, very powerful, which could make the nobility tremble in their châteaux . . . Vivent les Bretons! Vive la République!"[179] And there were jokes at the clergy's expense.[180]

Perhaps the most important organization was formed out of the desire to avoid the Manichaean dichotomy of clerical and anticlerical societies. This impulse certainly lay behind the founding of the Mutualité Bretonne and a second weekly newspaper, *Le breton de Paris*, which survived from 1906 to the early 1920s.[181] Its director and founder, Dr. René Le Fur (1872–1933), a physician from the town of Pontivy in the Morbihan, led the effort to provide a set of services very similar to those of the Breton parish, but with a more inclusive and social tone. The Mutualité created an information office, an employment agency, a bureau for financial aid in case of illness or accident, and aid in the fight against the "principal plagues of the moment," alcoholism and tuberculosis. Le Fur opened a clinic that favored Breton clients and shortly before the war, a clothing bank. It is for good reason that he is called "a great altruist" by the Breton historian Armel Calvé.[182] The son of a lawyer and Republican mayor who had acquired running water, a new slaughterhouse, and a new secondary school for Pontivy during his administration, Le Fur emulated his father by eschewing professional glory—in his case the role of the "prince of the scalpel" in Paris—in favor of a life of philanthropy and attention to the Bretons of Paris, who called him "the right man at the right place, as the English say."[183]

Le Fur's instrument for uniting the Breton community was largely the provision of news for "our numerous compatriots, the 200,000 Bretons of Paris and the banlieue." He noted that despite their numbers, Bretons did not yet have their own newspaper, and he aspired to rival the other regionalist journals such as *L'auvergnat de Paris* and *Le savoyard de Paris*.[184] *Le breton de Paris* went on sale in at least fifty-two kiosks throughout the city. Until the outbreak of the Great War it included four to six pages of news, features, and advertisements for commercial ventures and for Breton societies and activities. Subscribers would be listed in the *Annuaire des bretons de Paris* and had access to reduced prices at certain Breton businesses and for train tickets back home, medical care at the clinic, and free legal advice. *Le breton de Paris* had something for everyone.

Each issue included a sizable article of interest to Bretons and several short news items on the front page. News continued on the following pages, along with a list of delegates to *Le breton de Paris* from every arrondissement and banlieue of the city, many of them wine shop and restaurant owners—still key members of the Breton community. Letters to the editor and the "Carnet breton" followed—news of the engagements, marriages, and deaths of distinguished Bretons. "L'argus breton" featured documents and curiosities on Breton history; it was followed by a column reporting the activities of Breton societies in cities such as Le Havre and Bordeaux; then came a long section on news from home. One article or poem in the Breton language appeared in most issues. The publishers wanted to give the Breton language a place, but on the other hand did not want to forget that many readers did not speak Breton—in other words, enemies existed on both sides of the language question.[185] This was, in short, a regionalist publication, not a nationalist one. Stories from and about Brittany, advertisements, and a subscription form made it into each issue.

The folkloric concerns appealed to educated Bretons—advertisements for costumes, Breton language lessons, historical articles, features on political regionalism, and articles about and in the Breton language. The column "In a Breton Library" often included regionalist literature such as Charles Le Goffric's novel *Morgane* (1898) and *Âme breton*, his best-known work, and the *Grammaire bretonne du dialecte de Vannes* by Guil-levic and Le Goff.[186] The paper published poems by the author, per-former, and songwriter Théodore Botrel, another important regionalist figure in his prime during the Belle Époque. Historical articles focused on such issues as the Terror; but the marriages of Anne de Bretagne to Charles VIII and Louis XII at the end of the fifteenth century were of special interest because the terms of these marriages had determined Brittany's political relationship with France.

Regionalism itself was an issue and a political standpoint for the paper, defined not as particularism, an anti-Paris struggle, separatism, or re-action but rather as "a creative power stemming from the virtues of pride above all, in the elevated sense of the word."[187] Le Fur articulated the stance against particularism and for a shared Breton identity in his re-sponse to a letter from a reader writing as "the Great Druid" who clamed to represent Brittany itself: "We do not confuse Brittany with the bards," he replied. "In Paris, the Breton milieu is profoundly ignorant of them, insofar as they are discussed at all. . . . The true Breton patriotism, that is to say, regionalism, is greater than your personages and your work."[188] At a grand banquet at the end of December attended by Brittany's intellec-tual elite, Le Fur maintained that his "goal at the *Breton de Paris* is to make known everything that is Breton, to group together the Breton energies in Paris, to develop Breton patriotism, the value and the confidence of our race. . . . We have 300,000 Bretons in Paris."[189] The point was to unite and promote Bretons, breaking down barriers among them—"our motto should be: a greater Brittany in a greater France."[190] Thus *Le breton de Paris* affirmed a Breton identity, but a French identity as well.

Fundraising projects marked the pages of *Le breton de Paris*—and those of 1912 articulate the interests of the Breton community. Three stemmed from Breton pride—and first and foremost among these was a new statue for the capital city of Rennes to replace the "national shame" of the monument unveiled in the fall of 1911 depicting Anne of Bretagne on her knees before the king of France. The "Bretagne Debout" (Brittany Stand-ing) campaign was organized by Bretons of the highest stature, and thousands of signatures had been gathered to demand the replacement of this statue with another already designed by a distinguished Breton sculptor—a statue of the French king Charles VII kneeling in homage to Anne of Brittany. For those who contributed over 50 francs to raise money for the new statue, the paper offered a plaster miniature of the replacement statue; for those who contributed less, a photograph, a smaller photo, and a postcard, depending on the contribution. The campaign began on 14 January with a call for donations and a photograph of the statue; the contributions were subsequently reported (although many people donated one franc, Le Fur donated 50). By mid-April less than 450 francs had been collected—Le Fur asked his readers, "Bretons, have you no pride?"—and the project was subsequently dropped (as was the project for a *Bretons de Paris* airplane for the French army).[191] Yet this statue would remain an explosive issue for the next twenty years, as we shall see. Later in the same year funds were raised for a beautiful banner celebrating *Les bretons de Paris*, "a true marvel from the artistic and decorative points of view," emblazoned with regional symbols. Again a photograph was promised to those who made a donation (Le Fur offered 20 francs, Madame Le Fur 5), and by the end of the year nearly 420 francs had been donated and the banner realized.[192]

Charitable drives also fueled *Le breton de Paris*. As a physician, Le Fur was particularly keen on enabling Bretons to enjoy the same advantages as their peers, and for this reason he offered summer camps to the poor children of compatriots stuck in the city. Like the Oeuvre des Gares meant to save young women from danger at the railroad stations, the *colonies de vacances* were part of a wider rescue and charity movement.[193] The campaign began in February with a report on the other regional societies that sponsored summer camps and had managed to send about twelve hundred children to the countryside in the summer of 1911. Articles emphasizing infant mortality rates and poems about poor children in the city underwrote this effort. The names of needy children were solicited in the spring, and by the end of July the names of the chosen children—all girls and residents of the Eighteenth Arrondissement—were published and members of the society were urged to come to the train station to see them off. "Bonnes vacances, les petites Bretonnes!"[194] In the fall efforts moved to providing a Christmas party and gifts for poor little Bretons in Paris.[195]

Readers not only gave but received as well. Each issue advertised Breton businesses seeking to attract compatriots as customers, sometimes offering discounts, and businesses that offered Breton products such as cider. Notices appeared of fairs and fetes. Beginning in May, a great deal of space was given to advertisements for discount train tickets and holiday tickets to Brittany in August, with full schedules and prices.[196]

How was the home *pays* represented in *Le breton de Paris*? The sizable "Nouvelles du pays" featured in every issue offered a full, and fairly sensational, view of life at home, with stories from every département. Accidents and accidental deaths were rife in every département: a five-paragraph story described a fight between two friends in the Finistère, after which one died of gruesome wounds. In the same issue a carter met his death under the wheels of his own vehicle in the Ille-et-Vilaine; a brother-in-law was seriously injured with knife wounds in the Loire-Inférieure; a house burned in the Morbihan; and a child was seriously injured by a dog in the Côtes-d'Armor.[197] Village and small-town accidents far outweighed stories of local appointments. Vehicular accidents involving carts, trains, and automobiles were sometimes fatal; fires always caused gruesome and painful burns, and were sometimes fatal as well. Stories bearing boldfaced headlines such as "FILLETTE BRÛLÉE VIVE" recounted the deaths of children by drowning, fire, and felled trees, much to the distress of their loved ones. Family quarrels were dangerous to wives whose husbands—"entre époux," went the story—strangled, beat, kicked, or stabbed them in a "discussion tragique," or, in the case of one "violent," threw boiling water at her.[198] And young people disappeared, sought by their parents, like the naval official who looked for his fifteen-year-old son, gone two months, and the man whose seventeen-year-old son had left home six weeks earlier on his racing bike. It was the employer who sought a butcher's helper, aged thirty, last seen at a nearby railroad station on a Friday afternoon and seemingly unconcerned with a return to work.[199] Reports of theft and suicide completed the mix.

Drink was the cause of many a reported accident and death—that of the young mason passed out on the railroad tracks and run over by a train, the farmer killed by a drunken friend with an umbrella in the eye. Drink was assumed to have caused the death of the senatorial delegate found in an advanced state of decomposition weeks after disappearing; it was reasoned that under the influence of drink, disoriented, he wandered into the countryside and fell into the water. When a fifty-five-year-old woman from the Côtes-d'Armor was taken into jail dead drunk at 10:00 in the morning, her husband refused to take her home, claiming that she was fine where she was; the woman herself refused to leave the jail, where she died during the night.[200] On one hand, the reporting of strings of alcohol-related deaths and accidents may have been the result of the physician Dr. Le Fur's concerns. On the other, *Le breton de Paris* did not harp on alcoholism or point to it as often as the *Paroisse bretonne* or *Le breton de Paris* did. It recognized the problem of alcoholism, but also reported in an article titled "Bretons Are Not Degenerates," based on an interview with a physician from the French army, that although Bretons were reported to be alcoholics, they suffered less than their compatriots from Normandy from this plague.[201] Le Fur himself recognized the evils of alcoholism, but also wrote, "It's not cider that I denounce here, because cider, our national drink, only rarely gives birth to alcoholism"; it was hard liquor, absinthe, and adulterated drinks that were to blame.[202]

If news items did not depict Brittany as a haven of peace and safety, the poetry of *Le breton de Paris* certainly did so, contrasting the good air and peace of Brittany with the infecting and infected air of Paris. The poet Eugène Le Mouel wrote to the Breton child:

> Little man with sweet eyes, little guy of my race
> Paris, the great Paris is still too narrow
> For your blood to be pure, for you to grow straight . . .[203]

The message to women was even more dire than the one to children. *Le breton de Paris*, like other Breton publications and organizations, focused its concerns on the young woman new to the city. The poem "Restez au Pays" (Stay at home) warned of the hidden perils of city life: "Stay at home, carefree Breton girl," it opened.[204] News stories offered a more brutal picture, including the "lamentable adventure of a little Bretonne," an out-of-work maid of twenty who told her woes to a seemingly sympathetic woman, who in turn set her up to be robbed and mistreated by three male accomplices. The young Bretonne awoke the next morning, half naked on a bench in the place Gambetta in the Twentieth Arrondissement.[205] The dangers facing trusting young women were everyone's concern in an age haunted by tales of white slavery, but as Calvé points out, "Today's reader certainly has problems, since times have changed, understanding the degree of naivety, of timidity, and confidence of those who had food left their native soil for the first time, who, for many could only babble in a hesitant French, who had never had contact with the urban milieu—in a word who got off [the train] on another planet from the one with which they were familiar."[206] Just as the abbé Cadic explicitly warned girls against Paris, *Le breton de Paris* did the same, out of the same fear, and articulated the same core narrative of the lost and ruined girl. When this newspaper reduced its format with the outbreak of the Great War, it still made room in the issue of 14 August 1914 for a story titled "Les aventures d'une bretonne à Paris." This was the tale of Marie-Jeanne Floch, sixteen, who had arrived in Paris a week earlier and was staying in a hotel run by compatriots near the Gare Montparnasse while looking for work. A man who said he could arrange employment with a wealthy family took her out for a drink and was joined by a male friend. A little drive before dinner took them to the boulevard Masséna on the southern outskirts of town, where the two took her to an obscure hotel; Marie was subject to "all sorts of violence," robbed of her purse with 50 francs, and left locked in the hotel room.[207] With the outbreak of war at the end of the month, *La paroisse bretonne* added the news that there were few or no jobs for young women in Paris, and "the simplest thing was to go home."[208] Thus ended the Belle Époque for Bretons in Paris.

Bretons played a growing role in the city of Paris during the Belle Époque, testified by their increasing visibility and numbers, heralded in 1912 in an article in the popular daily *Le petit parisien* titled "The Capital Counts Nearly 300,000 Bretons."[209] This figure probably includes Paris-born children of Bretons and is also exaggerated, since the census of 1911 enumerated only about half that number of Breton-born people in greater Paris. Nonetheless this story in such a large-circulation daily paper reflects the importance that Bretons had come to have in the consciousness of the city. For readers of popular literature like *The Diary of a Chambermaid*, the Breton domestic lodged herself in the public mind, either as a beautiful woman without principles or a dull-witted bumpkin without talent. For child readers and their parents, the Breton servant was a lovable dolt who emerged as the comic character of Bécassine. The reader interested in the world of work found in the Bonneff brothers' story the Breton who preferred to work outdoors if he had to live in an urban environment, exactly like François Michel.

At the same time, social commentary about Bretons, while attacking them, focused on poverty at home as well as the vulnerability, poverty, ill-health, and alcoholism of Bretons in Paris. Some of the visibility of the Bretons originated in their reputation as the least fortunate migrants and

the least well-integrated into city life, a reputation that has been rein-
forced by scholarship since the Second World War. Measuring the residential segregation of provincial migrants in Paris in 1911, the social ge-
ographers Philip Ogden and S. W. C. Winchester found that within a
general pattern of integration, some newcomers were outliers—among
these the Bretons from the Morbihan, Finistère, and Côtes-d'Armor.[210]
Likewise, the historian Alain Faure, while effectively demolishing the
notion that immigrants to Paris were more subject to contract tuberculosis than Parisians, notes that immigrants from certain départements
were in fact more vulnerable to it, "the Breton departments especially."[211]
Although this research originates in fundamentally different perspectives
from that published during the Belle Époque, it finds Bretons' poverty
and ill-health worth emphasizing.

Less objective observers derided the religious faith and practice of
Bretons, alleging that they were superstitious fools under the sway of
their priests. This derision was characteristic of the age of separation of
church and state, when teaching congregations were being closed and
both nuns and priests left France in record numbers to serve as missionaries abroad or to resettle elsewhere. Nonetheless, many Bretons placed
their faith in people connected with the church, and the church was their
biggest defender. The impressively broad effort by Father François Cadic
and the Breton Parish provided work and material aid as well as spiritual
comfort, explicitly aiding women as well as men. Cadic was not alone, for
other church-oriented organizations like the Société La Bretagne came to
the aid of the poor and turned to Saint-Denis as well as the city.

Secular Breton communities also organized themselves and took action on behalf of the poor and middle classes in the period before the
Great War, becoming a visible force in Parisian organizational life. Under
the leadership of René Le Fur and the banner of the weekly *Le breton de
Paris*, the Breton community took on a voice. This voice articulated the
interests of many Bretons in Paris, provided a venue for literature and
political articles, a source of news of all kinds from home, and information
about special rates for vacation trains to Brittany. Finally, like newcomers
in cities throughout Europe and the Americas, Bretons themselves formed
organizations for mutual aid, charitable activities, regionalist interests,
sports, cultural development, and professional advancement.

These strands of evidence about Bretons in Paris offer different views
of these newcomers, each of which renders them somewhat distinct from

Parisians and other provincials. Marriage records complicate this picture by testifying to the striking differences between the experiences of men and of women, and to the social and economic integration of many Bretons into Paris life. Faure also reminds us that the city has long been a melting pot and that Parisian neighborhoods offered contacts and work that in turn provided a way out of the society of compatriots.[212] The city offered opportunity not only in the large numbers of jobs but also and perhaps especially in the occasion to connect with new people. This in turn testifies to echoes in postwar France, when many foreigners were greeted with suspicion, but nevertheless interacted with neighbors and came to be seen as members of the community.

Those who married in 1910 show us something of how some Bretons were able to emerge from their well-deserved reputation for misery. Both in Saint-Denis and in the Fourteenth Arrondissement they increasingly integrated with other French citizens, including Dionysians and Parisians. In the Fourteenth Arrondissement fewer Breton women than before had a child before their marriage. Bretons could increasingly sign their marriage documents in Saint-Denis. In both locations Bretons were likely to hold skilled and white-collar positions.

Yet these remain distinct communities with different labor profiles. Most Dyonisian grooms worked as day laborers or unskilled workers, their brides as servants, housekeepers, or day laborers. By contrast, men and women in the Fourteenth Arrondissement were able to obtain some skilled jobs, although many of these, even the secure jobs in the Métro system, did not pay laborers well. For women the price paid for the mobility offered by marriage with a skilled or secure worker was a late marriage—not the case for the women in Saint-Denis.

Marie Lepioufle and François Michel, Breton villagers from birth, hospital workers of the Belle Époque, and bride and groom of 1911, resemble many Bretons of the Fourteenth Arrondissement in their rural origins, the company of their siblings in the city, and their distinctly urban jobs—even though François Michel, a peasant's son, continued to work with horses to the end of this period. As we follow the couple into the Great War and beyond, we will see how they resemble and diverge from their compatriots. With the Great War in August 1914, the Belle Époque would come to an end and their lives would change. Nonetheless the Breton presence, now established in Paris, would continue.

CHAPTER FOUR

Between the Wars

The Great War did not begin for François Michel as it did for rural Bretons when the tocsin—the village church bell alarm—sounded, but rather when he reported to a railroad station in Paris to rejoin his army company in Brittany, with which he had served from 1903 to 1906. He left behind his wife of three years, a secure job, and a baby daughter. François was soon wounded in battle and served both combatant and noncombatant roles over the next few years. Marie remained in Paris, working in a hospital, and for some time her baby girl was sent back to Brittany to live with Marie's parents. She would constantly worry about François, and he about her—especially during the bombardments of Paris in 1918, after a shell from a "Big Bertha" claimed twenty victims at the maternity hospital in the Fourteenth Arrondissement, and then again when both mother and daughter were struck during the Spanish influenza pandemic. All three survived, however, and reunited after the war in the spring of 1919 to continue their life together in greater Paris and in the public hospital system.[1]

It is hard to imagine anything more different from the Michels' wartime experience than that of the fictional children's character Bécassine. In the Breton countryside at the outbreak of war, she was soon in Paris, in Alsace, and even behind enemy lines—an utterly ignorant and equally patriotic and well-meaning servant of France. She learned of the war when her mistress told her that all French people were worried, and Bécassine reflected that she was certainly French yet not worried, which is most puzzling; her confusion continued when she heard that there would be a war against the *Boches* (Krauts) but could find no Bochie on the map.[2] Once she knew the enemy however, Bécassine was implacably anti-German and protective of her countrymen.[3] She beat rugs with enthusiasm, pretending that they were Germans: "Take that, you dirty Kraut!"[4] Her real desire was to serve as a nurse, but her limited capacities caused dangerous mistakes. When her heart was broken at the news that she could not join the nursing staff, her mistress the marquise consoled her with these patronizing words: "You will be a nurse just the same, Bécassine—a nurse for the laundry, sweeping, making beds."[5] In Paris, to ease her mistress's expenses, Bécassine took a job with the tramways like many other women (but during a storm she drove off the tracks).[6]

Bécassine develops as a brave and patriotic adventurer—albeit one capable of the misunderstandings and blunders of the old days, as when she attacks an actor who goes after a French soldier, not understanding that she has interrupted the making of a propaganda film.[7] Major Tacy-Turn, a British officer who hates talking, forces Bécassine into an open airplane to take aerial photos of the enemy; our heroine vacillates between terror and a sense of adventure but takes useful photos, although the two are fired upon all the while by German guns.[8] She admires the soldiers, embraces the children of Alsace, and is astonished by the strength of the munitions workers at Billancourt.[9] She reports to the reader that she had chastised a whiny orderly, saying, "It will last as long as it lasts, we will suffer what we have to suffer—but the Krauts, we'll get them! The others all applauded me, and said that I spoke like a real Frenchwoman."[10] Bécassine is a thoroughly loyal citizen of France. This wartime fictional character for children both touched the realities of life during the Great War (by working on the tramways and experiencing the hardships of separations, for example) and made wartime less frightening with her zany adventures and new friendships. The wartime character of Bécassine could no longer be the peasant dolt of the Belle Époque. Breton soldiers demonstrated great patriotism as well. The pairing of Bécassine with the brave soldiers of Brittany seems to be an odd juxtaposition, but as we will see, it becomes an important one between the wars.

The memorable ringing of the tocsin that signaled the outbreak of war in the Breton countryside announced quick transformations—women and children took on the farming; shell and engine production geared up in Rennes and St. Nazaire; the clothing industry thrived as it produced uniforms; the worst unemployment and poverty declined; prisoners of war and refugees arrived; Allied troops landed on Breton shores.[11] But most memorable were the terrible losses. In April 1917 the Eleventh Breton corps lost 1,650 men in 24 hours. Bretons suffered disproportionately—at least 22 percent of the Bretons mobilized were killed, when the norm was between 16 and 17 percent for men from other parts of France, and many Bretons were drafted because Brittany had a particularly young population, with few engaged in industries that would exempt them from military service.[12] Whether the Breton losses are interpreted as a sacrifice for an ungrateful nation or as proof of attachment to the country, Bretons felt their loss especially keenly, and they noted the explicit appreciation expressed for their efforts by Marshal Joffre, who is said to have declared, "Napoleon had his guard, I had my Bretons!"[13] In the opinion of the Breton historian Joël Cornette, the Great War paradoxically bound Brittany to France: subsequently, much more than the holiday of 14 July, 11 November became an important day for Brittany.[14]

The populous department of the Côtes-d'Armor lost nearly 8 percent of its people between 1911 and 1921, but wartime losses accounted for only half of these. The others had left the department, many of them for the Paris basin.[15] This chapter focuses on these other Bretons: those in the Paris basin after the Great War, like François Michel and his family.

Demobilized in the spring of 1919, Michel returned to the public assistance retirement facility at Arcueil-Cachan, south of Paris, the Cousin de Méricourt, where he was the sole carter for the institution that had been built on the grounds of a château. It was to a peaceful, rural atmosphere to which François returned after the war. At Arcueil the Michels worked side by side with religious personnel—Marie in the kitchens and with the patients; François, as the only carter, picking up provisions, delivering laundry, and moving hospital goods to and from central stores in Paris. After the war he was most content working with the horses, keeping a few chickens, and cultivating a garden. The following year the couple's son Jacques was born and the family was complete—with the provision of private school and a piano for the daughter and trips to the department stores for Marie and to the Montsouris and Luxembourg parks for the children. There would be one more move, when the department of public assistance eliminated its use of horses in 1924 and therefore had no further need of a carter. The family then relocated to the enormous Bicêtre hospital, in the banlieue of Kremlin-Bicêtre just south of Paris, where Michel worked as a guard and carter while Marie took a second shift to be with the children until 3:00 p.m.[16]

This Breton family history has two striking features. As a family of *fonctionnaires*, it performed labor much more "modern" and regulated than the farm service in which Marie had spent her childhood and less grueling than the peasant work of François's family that was recounted in chapter 3. Although it is common to observe that newcomers to the city desired this kind of protected work, it is also true that in the long-term history of the labor force this move represents a transition from what we think of as an atavistic form of labor to a modern one.[17] Most fundamentally, this work allowed the Michel family to live together with their children—a privilege denied married domestics like Yvonne Yven, whose story illustrated chapter 1.[18] This hospital work not only allowed the family to pay for schooling, a piano, a family portrait, and other consumer goods but also allowed François Michel to build his own house in 1925. A key signal of this employment was that the Michel family could take vacations; in addition, François Michel could retire at fifty because he had served in the war, and Marie could retire at the same time because her health suffered from long years of work. Their working days ended in 1932.[19]

Their relationship with Brittany was complex. Marie's brother Auguste moved to Paris after his own army service in the mid-1920s; soon all the surviving siblings of both François and Marie lived in the Seine département. Although some aunts and uncles remained in Brittany, the family and its social life was essentially relocated to the Paris basin. Its members belonged to no Breton organizations and were not practicing Catholics. Although François was attached to the land and would have liked to retire in Brittany—his garden came to include a chicken coop and rabbit hutch as well as fruit trees and a vegetable garden—Marie refused to retire there, because her painful memories of childhood humiliations would not allow her to return. On the other hand, vacations would take the family to Brittany during the summer, where François enjoyed helping with the harvest. Finally, with the defeat of France in the summer of 1940, Marie left Paris for Brittany and François stayed to guard the house in Paris.[20] This was, in short, a Breton family transplanted in Paris whose primary social life was with relatives and that retained familial ties in Brittany, but did not develop broader social or political ties with Bretons in Paris.

How do François and Marie fit with the many Bretons in Paris after the Great War? Were other newcomers as fortunate as they? Did others eschew a Breton collective identity as well?

BETWEEN THE WARS

The Great War altered and traumatized Paris in ways that can only be touched upon here.[21] As a city with an unusually high proportion of migrants from elsewhere in France—most of them adults—it suffered from an immediate exit of over one million people with the outbreak of war and the aerial bombardment of the city at the end of August 1914. The government itself departed for Bordeaux that month, to return in December 1914. As refugees arrived from the north, mobilized soldiers like François Michel and many other provincials returned to their home *pays*. The departure of the bourgeoisie in particular spelled the loss of employment for many working people, particularly servants, so the immediate result of the war was considerable unemployment.[22] However, the "slow, massive reshaping" of the labor force that followed put people to work, and by the beginning of 1917, 20 percent more people worked in Paris than before the war.[23] Paris was the center of war production, and the inner suburbs were the site of most work, where French women and colonials worked alongside French men in munitions factories in a wartime economy "second to none" in 1918.[24] In suburbs like Saint-Denis and the center city, people suffered through dangerous working conditions, pay inequalities, skyrocketing food costs, fuel scarcities, and wartime dangers.[25] At the end of the war 77,000 people were again out of work in the spring of 1919; this unemployment crisis was quickly solved as women were pressured to leave munitions factories, foreign workers were laid off, and colonial workers were sent home.[26]

The years between the Great War and the German invasion of spring 1940 are less homogeneous or bland than the term "interwar period" suggests. The 1920s brought recovery and massive immigration, when French provincials and foreigners alike found employment in the nation's cities. By 1931 a record number of foreign-born lived in France, because it had encouraged the immigration of foreign labor after its wartime losses and decades of low birthrates.[27] Economic crises in the 1930s changed all that, transforming France from a welcoming and integrative liberal state into a suspicious and persecutory regime that would be marked by popular anti-Semitism and xenophobia.[28] By 1936 over 630,000 foreigners had left France, and the number of foreigners in Paris was reduced by a third. These were hard times for French workers as well, as one Breton exclaimed: "Work in town?! My poor friend, one hasn't been able to find work in town for a long time: the crisis there is more acute than in the countryside, and the misery greater."[29] Census data from 1921 to 1936, then, mask a complex reality.

The city of Paris grew to its maximum population of 2.9 million in 1921; Bretons continued to arrive: within the city limits alone there were over 117,000 in 1926 and over 125,000 in 1931. Those from the Côtes-d'Armor—already so numerous in the département of the Seine—increased from nearly 26,000 to 28,000 in 1931. Those from the Morbihan went from nearly 22,000 to nearly 27,000. Most striking: the most remote département of Brittany, the Finistère, shot from being the one with the fewest residents in Paris to the one with the greatest number in the thirty-five years between 1896 and 1931. By the early 1930s over 30,000 Finistériens lived in the capital. By contrast, the number of people from upper Brittany in Paris declined after 1911.[30] The newcomers to Paris after the Great War originated increasingly from Brittany's more remote areas.

These newcomers tended to concentrate in the peripheral arrondissements: the Thirteenth, Fourteenth, and Fifteenth on the left bank, and the Eighteenth and Nineteenth on the right bank; over eleven thousand Bretons resided in each of these five arrondissements by the mid-1930s.[31] Even more than the peripheral departments, the communes of greater Paris in the département of the Seine such as Saint-Denis grew between 1921 and 1936, attracting Bretons like the Michel family. And there they remained.

"Investing in the banlieue, these new urbanites invented a new way to live in the city," Elise Feller writes of retirees. "This Far-West was the banlieue where one found a sort of village economy and sociability while retaining the more individualistic and free manner of the big city."[32] Like the Michels, other Breton retirees who had found steady work in Paris could not do without their gardens on their modest retirement incomes. The pioneering generation of Métro workers hired before the Great War retired between the wars, and Bretons more than others did not return home after retirement, "marked forever by the poverty that work in Paris had allowed them to escape."[33] This is precisely the story of the Breton Métro worker Jean-Marie B. and his wife Eugénie, who arrived in 1905 soon after their wedding and lived in a hotel room where the first of their four children was born. The illiterate Eugénie cleaned houses, and the two saved enough to buy a little *pavillon* in the early 1920s in the banlieue of Sarcelles north of Paris, helped by earlier arrivals: a sister who worked as a domestic and a brother-in-law with the railroad. Farming their small plot, they grew and sold vegetables and fruits, expanding to the surrounding gardens with their retirement in 1933 and joining with their Italian son-in-law who bought land next door. Bad memories kept them away from Brittany, and the family transplanted to the good soil of Sarcelles.[34]

This generation of Métro workers, which included many Bretons, was primarily French and became even more so in the 1930s, when employment with the Métro was designated as municipal, requiring French citizenship. The regular and regulated work of the Métro employee—with a workday restricted to ten hours and given ten days of vacation, then restricted to forty-hour weeks and given thirty days of vacation in 1937—became the privilege of the French national. Many of these jobs, in the broad range from unskilled laborer to depot manager, paid little and did not require much education, but at every level they required literacy, good vision, and good health. As the Great Depression deepened, 517 applicants signed on for 100 available jobs, and in 1938 five years of residence in the département of the Seine became a job requirement. Despite these hard times and restrictions, over 16,600 men and women worked for the Métro by 1939, and among these, Bretons from the Côtes-d'Armor, Finistère, and Morbihan were the largest group.[35] Inclusion in the French nation, rough on those Breton children who were shamed when they failed to speak French in school, became a great advantage. Thus in the expanding years of the 1920s, and even in the hard years of the 1930s, Bretons became privileged by their status as French nationals.

ARRIVING IN PARIS

Scholars have produced interviews and testimonies of Bretons in interwar Paris that enrich perspectives on their lived experience and life trajectories. Françoise Cribier and her team of researchers interviewed a generation of Parisians facing retirement in the 1970s—a generation that included many provincial-born workers who had arrived in Paris between the wars. Catherine Omnès used retirement and employer records to study the historical experience of female workers born between 1882 and 1911. In the 1990s Didier Violain tirelessly interviewed Bretons who had arrived in Paris since the 1920s, gathering fresh and frank comments on their experiences.[36] By contrast, other sources are less revealing: organizations concerned with Bretons became less voluble in their concerns after the Great War and less descriptive of Breton lives, while census categories obscure detail. Consequently, information becomes less systematic but also more rich. And it is entirely clear that Bretons flooded to Paris in the 1920s.

The great majority of women surveyed by Omnès who arrived in Paris between the wars came to find a job (91 percent). This motivation was underwritten by family situations and poverty worthy of escape.[37] Even the Ministère du Travail knew that "Paris is the great center where all the young women chased from their home town by a sorrow, an abandonment, or misfortune come to seek refuge, anonymously."[38] Most biographies relate this combination of the desire to earn a living in Paris with an unwillingness to continue an unhappy life at home. Emma Girard was explicit: she came to Paris in the mid-1920s to work her way out of the poverty that had plagued her for years. The eldest of nine children born in 1906 in an inland village of the Côtes-d'Armor, Emma was given over to her grandparents early on, after her parents' worldly possessions were seized to pay off their debts. Her parents' marriage then dissolved, and she became acquainted with the shame of poverty and of her parents' separation as she worked on her grandparents' farm. Despite the pleas of the teaching nuns that she continue at school, Emma was kept working in the fields, the barnyard, and the house. At the end of the Great War, Emma worked for other farms and then in a hotel and restaurant nearby, finally finding work with a fair and prosperous car dealer, a widower with children in the département capital of St. Brieuc. She took the summer off to work in a posh tourist pension on the coast, where she saw luxury and kindness—but also a life of service. Back at St. Brieuc she grasped at a slender chance, asking one of the car delivery men who went to Paris weekly to find her a good job there, and soon she left to work in a restaurant near the Renault factory in Boulogne-Billancourt. One of her sisters came along. By the summer of 1931 she had married a restaurant customer: an electrician who worked for Renault.[39]

Did many Bretons arrive in Paris at this time knowing no one, like Emma? Or did newcomers operate within the migrant networks that are emphasized by migration historians? On one hand Paris was a well-known destination for Bretons, desirable for its employment (as difficult as were the jobs available), but on the other hand not everyone had a relative or a friend who had taken that path.[40] Over one-third of the women surveyed by Omnès born in 1901 (35 percent) arrived in Paris alone, and even more (40 percent) had no relatives in Paris—others arrived with their husbands (40 percent), many immediately after marriage.[41] Françoise Cribier studied men and women born in about 1907, of whom about one-fifth had come to Paris knowing no one (17 percent of the women and 22 percent of the men), but many had family in Paris (64 percent of the women and 59 percent of the men), and fewer had an acquaintance (11 percent of the women and 17 percent of the men); a third had married, many just before they moved.[42] Generally speaking, family had a greater presence than friends.

This is certainly true for those who told their stories of arrival to Didier Violain, like Jean-Marie Poupon from the Loire-Atlantique, one of ten children whose brother got him a factory job upon arrival in 1929, and Jules Trémel from a village in the bretonnant Côtes-du-Nord—also one of ten children—whose older brother would pioneer Bretons socialists in Saint-Denis.[43] When she boarded the train for Paris in 1927, Jeannette Favennec from the bretonnant Finistère, who had ten siblings, was responding to the urging of her two older sisters who had gone to Paris and had married there. "They talked to me about this city full of people, noise, and light and they had told me to join them. They had assured me that they would find me work and that they would put me up." Favennec recalls that her aunt had taken her to the nearby town to put her on the train "with my suitcase, my Pleyben *coiffe*, and my stomach in knots. I must have looked like a real Bécassine!"[44]

"But it was all so new for me," continued Favennec, who would marry a railroad worker and spend her life in greater Paris; "I had never been out of Pleyben and I was taking the train for the first time."[45] Indeed, the train to Paris was a great and memorable adventure, and the compartment a movable liminal space. Although most studies of migration neglect it, that journey was clearly crucial, even for those who stayed within their own country. For Favennec it was frightening: a man entered the compartment and brusquely closed the shades. Petrified, she grabbed her suitcase and went out into the corridor: "It was out of the question to stay alone with an unknown man, and even more so to speak to him. And besides I spoke French very badly." She saw two nuns on the fold-down chairs (*strapotins*) in the corridor, and in tears explained what had happened. They invited her to join them, and she did not leave their side until arrival in Paris.[46]

The train that carried newcomers from the Breton countryside to Paris seems to have been the space in which many people realized the import of their departure, and in many cases their lack of preparation for what was to come. Some were fortunate in their fellow passengers, like Germaine, who left her three siblings in Quimper in 1924 at seventeen, knowing not a soul in Paris; she was invited to follow her fellow passengers after arrival, and within hours she had a servant's job in the banlieue.[47] Many passengers spoke Breton and shared food.[48] The Breton historian Armel Calvé, cited in chapter 2, offers a reminder that because times have changed, it is very hard for today's reader to understand how naïve, timid, and trusting were those who left their native soil for the first time, many of whom could only babble a few words of hesitant French.[49] Young women remained a major target of concern at the railroad stations even after the war, when it would seem that naïveté would have been on the wane.

Those people interviewed by Didier Violain stayed on in Paris, making a life in the urban area without abandoning their Breton roots. Other Bretons studied by Catherine Omnès and those interviewed at the end of their working lives by Françoise Cribier did not demonstrate the same attachment to their provincial origins, and they too lived out their working lives in Paris and the banlieue. If there were long stays at home, these came at the height of the depression or during the Nazi occupation of Paris. It is impossible to know about the comings and goings of those who left, however. We only know about a few of the men—those covered by Jean-Claude Farcy's and Alain Faure's study of those born in 1860— and among the French, Bretons were more likely than any other group to leave the Paris basin after a short stay, usually in the banlieue rather than the city itself.[50] We know nothing about the women, except that the Breton migration to the city of Paris was in majority female and that women generally preferred city life.[51] It is clear, however, that many Bretons who arrived between the wars, like other newcomers, were mobile once they arrived in Paris. André Yhuellou was one, beginning in the Renault factory in Billancourt after his military service and then going on to run several cafés on the south side of Paris, in the Thirteenth, Fourteenth, and Fifteenth Arrondissements. Jean-Marie Poupon provides another trajectory: he started in metallurgy in a southeastern suburb, then laid rails, trained as a skilled carpenter, bought a little café, and ended his working life as a watchman in Saint-Denis.[52]

SAINT-DENIS

The wartime boom brought full production to Saint Denis, along with an increase in population, full employment, terrible working conditions, degraded housing, and unjust pay differentials, as well as the stench of industrial and human waste and widespread rises in the cost of living. A brutal reconversion to the peacetime economy followed in the spring of 1919, when colonial subjects, women, and foreign wartime workers were forced to leave the factories.[53] Companies such as Delaunay-Belleville, which had employed eleven thousand during the war, reduced their labor force considerably, but in general in the decade after the war Saint-Denis solidified its industrial infrastructure, whose success was due in no small part to the freight station on the plain that by 1939 was the most important in all of France. New industries were launched as the number of industrial buildings more than doubled in the interwar period. Established industries expanded: for example, a dyeing company that employed about 600 workers in 1900 employed 1,300 in 1925; a tannery that employed 250 in 1900 employed 750 in 1928; a construction company that contracted with the Métro and produced railroad cars went from 800 to 1,600 employees in the same period.[54]

Saint-Denis solidified its vocation of heavy industry and large factories. By 1929, 44 percent of its companies were in metallurgical industries and 25 percent in chemical industries; among the remainder, textiles were the most important. The basic shape of the industrial spectrum remained about the same as it had been since the turn of the century. More than ever, this was a city of big industry. In 1929 70 percent of its workers were in companies with over five hundred employees, 80 percent in companies of over a hundred. Its big metallurgical firms meant that Saint-Denis remained the "Manchester of France." And more important, perhaps, this was a workers' town: 68 percent of the employed population consisted of workers in 1921. With the depression this proportion was reduced to 60 percent because of the underemployment of women and the young, and Saint-Denis incurred a net loss of four thousand people. Nonetheless, this remained a quintessential worker city, even though the automobile town, Boulogne-Billancourt, outstripped it in size: in 1936 Saint-Denis had over 78,000 inhabitants, Boulogne-Billancourt 97,000.[55]

More than ever, Saint-Denis became a home to Bretons: while they were only 6.7 percent of the population in 1891, that figure reached 9.3

percent by 1936, and the largest group was from the Côtes-d'Armor. The provincial population settled into Saint-Denis and formed families there, so that by 1936 almost half the people there had been born in the département of the Seine.[56] With postwar prosperity, others arrived: as one Dyonisian remembered, "after the First World War . . . Algerians, Italians, Spaniards, Bretons, Africans, and many others came to the poor neighborhoods to move in, one on top of the other."[57] The memory of foreign immigration is important, because it would have such a bright future in Saint-Denis. Italians, already there in the 1890s, were 29 percent of the foreigners by 1926 and the Spanish, new with the Great War, were 30 percent of the foreigners by then. These groups performed unskilled labor, unlike the Belgians, Swiss, and Russians. At this time there were only a few hundred North Africans, who stayed on after the war—the poorest of all Dyonisians, they would later become the most important of immigrants. But between the wars the city had more Bretons than foreign-born.[58] Of all the social and mutual aid clubs in interwar Saint-Denis—sixty-nine of them, including veterans' groups, alumni groups, and groups dedicated to sports, music, and hobbies—only one was a regional association, and that was the Bretons of Saint-Denis.[59]

Bretons worked everywhere in this banlieue. Like the future leader Jean Trémal they labored for the railroad, and like his brother Jules they stained their hands and faces in the dyeworks; they cleared the way for new buildings and moved heavy stock. And some continued to work the land, like the grandmother of René Kersanté, who arrived in *sabots* from the town of Broons in the Cotes-d'Armor in 1924 to become a market gardener who sold her produce at the Halles of Paris.[60] A survey of electors in 1933 shows that most male Breton workers did not labor at an occupation demanding a real apprenticeship; they were rather, for example (in descending numbers), day laborers and unspecialized workers, gas company workers, factory drivers, earthmovers, carters, and layers of rail. Smaller numbers worked at jobs that required training, such as machinists, mechanics, electricians, skilled carpenters, and tanners.[61] Most Bretons in Saint-Denis were men, who made up more than twice the proportion of the Breton community in Saint-Denis as they did in the city of Paris.[62] But like the men, most Breton women held jobs that demanded little training; as Catherine Omnès has shown, women from the provinces paid dearly for their lack of education and apprenticeships.[63] Many found their first job in services: as domestics, waitresses, or shop cleaners. When Bretonnes went into industry their work was most often unskilled, like that of the workers producing pharmaceuticals and beauty products for the Thibaud-Gibbs company.[64]

This home to Bretons was notoriously ugly and unsanitary—more than ever, a contrast with its glorious royal past. In 1929 Daniel Halévy reflected on the irrelevance of the distinguished basilica in the city, on "the bitter human mold that now covers the plain of Abbeys and kings, giving to the ancient basilica the air of an enormous and enigmatic wreck—one of those mammoths that hunters sometimes find intact under the snow and ice of Siberia."[65] Others were more matter of fact, like Jacques Valdour, whom Alain Faure calls "the knowledgeable connoisseur of popular milieus of this period . . . who did factory work and lived in *garnis* just about everywhere in Paris."[66] After the war Valdour published *Ateliers et taudis de la banlieue de Paris: Observations vécues*, recounting his work and lodging throughout the Seine département. In Saint-Denis he took lodging in a *hotel garni* with about fifteen small apartments for young people, single men, and households—but children were rare. Dark, worn, drafty, and depressing, his lodging at the back of a courtyard was nonetheless swept clean. Upon entry, however, he was seized by the stench from the outhouses in the courtyard, which followed him upstairs and poisoned the entire building.[67]

The fascist and future collaborator Pierre Drieu la Rochelle described Saint-Denis in bitter and sarcastic terms when he visited the basilica in 1935, writing: "it's truly a Royal Avenue. Between the giant *gazomètres* going at full speed lay the open tombs of the forty kings who created France." And about the basilica: "an absurd beauty, lost, unbearable, disgusting, this beauty that has bubbled up into a foreign century."[68] For this author, who was not alone, Saint-Denis was a political anathema as well as an aesthetic one, for this "red city" was a powerful force among the socialist and communist municipalities that would make up the Red Belt around Paris. Jean-Paul Brunet has expertly related the dramatic political story of Saint-Denis, which elected a socialist city government in 1912 and communist councils beginning in the 1920s.[69] The politics of Saint-Denis were a nightmare for those who wanted to protect the souls of Bretons, as had the abbé François Cadic, and indeed the Bretons of Saint-Denis continued to be an articulated object of concern for the church in the Paris basin. Yet neither the Breton Parish nor the forces of conservatism had much success in Saint-Denis between the wars. Dechristianization was part of life in Saint-Denis as elsewhere in the Paris banlieue: although almost half the marriages in Saint-Denis had been matched by a religious ceremony in 1910–12, that proportion was reduced to 43.6 percent in 1920–22, then 42.7 percent in 1935–37.[70] The Pardon of the Bretons of Saint-Denis that gathered twenty thousand people in the first annual event of 1938, unlike the Breton Pardons that were penitential processions, was an entirely secular affair.[71]

For many Bretons, worker solidarity offered the best way to help their compatriots. These Bretons became part of the twenty years of workers' struggles, strikes, and demonstrations that in the end united the workers of Saint-Denis. Jean Trémel from the Côtes-d'Armor decided to take this path, founding the Groupe des Socialistes Bretons in 1898 and going on to be elected to the socialist city government and then elected adjunct major in 1912. As his nephew remembers, "Imagine what it meant for Bretons to be able to explain their problems to the adjunct mayor in their mother tongue!" Difficulties were considerable for Saint-Denis workers like his father, who had arrived to join his brother in Saint-Denis before he was fourteen years old and had labored at the Combes dye works with others who were recognizable on the street on Sundays by their stained hands and faces, working as they did without protection. The brothers Jean and Jules Trémel made a life's work of political and union organizing with a cohort of militant Bretons who helped to give Saint-Denis the reputation of a combative worker city and the capital of the Red Belt. Jules would be elected to the city government nine times, sponsored by the Communist Party beginning in 1925. In the 1930s solidarity and radicalism went hand in hand in Saint-Denis with the formation of the *amicale* of the Bretons of Saint-Denis in 1933 and the sale in the streets of the Breton communist paper, *War Sao (debout): Organe central des bretons émancipés de la région parisienne*.[72] When "Saint-Denis la Rouge" voted in a communist government in 1925, red flags began to decorate the marriage room of the city hall.

BRETONS MARRY IN SAINT-DENIS

Although more Bretons married in Saint-Denis in 1925 than earlier, the marriage records reveal less: children born before the wedding no longer appear on the record, and the law now called for only two witnesses. Neither age nor relationship to the bride and groom is noted for wit-

nesses, although relationship can sometimes be inferred from the surname. Furthermore, the capacity to sign the marriage records ceases to
distinguish one group from another because literacy was nearly universal
among the brides and grooms of 1925. Perhaps most serious, either the
brides or the city hall of Saint-Denis ceased to distinguish between housekeepers and women who were not in the labor force, so that nearly a third
of brides simply declared themselves "sans profession." This common but
frustrating title masks women's lives as effectively as the lack of notations
about children or about witnesses' relation to the couple. Yet the "sans
profession" of the poor *mère de famille* masked the busyness of her life:
bringing up coal from the basement, hauling laundry, raising children,
making meals, and an endless round of cleaning and washing, all in a
small space.[73] The legacy of the Great War added one new piece of information: the record notes decorated veterans. For example, when a meat
merchant from the northern banlieue of Stains, Henri Trochu, stood up
for his butcher brother at his wedding to a clerk from the Côtes-d'Armor,
it was noted that he had earned a Croix de Guerre, the medal awarded for
bravery in the face of the enemy.[74]

Other changes distinguished this group from those who married before the war. Brides in Saint-Denis had always been young to marry, and
continued to marry at the median age of twenty-three, but grooms married younger than ever before, at twenty-five; this was a sign of their
higher standard of living.[75] In this sense François Gourmelen and Marie
Morin are typical: both children of Breton peasant families from inland
villages, he a coachman on the east side of the city and she a nurse in
Saint-Denis, they married at twenty-five and twenty-three. Marie's sister,
brother-in-law, and parents came to the wedding—the sister from the
banlieue just southwest of Paris, the parents from their village in the
Côtes-d'Armor.[76] Younger grooms like Jean Cornet, a machinist from the
Côtes-d'Armor who married at twenty-two, and Georges Cervel, a chauffeur from the Finistère who married at twenty-three, tipped the balance;
both had fathers who worked the land and both married women who
were not from Brittany.[77] Other parents had come to work in this booming town. Some marriage partners married young because they were
living in the bosom of their family and had no need to support themselves
away from home before marriage—the same position in which young
Parisians found themselves (see Appendix, table 1).

The migration streams to Saint-Denis had shifted in the years since

1910, so that the Côtes d'Armor no longer contributed more than half of the Breton brides and grooms in Saint-Denis. They remained the largest group, but a quarter came from the Finistère, that westernmost départe-ment of lower Brittany, whose emigrants surged into Paris after the war. More came from upper Brittany as well, and about one in six was from the Morbihan. Thus Breton migration to Saint-Denis continued, but it was more varied. In the main, this remained a rural movement that only rarely included Bretons from Nantes, Brest, or Saint-Nazaire.[78]

Marriage with a compatriot decreased: whereas at one time two-thirds of Bretons married a fellow Breton, now only one-third did. This is one signal that the Bretons of Saint-Denis were becoming better integrated with the population of the Paris basin and the community that included children of Bretons. The Breton women in Saint-Denis married out more than before, as the women of the Fourteenth Arrondissement had in the past; in 1925 the largest group of marriages (40 percent) joined a Breton bride with a groom from elsewhere. They married men from Saint-Denis, from Paris, and from abroad, but primarily fellow newcomers to greater Paris. This group, which consisted primarily of day laborers, included Jeanne Guézénnec, from a family of laborers in the village of Plougonver that had sent so many people to Saint-Denis; she married a blacksmith from eastern France at twenty-five, attended by two day laborers at her address, one of whom was a relative.[79] Other Bretonnes had more spe-cialized work, like the several nurses living in Saint-Denis; these included Anne Chauvin, a mason's daughter from an inland market town in the Morbihan who at twenty-three married a mason from the Vienne, south-west of Paris; a fellow nurse stood up for her.[80] These women whose nursing career followed an established Breton pattern rarely married day laborers but rather more skilled masons, engine operators, machine fit-ters, and plumbers. We learn from such couples, once again, that social life in the Paris basin stretched beyond the neighborhood and regional companions. The city and its banlieue served as a melting pot that in-cluded Bretons.

In the 1920s some Bretonnes married men born abroad: this was a time when Saint-Denis attracted many foreign workers. The grooms, from Algeria, Italy, Martinique, and Mexico, fit no profile, except that none was an unskilled laborer. Vincent Ducini from the banks of Lake Como in northern Italy was among the southern Europeans drawn to Saint-Denis between the wars. A skilled wire maker, Ducini married Léonie Abiven, a seamstress and storekeepers' daughter from the town of Rosporden in the Finistère. The bride and groom were twenty-one and twenty-six. A fellow Italian wire maker stood up for Ducini, a salesman for Léonie. More than ever before, foreigners were part of the horizon of possibilities for all women in Paris.[81]

Nevertheless, some marriages reflect a close Breton community, like those of Louise and Melanie Poquet, sisters from a small town in the Finistère who married only minutes apart on a November afternoon—each with a worker in Saint-Denis from her home département. Louise married a fellow day laborer from her hometown at twenty-one; her sister, two years older, married a tramway worker from the next arron-dissement. The grooms were twenty-three and twenty-five. No parents were in attendance, but the sisters' widowed mother sent her consent. Their day laborer sister, or perhaps cousin, and her husband served as witnesses to both weddings, and everyone except the tramway worker lived at the same address in the crowded center city.[82]

By 1925 the Bretons of Saint-Denis had emerged from the insularity they had demonstrated at the end of the nineteenth century. Contacts among Bretons continued to stretch across Paris in the mid-1920s, joining the Breton men and women of Saint-Denis with partners in Paris and the banlieues. More likely to marry with people from other regions, they also came from a greater variety of home places—urban as well as rural, from the Finistère and upper Brittany as well as the Côtes-d'Armor. Nearly all, with the exception of one woman, signed the marriage document. Per-haps more important, the Bretons of Saint-Denis had better jobs than ever before. Only one-sixth of the men worked as day laborers, and 28 percent had jobs classified as unskilled labor—a dramatic decrease from 52 percent in 1910 (and 76 percent in 1890); the trend was similar for women. About one-sixth of both brides and grooms had a white-collar position like those in the railroads and tramways, business offices, and stores. Although many were unskilled laborers, as a group Bretons were no longer the dregs of the Saint-Denis labor force.

THE FOURTEENTH ARRONDISSEMENT

The Great War made its mark on the Fourteenth Arrondissement, begin-ning with the unemployment of domestic servants whose employers had left the city. François Cadic warned aspiring maids in the fall of 1914 that "job offers have been reduced to nothing . . . stay at home, oh, you who are in Brittany, you will live there much better than in Paris in this unhappy time of war."[83] Work for couturières entered a prolonged crisis, exacerbated by the more simple styles of women's dress.[84] As elsewhere in Paris, the mayor's office sponsored wartime charities, soup kitchens, municipal butcher shops and grocery stores, and clothing and heating fuel aid. Neighborhood solidarity responded to the German bombardment in April 1918 that killed twenty birthing women, newborns, and midwives-in-training in the maternity hospital on the boulevard Port-Royal. Unlike Saint-Denis, this arrondissement did not maintain the spectacular kind of wartime industry that made the banlieue thrive, but nonetheless the Fourteenth Arrondissement grew, filling out and filling in its rural spaces and seeing its population increase by over 7,700 to 171,292 in 1921.[85]

Change began at the margins, as the old city fortifications were destroyed after the war, exposing the "zone" just beyond the walls to city life. Home to gypsies and colonies of rag pickers, and known to be dangerous for its young "Apaches" and poor of all ages, the zone was an unregulated space of gardens, vacant space, shacks of wood and corrugated iron, caravans, the "Bois de Boulogne of the poor" on Sundays. By 1926 an estimated 42,000 people inhabited the zone around Paris—and the *zoniers* would not be removed until the 1940s. Gradually the city would settle and build up this space, beginning in 1920 with the massive Cité Universitaire project, a complex on nearly a hundred acres where fourteen international pavilions would add a student neighborhood to the arrondissement. Stadia and price-controlled housing would soon cover the rest of the space, and the Boulevard Périphérique would cut it off definitively from the banlieues beyond in the early 1970s.[86] A few farms that survived the interwar period sold milk and eggs in the neighborhood as the Fourteenth Arrondissement increasingly built up and crowded into the working-class Plaisance neighborhood around the railroad tracks. In 1919 most of the neighborhood—a long stretch of the Fourteenth Arrondissement along the railroad tracks—was officially designated one of the seventeen *îlots insalubres* of Paris for its unsanitary housing and high tuberculosis rate.[87] By contrast, large, distinguished buildings lined the boulevard Montparnasse and the other grand avenues; small houses of one or two stories lined smaller lanes, survivors of an earlier time.[88] But this was no country town: the Fourteenth Arrondissement was alive with entertainment and a significant intellectual and artistic life between the wars. Like Saint-Denis, it furnished movie houses and shows, bars and cafés, but in addition the Fourteenth Arrondissement was home to painters, sculptors, and singers from France like Georges Brassens and foreigners like Alberto Giacometti. The modernist art critic, poet, and author from Quimper, Max Jacob, began his Paris life in nearby rented rooms, but by this time had decamped to Montmartre. Montparnasse intellectuals gathered in famous watering holes like La Coupole, as well as places that would feed the poor artist, like the modest Chez Rosalie behind the boulevard Montparnasse. Those in search of fun had their choice in the nearby cabarets like the Jockey, and prostitutes were easy to find.[89]

Nothing if not heterogeneous, the Fourteenth Arrondissement carried the reputation of a Breton neighborhood. The wisest historians of Paris agree, however, that the city did not have an ethnic enclave in this period but rather was large and complex enough to house disparate groups side by side; indeed, Alain Faure demonstrates that the famous rue Lappe can be shown to have been remarkably Parisian, remarkably Auvergnat, or remarkably Italian![90] Nonetheless, the Breton population was increasingly important in the Fourteenth—growing from 9,455 in 1926 to 14,400 in 1936—an increase from 5.5 percent of the city's population to 8.1 percent —and the neighborhood near the Montparnasse railroad station has been called "little Brittany" by Bretons and historians alike.[91] Perhaps it is more accurate to think of the Montparnasse neighborhood as a "terminus and new beginning" for Bretons, as Didier Violain does, because although many lived there, it is important not to mistake the neighborhood for the totality of the urban experience, as Faure warns.[92] Yet undeniably, this area has a special meaning to Bretons between the wars.

Juliette Violain, from upper Brittany, testifies that "of course, it wasn't completely Brittany, but it wasn't really Paris either. Montparnasse oscillated between the two, ambiguous and ambivalent. . . . like all border zones."[93] Restaurants, shops, and cabarets in the neighborhood welcomed their Breton clientele. The well-known author Pierre-Jakez Hélias, whose book *Horse of Pride* explains Breton life at the time, explains: "One word we often heard was 'Montparnasse,' a district in Paris where the Bretons lived as a group, much as they had at home."[94] Childhood recollections from this period include the sight of Bretonnes in costume and coiffe coming to communion at Notre-Dame du Travail in the Plaisance. After arriving in Paris in 1924 and working as a cook, the Finistérienne Mélanie-Marie Tumet-Le Fur opened her crêperie near the boulevard

Montparnasse, in a neighborhood that increasingly had Breton hotels and cafés. Between the wars establishments with names like Au Rendez-Vous des Bretons, Hotel de Bretagne, and more specifically A la Ville de Douar-nenez and A la Ville de Pont-Aven dotted the neighborhood. Monsieur and Madame Beuzen, also from the Finistère, opened the best-known Breton café and nightspot, Ti Jos, in 1937. Clients could speak Breton in such gathering spots, as well as at street dances throughout the neighbor-hood; the door of the Pharmacie Principale announced, "aman e kom-zerhrezhoneg" (Breton spoken here). This welcoming community plays an important role in narratives of arrival for its café conversations and advice—as it did for Monsieur B., who headed for Montparnasse because he heard there were Bretons there, and picked up job advice from a fellow client in a Breton café, advice that got him lifelong employment with the railroad in the banlieue. The Fourteenth Arrondissement, and Montpar-nasse in particular, offered a new beginning to Bretons, but it was not simply a space for transient newcomers, or for workers alone: it also included shop owners, pharmacists, and restaurateurs who would remain and in some cases prosper.[95]

The Fourteenth Arrondissement offered many kinds of work between the wars. The abbé Cadic was among those who wanted women to return to domestic service, although women sought and preferred other kinds of jobs after the war: "You want to go to the movies every night, go dancing, play the role of fine ladies . . . the wisest among you have found the road back to domestic work, do as they do. Leave the typewriters and short-hand. It's better to amass some thousand franc bills as a domestic than to wander the streets of Paris looking for jobs that you will never find in commerce and in offices."[96] He was correct that Breton women would rarely find office jobs: even after the war newcomers from rural areas often began their careers in Paris as domestics, as waitresses, or in other service jobs, because they lacked the education and training that could prepare them for white-collar positions.[97] But many Bretonnes preferred the autonomy of having their own free time after working hours and the feeling of being with members of their own class rather than stranded in a bourgeois household. Thus women without training entered the factory —women like Camille, a Bretonne who worked in the Say sugar refinery in the neighboring Thirteenth Arrondissement from 1922 to 1945. Gruel-ing work damaged her fingers, but Camille found the long days bearable, beginning at 7 a.m. and concluding at 6 p.m., especially before 1936; after that the pace of work was set to a relentless machine, and conversations with friends were lost in the process.[98] Women were able to find non-service employment in the Fourteenth Arrondissement during the prosperous 1920s.

Breton men in this part of town continued to work in transportation and laboring jobs. The 272 Bretons living in the Thirteenth Arrondissement who were members of the conservative Catholic La Bretagne society afford some insight into how men made a living in 1931. Only about sixty of them had a profession that required real training, aside from the thirty-six railroad employees. The greatest number labored as *terrassiers*, the others as miscellaneous workers and day laborers; employees of the Métro, trams, and narrow-gauge trains numbered seventeen, and thirty-six more Bretons worked for the national railroad. Nearly two-thirds of these men were from the Finistère, the most remote department of Brittany, whose arrivals in Paris were most recent, and only about 8 percent were from upper Brittany; nearly 20 percent were from the Morbihan and about 10 percent from the Côtes-d'Armor—so these workers doubtless do not represent the most skilled members of the Breton community.[99]

Workers or not, it is instructive to analyze whom these men and women in Paris married during the prosperous 1920s, and the profile that they yield of Bretons in the city.

BRETONS MARRY IN THE FOURTEENTH ARRONDISSEMENT

Although more Bretons married in Paris in 1925 than earlier, the marriage records reveal less, as they do in Saint-Denis. As elsewhere, the legacy of the Great War was clear from the practice of identifying decorated veterans, even in the most humble cases: When Georgette Charpentier, a daughter of *cultivateurs* and a chambermaid, married a Paris-born machine operator, a family member who was a *valet de chambre* and probably her brother or uncle stood up for her, and records noted that he had earned a Croix de Guerre.[100]

The profile of Breton marriages changes discernibly. The Bretons who married in the Fourteenth Arrondissement in 1925, like those in Saint-Denis, did so at an earlier age than ever before. Breton women, whose mean age of first marriage had been nearly twenty-eight in 1890 and twenty-six in 1910, now married at twenty-five, with a median age of twenty-three; for Breton grooms, who had married at thirty and then at twenty-eight, the mean age of first marriage was now twenty-six, with a median age of twenty-five. People could afford to marry younger than ever before. Young women like the shop worker Marie Dejours demonstrate the new marriage pattern: from the village of Lambézellec just outside Brest, she married the Brestois machine operator Pierre Vantrou; at the time of their May marriage she was nineteen and he was twenty-four. Their widowed mothers did not attend, but a Breton sculptor and a workmate of Pierre from the neighborhood served as witnesses.[101]

Some Bretons married young because according to marriage records they, like many in Saint-Denis and like native-born Parisians, lived with their parents. Family migration and support facilitated early marriage because family often underwrote the occupational training, lodging, and social life that could enhance one's prospects. A couple from the town of Lorient in the Morbihan provides an illustration: Jean Kerlidou and Madeleine Goardet each lived with their parents in the Plaisance quarter of the Fourteenth Arrondissement a few blocks away from one another—he worked as an iron pipe fitter, and she as a bookbinder; their fathers were workers, their mothers housekeepers. When they married in January 1925 Madeleine was nineteen and Jean was twenty-two. A Breton couple from the northeast suburb of Le Lilas, plumber and dressmaker, witnessed the wedding.[102] Yet only a minority of marriage partners lived with their parents, and as of 1925 the majority of brides and grooms reported the same address as their partner at the time of their marriage—a notable trend for those who married fellow Bretons, as well as those who married outsiders.[103]

The largest proportion of brides and grooms come from the Finistère, continuing the surge in migrations from that département. They were now over a third of the Bretons who married, while a smaller proportion came from the Côtes-d'Armor. Fewer came from the two départements of upper Brittany—together about the same proportion as from the Côtes-d'Armor. Likewise, somewhat fewer came from the Morbihan. In contrast to previous wedding partners, these are emphatically more urban—especially those from the Finistère. Entirely rural in 1890, many of the men who married in 1925 came from the towns of Brittany—Brest, Quimper, Lorient, Rennes, and Nantes. A few brides had come from the towns of Guingamp, Saint-Brieuc, and Nantes all along, but in 1925 Saint-Brieuc, Brest, Quimper, Lorient, Nantes, Rennes, and Vannes all gave birth to more than one bride who married in the Fourteenth, and men were even more likely to be from urban areas. Most strikingly, Brest alone was the birthplace of eleven brides and fifteen grooms. Breton migration had not become urban, but it had come to include distinct urban migration streams: 30 percent of brides and grooms were from departmental and arrondissement capitals (see Appendix, table 2).[104]

Marriages between Bretons had risen somewhat, from 26 percent to 30 percent in fifteen years. This is contrary to expectations, because it indicates that in the Fourteenth there was not a smooth increase in intermarriages—which classically represent assimilation, or at least integration. Evidence suggests that the Breton men available in the 1920s were more attractive marriage partners: their urban origins mean that they did not represent the peasant life that women sought to avoid. Second, the jobs available to Breton men in the 1920s offered better work than in the past, and so attracted brides who would like to share their life with a compatriot. Machine operators from the Finistère city of Brest provide concrete illustrations. André Jaffré and Armand Davalan, born a year apart in Brest, both found work as machine operators in Paris, where they lived close to each other in the Plaisance neighborhood of the Fourteenth. They married on the same day in April 1925, both to young women from Brittany. Marie-Louise Trebuil, a factory worker whose parents also lived in the Plaisance neighborhood, married Armand Davalan; two of his workmates witnessed the wedding. Cook Marie Cabillic, whose widowed father was a worker in the Morbihan, married André Jaffré; a delivery man relative—probably her brother—attended the wedding, along with a female friend who worked as a waitress. At the time of the weddings both couples lived together, and the grooms were twenty-three and twenty-five years old, the brides twenty-one and nineteen. The young Breton couple whose story is told above—the shop worker Marie and the machine operator Pierre—lived in the same building as André and Marie.[105] These young men may well have worked in the railroad station, so near it shook apartment windows. Young couples like these gave the Plaisance neighborhood its Breton flavor, and Paris provided the work in these prosperous years.

Breton elites married in Paris as well, such as the Brestoise Augustine Henry, whose father was an inspector general in the Ministry of Public Instruction and wore the ribbon of the Chevalier de la Légion d'Honneur. At the age of eighteen she married a twenty-nine-year-old from Rennes who was a professor at the Faculty of Letters in Toulouse; his father was dean of the faculty of letters in Rennes. Another chevalier and professor signed as witnesses. Similarly, educated Bretons with a bright future came to Paris, like two pharmacy students, twenty-five and twenty-three—he was from the Finistère, with a customs inspector family witness. The student bride was from Pontivy in the Morbihan—her widowed father was a *lycée* bursar working in northern France.[106] The educated urban elite of Brittany had greater access to Paris by the 1920s and married there while on Parisian or more nationwide trajectories.

Nonetheless, 49 percent of the marriages joined a Bretonne with a man born outside Brittany, and these marriages continued to outnumber by a healthy margin those that joined two Bretons. These grooms were quite successful as well. More Bretonnes married Parisian men than ever before—well over a third of those who married someone from outside Brittany.[107] Typically, Louise Plessis from the Finistère married at twenty-two with a skilled worker—Georges Douet, a Parisian joiner whose widowed mother worked nearby as a laundress; the groom was twenty-eight. Plessis's widowed mother remained in the Finistère, but another relative who worked in the same town as a domestic—probably her sister—came to Paris to stand up for her.[108]

A few women from Upper Brittany married professionals, like the milliner Lucie La Barrière, from the chef-lieu of Fougères in the Ille-et-Vilaine, who at thirty-one married the Savoyard engineer Marc Landeau; his father was a responsible administrator in the department of Ponts et Chaussées in eastern France. Lucie's sister, who had divorced the previous year, stepped into a different social niche when she married an automobile chauffeur the following week. Their widowed mother, a shopkeeper living on the Norman coast north of their birthplace, did not attend the weddings.[109]

Seven Bretonnes married men born abroad in the 1920s—a very small proportion, but still an indication of changing circumstances when foreign immigration was substantial and there were many jobs to be had in the Paris basin. Léonie Le Roy, a daughter of cultivateurs from the Morbihan, followed a longstanding pattern by working as a domestic cook and delaying marriage, in her case to the age of thirty-eight. Yet her choice of husband came with the 1920s: Carlo Perrelli, a chauffeur from a small town near Venice who lived nearby. Marie's distinguished employer, whom she had probably served for years, Chevalier de la Légion d'Honneur and decorated veteran of the Great War, attended the wedding. Although marriage with an Italian may have been somewhat unusual for Breton women, most Italian immigrants were men, and likely to marry French women.[110] These foreign grooms did not fit in one mold: they included a metal worker, hotel employees, a mason, and a chauffeur, from Switzerland, Martinique, Algeria, Belgium, and Italy.

Breton networks continued to stretch across the Paris basin in the mid-1920s, joining the men and women of the Fourteenth Arrondissement with the area between the former city limits and the suburbs, banlieues such as Malakoff and Montrouge to the south and Saint-Denis to the north. Marie Le Morellec, from just outside Saint-Malo, married a Breton from an inland village of the Côtes-d'Armor who lived in Saint-Denis.[111] Arrondissement and city borders may have been drawn according to real barriers like grand boulevards, railroad lines, and the limits of the zone surrounding the city, but men and women did not hesitate to cross them.

Bretons who married in the Fourteenth in 1925 reflected a developing community in a prosperous age. They came from farther away than ever before—the tip of lower Brittany. Nonetheless, the Breton men were more skilled as a group than those who had come before: 40 percent were skilled laborers, with another 27 percent in white-collar and managerial work and an equal proportion in lower skilled work. Machine fitters, machine operators, skilled carpenters, and the like were more important than ever, and the horse groom had gone the way of the horse and buggy, although chauffeurs and carters remained. They worked in stores, offices, the tram, and the Métro. And over a quarter of the Breton brides had white-collar work in stores and offices, where two were typists and another two were telephone operators. Otherwise women's work did not offer chances for so much advancement; over a third of the brides worked in lower-skilled jobs and nearly another third as skilled workers. Bretonnes were still those who took jobs as cooks and domestics, and proportionally fewer than before worked as nurses and dressmakers.

Generally speaking, a larger proportion of brides and grooms came from Brittany's urban areas such as Brest. A greater number of grooms were from Paris itself, so intermarriage between Parisians and Bretons reached its peak with this group. Yet Bretons were also slightly more likely to intermarry than before the Great War, probably because they had more to offer one another. These younger and more skilled Bretons married earlier. Other Bretons followed the longstanding pattern of late marriage after a prolonged stint as a domestic servant. A smaller group, protected by the presence of their families and in some cases education and social standing, married early and seem to have set off for a life of relative comfort. Those with less social standing were even more likely than ever to live with their partner before the wedding. And everyone could read and write. By their choice of partner, Bretons in this part of Paris both attended to their own community and joined the city; they may have lived on the southern edge of the town, but they were by no means marginal in their family formation or their work.

As these Bretons set up a life in the city, middle-class girls and their families were exposed to a very specific Breton character in the comic character of Bécassine.

BÉCASSINE AND VICTORINE

Between the wars Bécassine's popularity reached a peak. The girls' magazine *Semaine de Suzette* sold up to 200,000 copies, and department stores prominently displayed the annual albums (on occasion, with a salesgirl dressed as Bécassine).[112] Bécassine products expanded to their greatest range as well: marketing began in earnest at the war's end, first with the trademarked Bécassine doll in 1919, advertised as the unbreakable "little Breton heroine" of the comic strip. A host of related items flooded the stores: charming stationery for children, songs, chocolates, and piggybanks. More dolls, plaster statues, jam pots, sugar bowls, children's play utensils, yarn boxes, umbrella handles, patterns from which Bécassine costumes could be made, and Bécassine yarns went on sale in the 1920s and 1930s, echoed by homemade dolls.[113] These derivative products gave Bécassine a presence in the middle-class home, primarily decorating the lives of her young fans.

This comic character combined the old-fashioned vocation of servant with the life of the modern consumer. In the first postwar album Bécassine returns to domestic work as a cook after a series of comic tries at the more modern occupations of model, sports guide, and antique buyer—"A servant in the old style! A pearl!" exclaims her employer.[114] She soon becomes the nanny for the marquise's adopted daughter Loulotte; it was in her role as nanny and companion to Loulotte, who (unlike Bécassine) grew a year older every year, that Bécassine had adventures for the next seventeen years, until the end of 1939. Bécassine acted as a loving and patient caregiver to the orphaned Loulotte and by extension to her young readers as well.[115] Her activities reflected those of the well-heeled bourgeois family: she used the telephone and gas stove, took a cruise, drove automobiles, skied in the Alps, joined the scouts, and went to the beach, all between 1927 and 1932. This series was kicked off by one of the most celebrated albums, *L'automobile de Bécassine*, in which she wins a fancy and powerful roadster, learns to drive, and takes a journey. This celebration of the new technology, mobility, and tourism reflected a prosperous, middle-class France.

Bécassine and her Breton roots represented a less prosperous and knowledgeable France. She could be regularly bullied, fooled, and outwitted; she made mistakes, suffered occasional confusion, and forgot crucial items. Bécassine revealed her peasant roots by relating her cure for the flu to her mistress, a cure that involved drinking a syrup concocted from slugs—one boiled up for each year of the sick person's life.[116] Peasants who came on the scene were by turn avaricious and amusing, maliciously trying to cheat urban travelers on one hand and sharing their wedding processions with geese and a pig, in the case of Bécassine's cousin Marie Quillouch.[117] A lovable nanny was Bécassine, but a fool.

As children read Bécassine, or as it was read to them, adults were snapping up a series of books by Roger Martin du Gard published between 1922 and 1940 under the collective title of *Les Thibault*. The author of this family saga would win the Nobel Prize for literature in 1937 for the portrait of an age, a "great sociological fresco" of the period between 1905 and 1914. It tells the story of lives divided by two worldviews, characterized at the prize ceremony as "that of the Catholic Church, and that of the freethinking, unflinching, humanistic philosophy of feasting and mastering reality."[118] As the historian David Schalk writes, "the simplest use that a historian can make of the novel is in obtaining background information about the social and intellectual atmosphere of an epoch." He also notes that "a great novel is read and understood differently in each successive generation," and draws on Carl Becker's observation that "each generation rewrites its own history, playing in new tricks on the dead."[119]

A minor character in this saga leaps out to the historian of Bretons in Paris—one who is first introduced as "a little slut of a maid I had here, a wretched brat of nineteen."[120] Hired from her seaside hometown, where her mistress had been on vacation, and brought back to Paris, this character fell in love with her mistress's lover—a compulsive womanizer who would set her up in rooms from time to time, impregnate her, and forget about her. Victorine Le Gad would not retain her name in this novel but would be renamed Cricri and Rinette by lovers and employers. The madam who took her on after her baby died exclaimed, "'Victorine' I ask you! So I changed it to 'Rinette.' Not bad, eh? . . . Colin's given her elocution lessons; she had a Breton accent you could cut with a knife; well, she's kept just the right dash of it, a bit of a foreign twang—might be English—delicious anyhow."[121] In a moment of bad conscience and temporary wealth, her former lover takes her out of a prostitute's room and puts her on the train for Brittany, exhorting her "to leave her finery behind, cast off the harlot's stock-in-trade, and begged her to go back, for good and all, to the simple ways, the purity of her former life," because, as the madam had declared, "She only has one idea: to collect a little nest egg and go back to Brittany, where her home is. Damn silly, but there you are! All Bretonnes are like that. A cottage near the village pump, the usual white streamers, and plenty of processions—just Brittany, in a word!"[122]

In Victorine Le Gad, Martin du Gard draws a character perfectly in keeping with a certain idea of Breton women: a bumpkin unsuited to Parisian life, naïve, sentimental, sexual, and on the slide from domestic service to prostitution. Other Bretons in *Les Thibault* fare no better. When one of the two heroes visits his professor at a later stage in the novel written in the 1930s, the door is opened by "a stupid-looking Breton maid"; catching his professor napping, he comments, "I certainly shouldn't have been admitted, if the maid had known her job." Martin du Gard renders those at home in Brittany as grotesque: the novel's physician recalls vacationing at a Breton seaport when a bicephalous child was born. "Father and mother had begged the local doctor to put an end of the little monstrosity, and, when he refused to do so, the father, a notorious drunkard, had flung himself on the newborn child and attempted to strangle it. It had been necessary to secure him, lock him up. There was great excitement in the village and it was a burning topic at the dinner-tables of the summer visitors."[123] Although these fine novels famously depict life in the Belle Époque, they also demonstrate that Bretons continued to be fair game between the wars for those wishing to depict naïveté, stupidity, and backwardness from the Parisian perspective.

THE BRETON COMMUNITY

The stereotypes of Breton troubles carried some truth. While other women were entering office jobs and desired shop employment or at least factory work, many Bretons were untrained, and so got their start as domestic servants or *terrassiers*. There was still great demand for each after the war, particularly during the good years of the 1920s. After all, Mélanie-Marie Tumet-Le Fur noted in an interview that she got her start as a domestic cook in 1924, and Jeanne Favennec first worked as a chambermaid in a clinic in the Fourteenth after she arrived in 1927, yet both women had long and successful lives in Paris. Likewise for Jean-Marie Poupon, who took every kind of job after his arrival in 1929, and for whom Paris work included laying rails with Portuguese and Poles.[124]

Other newcomers did not fare so well but slipped into alcoholism, became homeless, or earned their living in hotels "with no stars." Germaine Campion, a twenty-four-year-old servant from the Côtes-d'Armor whom a doctor's wife brought to Versailles in 1929 and then fired because she got drunk, spent alcoholic years doing odd jobs around the Halles, Pigalle, and Montparnasse before she recovered. Other young women worked in Montparnasse or on the rue Saint-Denis near the Halles, known for its prostitutes, turning their faces away as their compatriots passed and telling tales of good employment at home. As the Breton poet Glenmor later observed in his poem "Sodom," "they are pretty our country girls / that Paris sees so early in the morning / they no longer cry / for their faraway Brittany / they have the laugh of a child / Paris makes them whores."[125] For men alcohol was the greater temptation. The grandfather of Guy Caro, a Breton physician who combats alcoholism, recalls that his grandfather, employed by a gasworks in the banlieue, saw Bretons drinking up to six liters of wine a day. Caro himself reasons that the combination of displacement, depression, and the ready availability of red wine close at hand—rather than cider—made a devastating combination.[126]

Nonetheless, in the prosperous years after the Great War concerns faded with helping poor and vulnerable Bretons. The abbé Cadic, weakened by constant work and tuberculosis, had to leave Paris.[127] When he passed away in 1929 the Breton Parish did not survive him, and no equivalent organization was to take its place until after the Second World War. The task was left to the likes of curé Edmond Loutil of Saint-François-de-

Sales in the Seventeenth Arrondissement, journalist for the Catholic daily *La Croix* and prolific novelist under the name of Pierre L'Ermite. Loutil produced fiction with the intent of keeping the faithful on the road to virtue: a series of novels throughout the Belle Époque and interwar period such as *The Woman with Open Eyes* (1927). Here Loutil relates the story of a young Breton girl, Rolande, dazzled by Paris, who wisely took it as a sign that Paris was not the place for her when her dear aunt's purse and furs were stolen while the two of them were at the communion bar in the Sacré Coeur basilica. Rolande was quickly persuaded to leave by a priest and his old mother; she deserted her worthless Paris beau for a good boy back home and took the night train out of the city. One can assume that Loutil's *The Woman with Closed Eyes*, published the year before, had a less happy conclusion.[128]

Pious Bretons were less active as helpers than as worshipers, like those who joined the annual pilgrimage to Sacré Coeur in Montmartre; over a thousand of these were Finistériens in national costume in 1923. Two years later a special train brought over five hundred costumed peasants to a series of services in three churches, ending in the company of the Maréchal Foch at the Arc de Triomphe at the tomb of the unknown soldier.[129] The standard-bearer for a more secular Breton care and solidarity, Dr. René Le Fur's weekly *Le breton de Paris*, ceased publication in May 1923.

I do not suggest that the Breton community became less numerous or coherent. On the contrary, it grew to an estimated 200,000 in greater Paris by the mid-1930s.[130] Interwar Bretons in Paris included more self-conscious, educated, skilled, and powerful Bretons than ever before, and a smaller proportion of the unskilled rurals who had come to clean the kitchens and build the Métros of Paris, those who had been characterized as the "pariahs of Paris" in 1898.[131] The black-and-white Breton national flag—which would have a bright future—was designed about 1923. The Breton press in Paris was energized that same year when Louis Beaufrère began to publish the weekly *La Bretagne à Paris*, modeled on the paper of Le Fur and equally interested in promoting Breton identity and solidarity. Called "the official organ of the federation of Breton societies in the Seine," the paper gave free publicity and news of Breton societies—and these increased in number as associative life grew. The federation included all sorts of groups: those organized around département of birth, literary interests (La Pomme), athletics (Le Club Sportif des Bretons des

Paris), student life (L'Association des Étudiants Bretons de Paris), and professional life (L'Amicale des Médecins de Bretagne). Most of these were only active within the city limits, but the sports club drew from greater Paris and grew quickly after it was founded in 1925, adding teams for football, tennis, basketball, cycling, and various forms of wrestling. The growth of the sports club indicates that a certain number of Bretons were not too exhausted by work to be able to play. Or to dance—for street dances throughout the city and in the banlieue included *Bals bretons* on the national holiday of 14 July and throughout the warm-weather months, where Bretons met and mixed.[132]

Bretons founded thirteen other groups in the banlieue, like Les Bretons d'Aulnay-sous-Bois. The Amicale des Bretons de Saint-Denis stood apart for its power and explicit leftist politics. It organized the Pardon of Saint-Denis beginning in 1936—a gathering and manifestation based on the Breton tradition of the religious Pardon, but completely secular. Thousands of Bretons attended: an estimated twenty thousand in 1938 and thirty thousand in 1939. Other organizations stood outside the federation: the creative group of artisans called the seven brothers, "Seiz-Breur," and creative groups such as the Clairière Parisienne, for "druids, bards, and *ovates*."[133] These groups belie the Breton stereotype of individualism and inability to organize.

Two years after the founding of the newspaper *La Bretagne à Paris*, the annual election began of a young woman to be the Duchesse des Bretons de Paris, sponsored by the federation of Sociétés Bretonnes de Paris. This was the doing of the newspaper editor, Beaufrère.[134] Hearkening back to the Duchess Anne of Brittany, whose marriage to two French kings joined the province with the nation of France, the postulants wore impeccable Breton garb. Delegates from each society voted in a two-round election, and the final round was held at a dinner dance on the left bank, at which the duchess—she who had a clear majority—was crowned. The elected young woman led the procession to the celebration of Saint-Yves each year on 19 May, and then on to Mass, riding a white horse and dressed in sixteenth-century robes.[135]

Nonetheless, neither Breton organizations nor celebrations suited every Breton in greater Paris. Many who attended the festivities surrounding the annual Saint-Yves celebration in May or the warm-weather street dances abstained from Breton associations. None of the interviewees of Françoise Cribier belonged to regional associations. Neither

Yvonne Yven (chapter 2) nor François and Marie Michel (chapters 3 and 4) associated themselves with Breton organizations. Organized Breton identity was a part of the world of Bretons in Paris, yet only a part.

For members of the Breton nationalist movement, this identity was fundamental and political. Centered in Brittany, the Breton movement was affirmed and politicized between the wars. This movement's long-standing and complex history dates from the founding during the Belle Époque of the Union Régionaliste Bretonne, led by the Marquis de L'Estourbeillon, a legislative deputy who played an important role as president of the Société La Bretagne described in chapter 3. The URB represented the conservative, aristocratic, and clerical interests that emphasized Breton language and literature. After the Great War the second Emsav, or uprising, began with the founding of the Groupe Régionaliste Breton in 1918. The Breton nationalism of the 1930s was rooted in several organizations with some publications, the most important of which was *Breiz Atao!* (Brittany forever), and drew primarily from the extreme right. This regionalism would reflect the important ideologies of the times, including socialism, but also fascism and racism for a Breton nationalism that looked to Ireland—and then Germany—for inspiration.[136]

Breton nationalism became visible in the Paris of the late 1930s, at a time when the French state would come to explicitly support regionalism. Violent action brought national attention, first in 1932 when members of a secret society blew up the statue of Duchess Anne kneeling before the King of France in front of the Rennes City Hall. This statue had long been a sore point with Breton loyalists; *Le breton de Paris* and René Le Fur had campaigned for a replacement in 1912 because it symbolized the joining of Brittany with France in a way that demeaned Brittany. The statue finally met its end in August 1932, when President Édouard Herriot was in Brittany to celebrate the four hundredth anniversary of the union of Brittany with France. When Herriot returned in November for a similar celebration, the railroad lines were sabotaged on the Franco-Breton border. These actions held importance for many nationalists but remained irrelevant for most Bretons; and for the educated like the famous Breton writer Pierre-Jakez Hélias, then a student in Rennes, it was an old, irrelevant story.[137] Some Breton nationalists, writers, and organizers would take up residence—at least part time—in Paris. Herry Caouissin, who plays an important role in this history, arrived in 1932.[138]

BÉCASSINE LEAVES THE PRINTED PAGE

By 1935 Bécassine had been published for thirty years, and perhaps the creative energies of the author, Maurice Langereau, were running low as he approached the age of seventy. The stories published after this date, such as *Bécassine en roulette*, lack the energy and sparkle of earlier ones. Moreover, the last three albums of 1937, 1938, and 1939 came up shorter than the others by some fifteen pages. In any case, with the late 1930s the realities of Bécassine's era were passing. The economic depression and the democratizing measures of the Front Populaire government of 1936–37 spelled the twilight of the class-bound society in which the Marquise de Grand'Air and her friends ruled, while ignorant country folks could be ridiculed at will.

Yet on the street Bécassine still had meaning: Bretons continued to be ridiculed with the name Bécassine, and its male variant Bécassin. This was a thorn in the side of young women especially, subjected to comments like "Look, Mama, it's Bécassine!" from the mouths of children who saw Breton dress in the streets of Paris. Especially painful because domestic work became perceived as increasingly humiliating after the Great War, Bécassine was most offensive when she left the anodyne printed page of children's stories.[139] The colonial exhibition of 1931 was to feature a children's area with nursemaids dressed as Bécassine, until *La Bretagne à Paris* and the Breton newspaper *Ouest-Éclair* sounded the alarm in imperial terms: "We can't give such a negative image of Bretons to the children of Indochina and Algeria!" Finally the exhibition organizer and imperial warrior Maréchal Lyautey intervened to prevent the appearance of Bécassine nurses, assuring that there would be no "Bécassine coloniale."[140]

Changes in attitudes toward French regionalism and folkways in the interwar period underlay objections to Bécassine. Among the Breton activists who moved between Brittany and Paris were writers who participated in the regionalist literary movement analyzed by Anne-Marie Thiesse in *Écrire la France*.[141] One of these was the artist Herry Caouissin, who produced a striking postcard cartoon of a Breton peasant literally kicking Bécassine out of Brittany, sending her and her illustrator Pinchon scurrying back to Paris.[142] Caouissin, along with the author Léone Calvez, wrote a virulent, emotional anti-Bécassine play at the end of 1936— initially performed by students at Notre Dame de Lambader in front of the president of the Bleun-Brug, the Catholic Breton nationalist association. Performances were in the Breton language, and a French-language publication appeared in 1937.[143] *Bécassine vue par les bretons* (Bretons' view of Bécassine) features a vivid color illustration of a distinguished Breton woman standing on the small of Bécassine's back, effectively breaking it—similar but much more virulent then a cartoon in the Breton paper *Briez Atao* titled "The True Brittany Crushes Bécassine."[144] The remarkably dramatic rhetoric and plot of the play deserve a brief summary.

Bécassine vue par les bretons begins when the grandmother of a noble young woman named Mona mourns her departure for Paris. The grandmother had already lost her husband to the sea and three of her four sons to the Great War when her remaining son and grandson drowned. Of her six orphaned grandchildren the eldest, Mona, has agreed at the age of fifteen to work for a bourgeois Breton family in Paris, having arranged through her priest to keep her younger siblings at school. Mona departs in her beautiful local costume, having rejected her employer's request to discard it. In Paris, Mona serves as the maid for a spoiled adolescent of her own age, Nicole. As Nicole gathers with her equally spoiled friends, one offers Nicole a Bécassine doll and all begin to make fun of Bécassine as a typical Breton; when Mona enters the room, one friend declares that she looks ridiculous in her medieval outfit, and another that she is nothing but a savage from a backward region. In her outrage Mona ridicules Bécassine and recounts the ignorance with which the hurtful insult is used in the streets. She articulates a stirring defense of Brittany, recalling that without Arthur de Richemont and his Bretons, Joan of Arc could never have saved France, and that the Breton sacrifice in the Great War had been recognized by Joffre, who claimed that "Napoleon had his guard, I have my Bretons!" Without the Bretons, Mona continued, Paris would have been taken by the Germans. She finishes with indignation: "And you have the courage to treat like Bécassine the mothers, the wives, the sisters and the daughters of these heroes to whom you owe your national independence."[145] The girls are effectively shamed. The denouement: Mona, having received a discarded lottery ticket as a gift from Nicole, wins the national lottery; when the family soon goes bankrupt, Mona intervenes to save them and declares her intention to return home to Brittany.

The contrived plot and virulent rhetoric of *Bécassine vue par les Bretons* express the outrage of Bretons at the nasty insult that the figure of Bécassine had come to mean to them. Certain Bretons were alert to insults in the public realm, and Henry Wulschleger's film *Tout va très bien, Madame la Marquise*, released in late 1936, lit the flames of ire in January 1937. The front-page editorial of *La Bretagne à Paris* called the film an odious and inept attempt to smear Brittany and its people—the film included a Breton hotelier serving spoiled fish and a snot-nosed, louse-covered child. Deputies to the chamber, along with some forty students, demonstrated in front of the theater where the film was shown. The film was withdrawn at the end of its first round but could reappear on other screens. Albert Le Rail, a deputy representing the département of the Finistère, sent a letter to the prefect of police signed by most Breton deputies; in response the police agreed to have the injurious words cut from the film. Meanwhile, Breton theater owners refused the film outright, and the mayor of Le Havre proposed a national boycott.[146] When the film was shown in the Breton neighborhood of the Fourteenth Arrondissement, students and club members hooted and whistled so loudly that the film could not be heard; the police were called—"good boys who were not too severe, because there were certainly a good number of Bretons among them," according to Beaufrère—and the show continued amid shouts and whistles until the audience sang, at the end, "Bro goz ma zadou" ("Vieux pays de mes pères"), the Breton national anthem. After demonstrations at the theater, Beaufrère reported that in its newly cut version, only 1,400 of the original 2,500 meters of film remained.[147]

In this year of 1937 the French state honored the blossoming of French regionalism, first by opening the Musée des Arts et Traditions Populaires in the Trocadéro Palace on 1 May, indicating a respect for the usages, costumes, and lives in the former provinces.[148] The Exposition Internationale des Arts Décoratifs et Industries Modernes was to commence on the same day—an exposition perhaps most widely known for the heroic structures of the Soviet and German pavilions facing off alongside the Seine, and for the exhibit of Picasso's *Guernica*. Nonetheless, unlike other world's fairs that emphasized the new and modern, this exposition "also celebrated rural life, regionalism, and folklore."[149] A rural center, a model village, and twenty-seven regional pavilions lined up along the Seine alongside national exhibits from throughout the world.

The Breton pavilion opened with fanfare and joyous celebration on 30 July, an inauguration that brought all Breton organizations in Paris to the scene. The pavilion held pride of place along the Quai d'Orsay, its interior and exterior the result of competitions and struggles among

Breton architects, artisans, and intellectuals. Signaled by pointed use of the Breton language with the sign Ty Briez (Breton House, Maison de la Bretagne), the building had a modern look that also echoed Breton architecture. A Celtic column ten meters high dedicated to the history and virtues of Brittany decorated the front, and a fresco was at the entrance. The most remarkable and memorable part of the pavilion was the largest ceramic sphere ever created, a globe of the earth illustrating the glory— and the routes—of Breton navigators. Ti Briez combined exhibits of traditional pottery, dance, and costume with more modern artisanal creations featuring work of the Breton Seiz Breur.[150]

Despite this honoring by the state and the international community of Breton culture in the form of artisanal, folkloric, and architectural accomplishments, the Breton Bécassine remained the butt of jokes. Late 1938 brought news of a film about Bécassine starring the pretty young starlet Paulette Dubost. In an article about a new offense to Bécassine, Beaufrère of the *Bretagne à Paris* warned that if the filmmakers went ahead with the project there would be a movement against it, like that against *Tout va très bien* two years earlier.[151] Nonetheless, *Bécassine* was filmed in two Breton locations and a studio in Paris, although even in the eyes of Bécassine's greatest defenders the film violated the cartoon character's innocent spirit. The film showed Bécassine taking a piglet to bed with her and feeding potatoes to the pigs while giving peelings to little Breton children —this last echoing the taunting couplet "les pommes de terre pour les cochons, les épluchures pour les Bretons" ("potatoes for pigs, peelings for Bretons").[152] Meetings were organized to protest the filming in Brittany, and representatives of Breton organizations throughout France, from Lyon to Le Havre, wrote indignant letters to deputies and to *La Bretagne à Paris*.[153] Herry Caouissin, his brother, and a couple of friends plotted to kidnap Dubost during filming in Brittany—after tying her to a tree they were to notify the press and then take her to dinner in the evening—but their plot was foiled by the departure of the film crew. The filming went on, and when *Bécassine* was released, the main character danced across the advertising poster, a pig dancing right behind her.[154]

The film could not be shown in Brittany; in Paris additional repercussions ensued. On 18 June three Bretons living in the capital—an electrician from Rennes and two students from the Finistère, all in their twenties—entered the Musée Grevin, the popular wax museum of Paris, and smashed the wax likeness of Bécassine, in their words "an idiotic-looking wax statue."[155] Press comments reflected a variety of opinions: *Le breton socialiste* called it "a joke in dubious taste," while *L'Ordre* labeled this an "imbecilic gesture." The popular illustrated daily *Excelsior* noted that the three were members of the nationalist organization Breiz Atao and suggested that the newspaper of the same name had doubtless egged them on, but "in any case, Brittany is rising—she hates Bécassine."[156] When the police asked if the three were part of a separatist movement, one replied, "It was in no way a separatist act. We read in the *Bretagne à Paris* that an odious cinematographic production was going to ridicule our Brittany once more. In breaking the wax statue in the Musée Grevin it was, in our thinking the Bécassine in the new film . . . that we wanted to get at and that we, the young people, will no longer tolerate what they put on the screen, or even a simple effigy of the awkward and foolish Breton we know. Our mothers, our sisters, and our fiancées do not deserve to be made fun of like this; and as for our grandmothers— those stoic and upright grandmothers, many of whom lost their sons in the Great War—we demand on their behalf respect for their *coiffes* and traditional costumes."[157] This was of course reported in the *Bretagne à Paris*. In July, Breton senators and deputies sent a delegation to the president of the Conseil d'Etat demanding that the *Bécassine* film be censored. Others wrote to the minister of national education, Jean Zay, and the minister of selected justice, Paul Marchandeau, reminding them that this film was an insult to the Bretons, who were one-sixth of the victims of the Great War.[158] In Brest "this abhorrent caricature of Breton women" was burned in effigy on 2 July.[159] The *Excelsior* was correct: Bretons now hated Bécassine. They directed their hatred to the usage of the term "Bécassine" as an insult, a derogatory nickname for Bretons and especially Breton women. In addition, disrespect for Bretons carried the more male, and political, insult to those who were more keenly aware of their role in French history and especially to Breton sacrifice in the Great War. Breton anger took its toll on Bécassine products, which became intolerable to Bretons. Not only the film but also the magazine *Semaine de Suzette* and Bécassine albums disappeared from Breton shops, as did Bécassine yarn.[160]

The author, Maurice Langereau, was shocked by this anger at his beloved character: "Bécassine provokes laughter by the blunders that her naïveté gets her into, by the adventures and misadventures that result. But while they are laughing, children murmur 'that good Bécassine!' And they pronounce these words with a tone of profound affection. Goodness is in fact the basis of Bécassine. Constantly she neglects her own pleasure and her own interests."[161] Langereau was doubtless sincere, but he did not understand the way Bécassine had been used on the street or what her legendary stupidity had come to mean to Bretons. And it is undeniably true that Bécassine had proven to be a profitable venture for Langereau and Pinchon: the twenty-four albums based on the stories in *Semaine de Suzette* had sold 1,864,000 copies, and an alphabet book had sold 370,000. This brought Langereau 35,316,000 francs—in addition to 250,000 francs for allowing Bécassine's name to be used in the film in 1939. In any case the French state was unwilling to prosecute the three young men who had vandalized the wax museum Bécassine in June 1939, because more important matters were at hand.[162] The Second World War put an end to Bécassine; the German occupation forbade owning or reading Bécassine albums.[163] Further, 1939 marked the close of the era of marginality for Bretons in Paris.

The interwar period saw a sea change in the public image and discourse about Bretons in Paris. On one hand real slights remained, directed to minor characters in the finest fiction of the time, such as *Les Thibault*, and to Bécassine in the film. Although this film was hardly in the same league as Jean Renoir's *Rules of the Game*, released the same year, as an insult it had the power to arouse Breton ire for sullying this character. Yet on the other hand, a strong contingent of literary and skilled Bretons took it upon themselves to reply to such insults with literary and public action: an anti-Bécassine play and the destruction of the wax museum statue. An equally skilled group of Bretons produced a provincial display at the World's Fair in Paris in 1937 that was not a folkloric caricature, as it had been in 1900, but rather a demonstration of Breton modernity and skilled craftsmanship.

The church remained vital. Events such as Pardons in Paris and pilgrimages to the Sacré Coeur basilica gathered Bretons by the hundreds. Writers like Monseigneur Edmond Loutil continued to publish literature on the evils of the city. Nonetheless, there were also signs of a fading influence. In the 1920s the Paroisse Bretonne lost its life force when François Cadic left the city. The Pardon of Saint-Denis was a secular affair that matched the declining influence of the church in Saint-Denis.

Likewise, the Breton community lost the leadership of René Le Fur and the thoughtful traditions of his publication, but it also gained sources of support. The first was a new weekly newspaper with a young editor, the second a strong associational life with the proliferation of clubs of all kinds. Finally, some Parisian Bretons were influenced by, and important to, the burgeoning nationalist movement, the Emsav. The voices of the Breton experience sound more clearly for this period, and they allow us to hear more acutely the range of experience, from loneliness and isolation to a close-knit familial and working life.

The nuptials of Bretons in Paris during the prosperous 1920s record how the changes in this community had accrued since the 1870s and draw a powerful portrait of changing lives in the varied urban environments of the Paris basin. In both Saint-Denis and the Fourteenth Arrondissement, Bretons joined the broader social trend of earlier marriage, no longer following the prewar pattern of early marriage to a fellow rural in Saint-Denis or late marriage following years of service as in the Fourteenth Arrondissement. Rather, more secure and lucrative work prompted earlier marriages in the 1920s. Moreover, the Bretons of Saint-Denis became more fully integrated with other men and women in the Paris basin as they became more likely to intermarry, while men and women in the Fourteenth Arrondissement also chose mates from across a wide spectrum, including fellow Bretons. Within the melting pot of greater Paris there did remain a community of Bretons who chose to marry with one another.

And for the most part, they would stay on in the Paris basin. Like François and Marie Michel, and the Métro worker Jean-Marie B. and his wife, Bretons often settled outside the city limits, where they could have a garden and a little house. In any case, memories of a difficult life in Brittany, the death of family members there, the relocation of siblings and cousins to the city, and the attractions of the Paris basin kept Bretons in Paris or the banlieue. These patterns in work and residence would continue in the postwar decades.

By the late summer of 1939 a trilogy of forces worked to end the days when Bretons could be considered pariahs. An expanding labor force and the booming Parisian economy of the 1920s allowed Bretons access to jobs that demanded more skills and in some cases offered employment security. In other words, many people from Brittany were able to enter the labor force that we consider modern, as skilled and sometimes unionized workers, state employees, and white-collar workers.

In addition, the Breton community included politicized men who were willing to bring to Paris their Breton identity, awareness, sense of historical wrongdoing, and anger at insults like the famous cartoon character Bécassine—students, intellectuals, and skilled workers like the three young men who broke apart the statue of Bécassine in the wax museum. These members of the community had the time, energy, and willingness to be disruptive on behalf of Breton power and identity.

Finally, the political inclusion that had Bretons smarting from the forced learning of the French language in earlier years came to be a benefit in the 1930s. Municipal jobs such as work for the Métro system became reserved for French nationals. With the Great Depression, hundreds of thousands of foreign workers—welcomed and even recruited in the boom years of the 1920s—were victims of what Janine Ponty calls "conjunctural xenophobia." They were encouraged or forced to leave the country by processes that varied by immigrants' national origin and location in France. The tracking of foreigners, perfected by the Paris police in the interwar period, served to expel unwanted newcomers and colonials. These departures reduced France's principal foreign-born groups by over a half million between 1931 and 1936 alone and left the labor force more exclusively to French workers.[164] With the deepening of the Depression and worsening xenophobia that came with the influx of refugees from fascism in Italy, Spain, Germany, and points east, attention would turn to non-national outsiders: most especially, foreign-born Jews would become the target of exclusion and persecution.[165] This exclusion of others created the context for greater inclusion of the derided pariahs of yore.

CHAPTER FIVE

A Long Resolution in
Postwar Paris

When François and Marie Talabardon came to Paris in 1947 from the inland countryside of lower Brittany with their two young children, they began by popularizing Breton specialties from a grocery in the Fourteenth Arrondissement, then a few years later took their savings to buy a café-hotel in the Plaisance neighborhood. In 1966 Monsieur Talabardon figured among the founding members of the Breton Association, gathering natives from his home canton. The couple's children, Jean and Annaïg, grew up playing with other children nearby, and the family quickly became part of neighborhood life that Madame Talabardon and Annaïg recall with great fondness. Part of the Breton community, their café became a gathering place for compatriots. Such was the success of the enterprise, and the force of urban renewal in the neighborhood, that the family left the hotel in 1970 and together with their son-in-law Titi Gallo opened a large brasserie across town on the place de la Nation.[1] The Talabardon family number among the many Bretons who began their time in Paris after the Second World War and led successful Parisian lives while remaining conscious of their regional origins. Theirs is part of the complex history of Bretons since the war that has reflected the broader social changes of postwar France.

Before the arrival of the Talabardons, wartime Paris was of course less welcoming. An uncounted number of Bretons like Marie Lepioufle Michel went home to relatives, where it seemed that life would be safer and food more accessible; others like her retired husband François stayed in the Paris basin to guard their home. Still others, like their son Jean, were initially conscripted into the French army and then later sent to Germany as laborers.[2] Although wartime Paris was hungry and dangerous, Métro company records from 1941 and food rationing cards from 1943 give some indication of the means by which Bretons could earn their way, because sources list the provenance of Paris workers. In November 1941 nearly 580 Métro employees came from the Côtes-d'Armor, especially from the southwest Bretonnant cantons of the département. But wartime rationing cards show a more heavily female population, because relatively few men were counted among emigrants from the Côtes-d'Armor two years later in 1943—some 37,000 men had registered, but so had over 60,000 women. Thus, during the war Bretons in Paris were more than ever women. What did Bretons claim as employment in this very particular time? One-seventh of the men listed themselves on rationing cards as functionaries, including retirees like François Michel; this wartime labor force included workers for the police, the *garde mobile*, the gendarmerie, the postal service, the railroad, the Métro, and hospitals. An equally large group consisted of employees of all types, and over 40 percent were listed as laborers. Of the women, a quarter worked as maids, cleaning women, or housewives, but one-eighth worked in commerce, at an office, or as unspecified "employées." Over eighteen hundred women were nurses and nearly eight hundred functionaries.[3] Although Breton women were still domestics during the war, the proportion of women who had this kind of work had diminished.

THE FIRST POSTWAR YEARS

Bretons surged into Paris after the war—indeed, the first years of the "trente glorieuses" witnessed a burst of Breton immigration, since this region sent far more provincials to Paris than any other—nearly one in six of all new arrivals between 1945 and 1960.[4] The proportion of Bretons who departed was higher than before the war and the highest in France; Jean-François Gravier showed special alarm over the depopulation of central Brittany and emigration from it in his book *Paris et le désert français* (1947).[5] The origin of French provincial migration to Paris had shifted to the west, away from the Savoie and the Massif Central, which had been so important a century before. Bretons were in many ways the archetypical new arrivals to Paris after the war. For example, it was predominantly rural Bretons who came, and who came straight from their birthplace; the stronger the attraction to Paris, the fewer the stops en route, concluded the demographic researcher Guy Pourcher.[6] Another, smaller stream entered the city after an initial move or two, or came from towns. When asked why they had left, Bretons cited economic reasons: to escape a region without economic prospects and seek professional advancement—by contrast, marriage, family, and schooling played a smaller role for Bretons than for other newcomers.[7] Women were in the majority, as were singles, and here again the Bretons are emblematic: while women accounted for 56 percent of newly arrived provincials in Paris, the comparable figure among Bretons was 62 percent; as for the unmarried, they made up 62 percent of all newcomers and 69 percent of Bretons.[8] Paris was welcoming, because more than most newcomers, Bretons knew someone who could help them in the city; in addition, the job market was open in postwar Paris, and Paris was considered the center of France.

The social reality of the capital city at this time was the fruit of a long tradition of French provincial immigration. "Paris is in truth a city of migrants" was the word from demographers in 1964.[9] This statement reflects the concern of the National Demographic Institute with provincials in Paris, but Paris was also becoming a destination for foreign newcomers at the same time. Italians, Spaniards, and Poles maintained a strong presence in France in the early 1960s, when Pourcher surveyed provincial newcomers; after the war the small number of Algerians in France had expanded to over 200,000 in 1954 and over 300,000 in 1962. Nonetheless, foreigners and former colonial subjects were not yet the articulated public concern that they would become in the 1970s; it was not until 1988 that a French scholar, Gérard Noiriel, pointed out in *The French Melting Pot* how France had ignored its history of immigration.[10]

Provincial migrants in Paris moved along two tracks: a majority of service workers, laborers, and artisans who arrived in their twenties and made relatively modest careers, and a minority who arrived later in their lives to take up white-collar and professional work. Bretons entered all areas of the urban labor force, some heading to Saint-Denis, where the press described insalubrious housing in 1946 that made "vermin, bugs, and fleas the queens of the area"—no better than before.[11] Others like the Talabardons went into the city of Paris and entered commerce and services, some driving taxis and working as hairdressers. From the rural perspective the most successful were the most secure, like the 3,300 Bretons who served as permanent employees for the Chemin de Fer Métropolitain in 1948—one in ten of all Métro workers.[12] Some Bretons attended the Sorbonne.[13] This was not a dichotomy of rich and poor but rather a spectrum of well-being. Bretons' role in the history of the European labor force paralleled that of others who moved from farm service through domestic service to more protected and secure employment.

Nonetheless, many women continued to begin their Parisian life as servants, and a few cleaned houses all their working lives, aided by the postwar arrival of Suzanne Ascoët, a spirited pioneer of syndicalism for domestic servants who set out to "revolutionize Bécassine."[14] Her trajectory reveals the possibilities for young Bretons in the 1940s: orphaned by the age of sixteen in 1942, Ascoët left the Finistère during the war for Rennes, where she worked as a maid in a clinic and found militant friends through the Catholic worker youth association (the Jeunesse Ouvrière Chrétienne, since other groups were proscribed by Vichy), then a better position as servant in a bourgeois home. At the war's end Ascoët helped to found the first servants' union in France and then returned to Quimper in 1947; she left the struggle to organize domestics in 1953 and took cannery work near her birthplace, "but it was seasonal," she explains, "so finally, like all *Bretonnes*, I went to Paris."[15] Ascoët would spend her career working for the legal rights of servants while continuing to work as a domestic herself. Arriving in the fall of 1954, she was without work or lodging until the Breton Mission and the abbé Gautier found her work with the family of a teacher from the Côtes-d'Armor.[16]

The abbé Élie Gautier, like François Cadic at the turn of the century, was a man of the cloth and writer who would dedicate himself to Bretons in Paris. Once again, the Breton community, and specifically a Breton Mission, came to life in Paris after the war; the abbé Gautier founded the mission just after arriving in the capital in 1947, the same year as the Talabardons. Born in 1903, Gautier had worked for years, teaching and writing in his hometown of Dinan in the Côtes-d'Armor, before he completed an extensive two-volume dissertation at the University of Rennes under the titles *Why Bretons Leave: A Century of Indigence* and *The Hard Life of Peasants*.[17] As a scholar Gautier was in contact with Louis Chevalier, demographer and historian of Paris who would soon move from the National Demographic Institute to the Collège de France to begin a long and important career as a historian of Paris. At the time Chevalier was writing his well-known study *La formation de la population parisienne* (1950).

The Breton priest and the secular historian both emphasized a history of Breton marginality and poverty in Paris. Chevalier cites Bretons' historically degraded position, quoting a personal communication from Gautier to the effect that Bretons were considered the "pariahs of Paris" at the turn of the century. He explicitly contrasts Bretons with the successful and hard-working Auvergnats, citing Bretons as social and economic failures who were, in the words of François Cadic, spendthrifts incapable of saving.[18] Chevalier wrote the foreword to Gautier's study *L'émigration bretonne: Où vont les bretons émigrants: Leurs conditions de vie* (1953). Gautier's study is a document, Chevalier writes, because it draws on the insights of priests who deplored the fate of their compatriots and because the author, as a Breton and a confessor, had access to the intimate milieus of Bretons in southern Paris and Saint-Denis. The study documents an emigration "profoundly different from others," Chevalier continues. The principal problem was a lack of success: "In Paris, finally, and in the Paris *banlieue*, Breton emigration presented the greatest contrast with other emigrations and particularly with emigration from the Auvergne or Normandy."[19] Gautier's study summarizes Breton temporary and definitive migration, within France and abroad, with an emphasis on Paris; he then turns to historical and present-day social conditions and practical suggestions for improving Breton conditions. His argument corroborates Chevalier's observation about Breton historical poverty. However, Gautier also makes it clear that by the end of the war Bretons had a significant place in the best-supported and most secure segments of the Parisian labor force. Gautier himself had a hand in this, having placed over 350 men in the Métro system.[20]

The abbé is most fondly remembered for his work with the Breton Mission and his aid to innumerable Breton newcomers after the war. Knowledgeable and concerned about Bretons away from home, Gautier founded a mission with similar goals as the Breton Parish a half-century before: to support young Breton immigrants, especially young women, to "keep them from falling into dangerous hands, help them to find housing, to find work and especially to meet other young people."[21] To this end a striking poster appeared in the Gare Montparnasse in 1950, picturing silhouettes of a young woman with a suitcase shadowed by a menacing figure in a raincoat: "Young people—dangers lie in wait . . . where will you stay? Where will you work? Reject misleading offers" (see figure 3).[22]

Gautier was unable to protect religious practice, however. Just at this time, in the early 1950s, one of the founders of the sociology of religion

JEUNES

DES DANGERS VOUS GUETTENT...

OU LOGEREZ-VOUS ? OU TRAVAILLEREZ-VOUS ?

DEFIEZ-VOUS DES OFFRES TROMPEUSES

Tous renseignements (Paris-Province)
une adresse :
ŒUVRE des GARES
21, Avenue Général Michel-Bizot, Paris 12ᵉ

Accueil et Loisirs :
MISSION BRETONNE
45-47, rue La Quintinie
Paris 15ᵉ Métro : Vaugirard
Vau. 20-94 - 62-77

Edité par les EQUIPES d'ACTION contre la traite des femmes et des enfants
21, rue Sainte-Croix de la Bretonnerie, Paris 4ᵉ

3. Poster for the Breton Mission, 1950s

spoke with feeling about Bretons' loss of faith in the city. Gabriel Le Bras, a professor at the University of Paris from a coastal town in the Côtes-d'Armor, opined that ninety out of a hundred rurals who emerged from the Gare Montparnasse ceased religious practice. The threshold of the station was the threshold of non-belief, in his opinion, and even his estimate that 10 percent remained faithful was generous. He told of twenty-five Breton maids—all practicing Catholics at home, some even active in the local fellowship—none of whom went to Mass in Paris and one of whom even became a dancer in Pigalle.[23] The fears of the church were well founded; religious practice faded in Paris for most Bretons.

Religious practice aside, the impulse to build an active community meant that social and public events for Bretons expanded. The 1950s and 1960s are remembered as the golden years of Breton associational life in Paris. Sunday dances at the Breton Mission complemented neighborhood and café dances, and perhaps eight hundred people attended on Sundays; theater companies performed at the mission. Gautier also worked to create the fête of Saint Yves each year on 19 May as a large ceremony for Bretons celebrated in the Arènes de Lutèce, the Roman arena unearthed and restored in the 1860s near the Latin Quarter.[24] This memorable event garnered a large audience of Bretons who ordinarily did not participate in events with compatriots. Venues for musical performances and dances included the *mairies* of the Fourteenth and Fifteenth Arrondissements.[25] One climax of the year would be the crowning of the Duchess of the Bretons of Paris, a position neglected after 1938 but revived in 1946. The annual Breton Pardon in Saint-Denis revived, as secular as ever. The federation of Breton associations began a renaissance in 1945, so that by January 1948 there would be thirty-five associations, with forty-two a few months later.[26] For the Breton-identified community, ceremonies, public occasions, and small meetings proliferated, promoting Breton culture and a dignified identity.

Three threads created public understandings of Bretons in Paris during these years: studies of Brittany, writings and studies by Bretons, and the Breton movement itself.

NEW UNDERSTANDINGS

Yet old images died hard. At the close of the war the geographer Jean-François Gravier painted an arresting portrait of Brittany in *Paris et le désert français*, comparing it to the Deep South of the United States: "Like the American South, it gives the impression of an enclosed space, mysterious and distrustful of the outside world. Physically it is the *bocage* almost everywhere . . . hidden and dispersed farms, often sunken lanes. In human terms it is the country of tradition, of landed nobility, where the Vendée and the Mauge [regions] remember 'the Great War' of 1793." Like the South, Brittany was losing people. Only since 1950 had a few industries been developed—and by outsiders.[27] The newsmagazine *L'Express*, a politically engaged left publication at the time, sent a reporter to explore and conduct interviews in villages and hamlets of the Morbihan in 1960, echoing government interest in this region that was losing so many people.[28] After a disparaging account of his entry into what he called a medieval territory, the reporter, Jean Cau, described the home of "an ageless peasant woman. Five children. This one is visibly an idiot. . . . The father has the fixed small eyes of an alcoholic rat. The farmhand is equally idiotic and smiles beatifically from her wet lips." Cau went on to write: "Like fools in some lands, drunks are sacred here. You don't touch them, you don't disturb them, you don't give them a bad time." He interviewed a village mayor who explained massive departures: "After the army, the guys don't come back. Fifty have left; they are in Nanterre. Laborers. . . . Those who stay can no longer find a girl to marry. . . . . They become maids in Paris, waitresses or aides, workers if they have a little luck."[29] Cau depicted, in short, a region of degradation and particularly of alcoholism, offering a similar portrait to that in the *Assiette au beurre* over fifty years earlier. Bretons were outraged by this report's calumnies. However, one wrote reasonably that alcohol was in fact a problem in Brittany, as elsewhere, and that the author had confused a lack of sociability with tradition. "The error of Monsieur Jean Cau was to willfully ignore Morbihan as he visited it," one mayor wrote.[30]

More careful, exhaustive, and scholarly studies would follow in the 1960s. Attention turned to Brittany in 1962 when Plozévet, in the pays Bigouden of the southern Finistère, was chosen as a site for important academic studies, underwritten by the national Délégation Générale à la Recherche Scientifique et Technique. Plozévet was the scholars' choice, not because it was considered backward or isolated but on the contrary because it had well-kept archives as well as a characteristically rural high rate of endogamous marriage. In addition, its diversity of settlements— the center, agricultural hamlets, and fishing hamlets—made the commune of Plozévet and its 3,700 inhabitants particularly rich for research.[31] And researched Plozévet was: nearly 100 researchers combed the 6,670 acres of the commune beginning in 1961—and a few projects remained after seven years, by which time forty articles and reports and six hours of film had been produced by anthropologists, sociologists, historians, and other scholars in the biological and social sciences.[32] This lower Breton commune near the tip of the Finistère became the most studied village in France.

Most researchers focused on postwar life in Plozévet; the first widely disseminated result came in 1967 in the form of an ethnography of response to modern life from the distinguished sociologist Edgar Morin, translated three years later as *The Red and the White: Report from a French Village*.[33] This English title betrays the focus on contrasting worldviews and on the dialectic between the old and the new in the 1960s, as well as a keen understanding of the importance of the period 1880–1910 that brought secular education, economic growth, and flourishing Radical Republican politics. Like other observers and students of rural life elsewhere, Morin saw that the women of Plozévet were loath to marry a peasant, writing that they were, despite appearances, "the secret agents of modernity."[34] In lively and warm prose, Morin's study tracked a social structure from the poor and dispossessed to the bourgeoisie of the commune.[35]

The task of writing a volume that would summarize the entire enterprise, *Bretons de Plozévet*, fell to the anthropological historian André Burguière. His study, published in 1975, came on the heels of many specialized reports and two passionate successes: Morin's *The Red and the White* and Pierre-Jakez Hélias's *Horse of Pride*, which I discuss below. Burguière managed to summarize the findings of primary research in biology, demography, space, politics, culture, and the future of the peasantry, and to put these in the "unjustified but indispensable" context of the commune's history. He also provided a critique and reflection on the study in this most nuanced and responsible book.[36] In the end Burguière produced a sensitive study—and a summary of a project that had imposed itself on the people of Plozévet for many years—bearing no resemblance to earlier efforts that had made a caricature of the people of Brittany.

Pierre-Jakez Hélias, a Bigoudin, articulated the Breton experience for a broad audience with *The Horse of Pride*, first published in 1975. A vivid and humane memoir of growing up only a few kilometers from Plozévet, Hélias's tale of childhood, family, education, moeurs, work, and encounters with the French language at school became a bestseller, speaking to the French and then to international audiences in translations into some twenty languages.[37] A professor of Celtic and a Breton public intellectual about to retire at the time of publication, Hélias wrote the book in Breton, then translated it into French, as he had done with some of his other works. Folklorist, playwright, and poet who would go on to write novels in his later years, he worked in both languages. This memoir confirmed the experience of the Republic in its description of Hélias's move between Bigouden and French national cultures. The American scholar Laurence Wylie articulated the general enthusiasm for *The Horse of Pride* when he wrote that it "is an epic, an epic of peasant life in Brittany during the first half of this century. It is also an ethnographic description of a culture that has all but disappeared. It is an intimate social history of the Third Republic. It is a case study in the quarrel over ethnicity. It is an account of a childhood. Above all, it is a gripping tale."[38] In any case, Bretons were its first and most avid readers, as those who studied Bretons in Paris were to realize.

When *The Horse of Pride* appeared some thirty years ago, a pair of ethnologists was at work learning how Bretons formed a life in Paris, using long and repeated interviews with seventy men and women who had moved to Paris from the Morbihan.[39] Guy Barbichon and Patrick Prado remark that a Breton railroad man was probably a typical reader of *The Horse of Pride*, which was sitting on his table as they conversed. The man, who had come to Paris thirty years before from an impoverished agricultural family, explained that "Bretons love their *pays*, but I don't think they are nostalgic. I believed they have taken root in Paris. Our life, those of us who left, is preferable to that of those who stayed on."[40] This manager and his fellow interviewees allowed Prado and Barbichon to create a rich portrait that resonates with and reveals the evolution of Bretons in Paris as the postwar era took shape.

The portrait that emerges is one of success. Every one of the Bretons who arrived in the first years after the war owned his own villa or apartment. Like Marie and François Michel, who lived not far from the hospitals south of the city, and the family of Jean-Marie B., who had retired before the war and were able to obtain land and a little house in Sarcelles north of Paris and Saint-Denis, Bretons had the security and higher standard of living that came in part from owning their home.[41] Nearly a third were torn between their home area and Paris, content in neither place, and a little over a third enjoyed and confirmed Paris as their permanent home.[42] Even those who felt that they would delay happiness until retirement expressed a keen understanding of a material life better than the one they had left behind. Most had successfully sought to avoid the factories, opting instead for public employment in the railroad, post office, police department, Métro, parimutuel betting system, or social security system, work as concierges and in the construction trades, or more prestigious positions in commerce, the *cadres*, education, and nursing.[43]

Nevertheless, because old images are slow to fade, in the 1970s newcomers reported that they occasionally faced objectionable stereotypes—as slow-witted hicks, as Bécassines, as whores. Along with these came more acceptable images—of being proud, hard-working, courageous, and faithful. In the end most expressed pride at being a Breton.[44] Yet men and women who had arrived earlier carried the bitter memory of insults and prejudice, of being hailed as a Bécassine or a *plouc* (yokel), that were part of a widespread cultural memory.[45]

Many Bretons experienced a sort of nostalgia—connected with their home *pays* in a variety of ways. Some made regular, enthusiastic visits to Brittany or built a vacation home there. Some wanted nothing more than to return, like students who received training for jobs available at home or railroad workers who put in their five years so that they could request a transfer back to the west.[46] Others found a way to balance their lives, like the regular visitors to inland villages, including a man who lived with his "feet in the city, his head in the village" because it was only there that he felt at home, and the school employee H., whose vacations allowed him to live with "feet on the earth, his head in the city" as he helped his brother on the farm every summer.[47] Content with city life or not, the connection with Brittany was there for most.

What set one Breton newcomer apart from another was gender—even more than their origins with a peasant, artisan, or small-town family—so distinct were the attachments of men and women to home, their role in the move to Paris, and their attachments to urban life. Men had a palpable desire to escape poverty, but their relationship to property ownership was stronger than that of women, who were less attached to the land and often felt an active revulsion toward farm work and rural life. Attraction to city life, especially Paris, was a "feminine phenomenon," bred by schoolteachers' reports, fashion, television, and returning visitors. "When I left, for us young people, Paris was paradise," remembers a rural woman who left at seventeen in 1959. And independence was in the offing.[48] For men, moving to the city enhanced their chances of marriage, so reluctant were women to spend their lives in the countryside.[49] While many men viewed the city as a training ground, women were more inclined to stay on—which bred conversations about retirement like the following, in which the husband contended, "We'll be happy, there will be groups of friends there," and the wife replied, "In the village, there are four, five farms, no stores, nothing." Women were most preponderant in the largest group of interviewees—those who were committed to and content with urban life.[50]

Like the women interviewed by Françoise Cribier and like Marie

Michel, most female postwar arrivals preferred to live permanently in the city rather than retire to their childhood sites of poverty and humiliation. As Michel's son put it, "it was the misery of her first years, the humiliations she sustained. Also, she preferred the city, the synonym for a better life."[51] And for Parisian residents who did visit home, their visits changed as life went on, as they did for the Morbihonnaise Madame Le Guen, who left her village after her wedding in 1927, but then returned to bear her daughter at home and then regularly for vacations beginning in 1936; she then spent the war years at home, caring for her parents and the family business. After her return to Paris after the war's end, vacation visits and trips for family reunions, weddings, and baptisms were occasions to speak Breton with old neighbors and stay in the childhood home. By the 1980s it was only funerals that occasioned these visits; the childhood home was gone, and there was no point in making a definitive return. This helps to explain that the rate of retirement departure from greater Paris for Madame Le Guen's cohort—those who retired in 1972— was only 25 percent for Parisian workers born in the provinces, and higher for men than for women.[52]

A common pattern marked the process of forming a new life in postwar Paris. Half the newcomers interviewed by Prado and Barbichon had spent time at an intervening destination, a small town or the fields of the Paris basin, and then continued to Paris. For most newcomers the initial period of finding housing, work, and a contact or two was mediated by individuals—often family and friends from home. If family, it was most often women—sisters, sisters-in-law, cousins, and aunts—who introduced them to the city. Subsequently, exploration of Paris brought out a newer and wider network that often let relations with the first family member fade as other Bretons and, especially in the 1940s and 1950s, Breton associations and dances attracted young newcomers. If and when single newcomers married, patterns shifted as some became more deeply enmeshed in Paris's Breton community and others more peripheral, depending on their marriage partner and social status. This is where sociability began to diverge.[53] For most families, again like Marie and François Michel, society consisted primarily of a circle of relations.[54]

When these postwar Breton arrivals married in Paris, they still married fellow Bretons, or descendants of Bretons born in the city, in the majority —but this general pattern veils a predictable but important disparity. Women who were not from peasant families tended to marry Parisians and other provincials; they echo the pattern set by the women who had married in the Fourteenth Arrondissement since 1890. These newcomers were the very women who were the most positive about the move to the capital and who had made the clearest break with their home. By contrast, most men married a Breton, whatever their origins. And all the single men from agricultural families met their wives in Paris.[55]

By the late 1970s the Breton community consisted of many organizations, more and less formal. Among the informal were village-centered networks, evolving groups that provided news from home and transportation to and from home. Others were, or became, groups centered in Paris that combined compatriots near and far. In addition, many kinds of formal associations spread across the city, revived after the war. Most were groups that met once a year for a banquet and dance. By 1978 twenty-four associations, most based on a shared home place, and twelve Celtic cultural organizations known as *cercles* made up the Fédération des Bretons de Paris. Groups with other interests, nationalist and socialist, formed other clubs. The Breton Mission served a wide range of people because it had a fixed location and open spirit. Finally, social aid organizations were at the ready to help destitute newcomers.[56] Tellingly, two of the largest and most active groups were outside the city limits in the 1970s. To the west, the Bretons de Puteaux sponsored a modern dance, a traditional musical occasion (Fest Noz), and a crêpe banquet, in addition to bus trips to Brittany and celebrations of Twelfth Night (la Fête des Rois). Supported by the municipality, this group was formal and organized. To the east, in Pré Saint-Gervais, was an ad hoc convivial village. Here the founder's home served as a center that had welcomed his aunt, uncle, and sister, who in turn welcomed other fellow villagers. But this was not exclusively for Bretons: a Parisian from Belleville and "even an Auvergnat" were also welcome. Two activities animated this group: car repair and food—meat from the Rungis market, and rabbits and chickens from the hutches in the yard. "Festive meetings prevailed over work, affective relations over material interests."[57]

For those who arrived in the 1940s and 1950s formal associations were crucial: over half the interviewees who arrived before 1966 became members. And the Breton dances were even more important, gathering hundreds, especially Chambronne in the Fifteenth Arrondissement and in Saint-Denis. These dances provided the meeting places for nearly all the rural newcomers interviewed and their future spouses. Dances and associational life gave a chance at finding a wife to someone like H.—son of the soil, a school employee who had come to Paris in 1962, at forty, without marital prospects.[58] After about 1966 this changed dramatically: only a few newcomers interviewed attached themselves to an association, and the leaders deplored the disaffection of the youth.[59] Newcomers to the city were now more sophisticated than those who had arrived on the heels of the war, and they often enjoyed the aid of educational institutions and employers upon arrival.

Breton sociability was undergoing dramatic changes. With the arrival of the young abbé Quéméner to replace Gautier in 1966, the Breton Mission would shift from giving lessons in math and French to lessons in the Breton language and bagpipes; the mission's name would change, adding the words *Ti ar Vretonned* (Breton house) to suggest a less religious orientation.[60] After the Saint Yves celebration in May 1968, when a parade of nearly fifteen thousand Bretons traversed a silent Paris, stilled by transport strikes, the election of the duchess became less popular. On one hand, many such traditions had less cachet than before, and on the other, Breton nationalists saw the celebration of the Duchess Anne and by extension the joining of Brittany to France as degrading to Brittany. The ceremonial parade waned, and the election of the duchess ceased after 1975. Publication of the weekly *La Bretagne à Paris* ceased in 1988.[61] To be Breton was increasingly associated with music, with language, with folklore; moreover, the spirit and energy of May 1968 breathed life into Breton music and protests in Brittany at conditions there.[62]

A new, broader, and more historically and culturally oriented Breton identity was in the making, marked by an interest in Celtic culture. Localism and universality converged, enlarging the horizon of Celtic culture to an international inclusion of Scottish, Irish, and Welsh music and literature. *Festou-Noz* proliferated, bringing dances and performances of Breton and other Celtic music to Paris. The poet, singer, and writer Glenmor began by "defolkorizing" Breton song and music—"jostling tradition without disowning it," in the words of the historian Joël Cornette —for a public that was new and cognizant of Breton identity. Alan Stivell brought Celtic music to the wider world in the prestigious Parisian venue of the Olympia, in early 1972; one fan reported that "the temple on the Boulevard des Capucines will not forget this night of recognition." The Celtic harp and its companion instruments were beginning a new day, played by a host of young musicians.[63] "It is thus that Brittany in the space of a few seasons at the beginning of the seventies came into fashion, to the sound of electric guitars, Celtic harps, talabards, drums."[64] Celtic clubs thrived; in 1973 the Breton book and music store Librarie Breizh was founded in the Fourteenth Arrondissement.[65]

Room remained for stronger and more specific identities. Paris remained the destination for Bretons with literary ambitions like Charles Le Quintrec, a poet and novelist who arrived in 1948 and maintained a strong Breton identity throughout his distinguished career. Longstanding Breton activists, like the Caouissin brothers, who had plotted to kidnap the starlet of the Bécassine film so long ago, in their twenties, retained a presence in Paris.[66] Helping organizations and nationalist venues existed side by side. For some Bretons, to speak French was to speak modern, and Breton was only a dead language; but for others, learning Breton remained a key to conviviality with friends and even to their identity.[67] Particular gathering places and cafés would always be important, but also ready audiences for Celtic events—with a strong Breton and Breton-descended audience—gathered from throughout greater Paris. Prado and Barbichon conclude that "a Breton village has been founded in a new form by migration, which is not the recreation of the home village, but a community of which the residences are dispersed over a vast urban landscape."[68]

The negative image of Bretons belonged in the past. The historical accounts of poverty and backwardness, of unfavorable comparisons between Bretons and other provincials in Paris such as the Auvergnats, were just that—historical.[69] They had no place in the Paris of the 1970s.

BÉCASSINE: ENCORE ET TOUJOURS

The rehabilitation of Bécassine began in this atmosphere. Although neither a book with a new author and illustrator, *Bécassine Returns* (1959), nor a television pilot in 1962 was a success, the original Bécassine albums continued to sell after the war, and the publisher modernized the covers and brightened the illustrations.[70] Later the original albums were reprinted. At the end of the 1960s objections to Bécassine found a new voice: Breton nationalists appropriated and transformed the "ridiculous but well-disposed" Bécassine in the early 1970s, reversing her adoption by Parisian and middle-class culture to create a symbol of leadership to Bretons. In the short-lived monthly *Bretagne révolutionnaire*, a cartoon Bécasssine invited a couple praying at the Angelus, "Comrades, join with

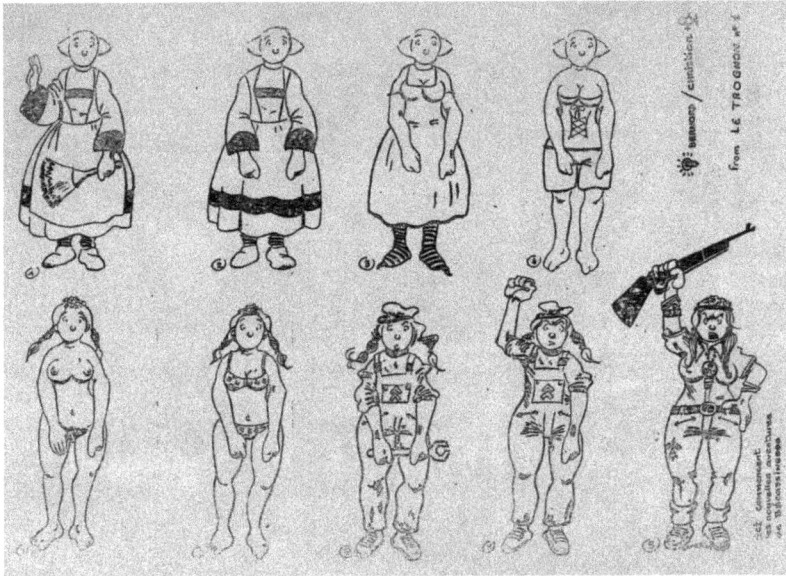

4. Bécassine in Revolt, 1970s. Collection of the author.

us," then led them out of the field in three frames. A widely distributed caricature illustrated the evolution of Bécassine from a classic servant to an armed guerrilla in eight frames.[71] Thus the cartoon—the ridiculed symbol of Brittany—retaliated (see figure 4).

At the same time, standard national culture welcomed Bécassine when she was listed among the *personnes célèbres* in the dictionary *Petit Larousse*. Described in 1979 only as a comedic Breton servant character, in the 1980s she saw her entry enlarged to acknowledge her role as one of the first comic strip heroes, created in 1905.[72] More tolerance for Bécassine manifested itself in the 1980s, even in Brittany. The singer Chantal Goya performed her popular "Bécassine is *ma cousine*," celebrating the character as a companion, not an object of ridicule, to applauding crowds at a mid-Lenten fair in Brittany in March 1980; a float at the same event carried not only a statue of Bécassine but also girls dressed as their "heroine"—a far cry from the burning in effigy of 1939.[73] When the old *Bécassine* film was shown in its fiftieth year at a Breton film festival, the audience was more curious than revolted.[74] Meanwhile, in 1983 the Centre Culturel de Marais in Paris mounted an exposition of the illustrator Pinchon's drawings.[75]

By the beginning of the twenty-first century a full-scale transformation of the Bécassine who had been so wounding to Breton women was under

5. Bécassine Commemorative Stamp, 2005. Collection of the author.

way, based on the reconstruction of the character as a childhood heroine with a heart of gold. Her blunders had been forgotten and her lovable nature had even become part of her (now illustrated) dictionary entry, which described her as a naïve and devoted Breton who embodied the faithful servant.[76] In some quarters the use of Bécassine dolls and albums continues to be seen as treason, but the economic prosperity and cultural popularity of Brittany in the past decades have rendered Bécassine harmless.[77] Once again it is entirely safe to put Bécassine up for sale. Bécassine dolls of every size, statuettes, mugs, bowls, aprons, dishtowels, potholders, stationery, calendars, books, postcards, alarm clocks, and teapots are in shops—the list is endless. Albums printed before the Second World War demand an especially high price.[78] Bécassine now enjoys a prolonged life as an anodyne commercial figure.

The character of Bécassine has become an object of study as well; she appears alongside Pinocchio and Robinson Crusoe in a book on survival heroes for children.[79] Two knowledgeable, loving fans of Bécassine have written studies of her life and the commercial and noncommercial artifacts inspired by her.[80] The Centre National des Recherches Scientifiques published a colorful paperback of the dissertation *Bécassine inconnue* in 2000.[81] As her centenary approached, a rather official—and lavishly illustrated—history, *Bécassine: Une légende du siècle*, was published by Gautier / Languereau under the Hachette imprint and the authorship of the Breton Bernard Lehembre. A two-page review essay in *Le Monde* celebrated the book.[82] As the French national gesture to this character, the postal service issued a large, red commemorative stamp celebrating the birthday that pictured Bécassine carrying a giant birthday cake (see figure 5). Her most durable manifestation may not be the stamp but rather her giant colorful plastic likeness on the wall of a Métro platform at the Tuileries. There Bécassine is described as a successful migrant woman —the country cousin come to Paris, where she had great success. Not only is the day of the stupid Breton in the past, but so is the image of the rural French woman, inept, slow, and bumbling. This shift can be read as a vindication of the hundreds of thousands of young women who have come to Paris to work as domestic servants and in other lowly jobs, and more broadly of all Bretons.

🦋

Postwar Paris provided avenues of integration for Bretons that resolved and transformed their former image. Immediately after the war the studies that emphasized Bretons focused either on the past or on rural Brittany. The region was depicted as a most backward and insular part of the "French desert," while the close study of Bretons in Paris by the abbé Gautier emphasized earlier times. Subsequently, serious study of Breton communities began as the people of lower Brittany opened their homes to researchers beginning in the 1960s.[83] Alongside academic reportage, the best-selling memoir of the 1970s, *Horse of Pride*, introduced France and the rest of the world to Breton childhood. Although this was part of a genre that continues to this day, this Breton memoir found a particularly wide audience.

The church revived an aid organization for Bretons, prompted by the great number of arrivals soon after the Second World War, when the abbé Gautier founded the Breton Mission. Responding to needy newcomers, the mission offered the same kinds of services that François Cadic had helped to organize at the turn of the century, providing help with jobs, a community, and protection for young women. The Mission was complemented by a growing number of clubs and societies, seemingly for newcomers from every point of origin and interest. Breton organizations began to cater to a less young and less needy group in the 1970s, as their focus settled on a common past and common interests rather than mutual assistance. Like the church, however, Breton associations attracted relatively few of the many Breton-born people living in greater Paris.

The resolution of Bécassine's history as a fictional character for children, a symbol for Bretons, and a commercial product provides a lesson in contingency and the flexibility of a historical image. Bécassine's life as a storybook character was revamped with more colorful reprint albums. At the same time, Breton nationalists inverted the image of Bécassine from a shameful symbol of stupidity to a symbol of leadership. The state—both the postal service and the Paris Métro—offered amends by creating colorful positive images on her centenary. Bécassine's longstanding role as a commercial product has expanded, so that she occupies more space than ever on the boutique shelf.

Bécassine remains a distinctive part of the Breton story. Unlike her fellow Breton character, the wily Gaul Astérix, and other French cartoon characters, she is a creation of a bourgeois Parisian Belle Époque society whose existence predates inspirations from the United States.[84] Because Bécassine appeared in Paris just as Breton women were migrating to the city in great numbers, her creation is rooted in the social understandings of that age. Moreover, the illustrator Pinchon's sensitivities to costume provided his audience with a portrait of changing fashion for the two decades before the Second World War—except Bécassine's costume, which was constant.

Interviews with and testimonies from Bretons who arrived in postwar Paris demonstrate the continuation of a theme that emerged from the earliest marriage records of Bretons in the Paris basin. New arrivals in the city found their way—or did not—connected to a particular set of compatriots or contacts. As much as perceptions of them may have been colored by stereotypes or images, these images did not have the power to make a tidy prediction of the future for newcomers to the city. More than ever before, newcomers had the power to define what it meant to be a Breton in Paris.

The city of Paris has served as a melting pot in which Breton identity is no longer denigrated. This history of "national assimilation," to use the words of Gérard Noiriel, is the work of a state that has privileged its own citizens, but also of the ups and downs of the urban economy, of changing immigrant groups, and of the Bretons themselves, who in many cases chose to make their most intimate life outside their compatriot group.[1] The sort of life trajectories visible in marriage records reveal the complex and multifaceted choices grasped by newcomers in their twenties and thirties. These contradict an image of smooth integration, the stereotype of a community apart, and the "black legend" of wholesale migrant failure.

As the twentieth century drew to a close, Breton culture and Bretons experienced a certain visibility in greater Paris. Saint-Denis elected a mayor of Breton descent named Patrick Braouezec in 1991, a communist who well remembered family stories of prejudicial treatment toward Bretons. Braouezec skillfully negotiated with the conservative national government to bring about the destruction of the huge gas structures in Saint-Denis and their replacement with a great soccer stadium, the Stade de France, built in time for the World Cup of 1998.[2] Two important studies of Bretons in Paris appeared in the 1990s. The first, by the Paris-born author Armel Calvé, *Histoire des Bretons de Paris*, emphasizes Breton associational and commercial life. The second, by Didier Violain, a Nantais who had lived in Paris for over fifteen years, was *Bretons de Paris: Des exilés en capitale*, which presents a selection of interviews and memoirs interlaced with lavish photographs that illustrate the joys and heartbreaks of moving to and living in Paris. This book proved so popular that it was published twice, the second time by the French book-of-the-month club.[3]

Fiction, memoirs, and histories of the present century demonstrate a positive and accessible approach to Bretons. After taking on the history of Auvergnats in Paris in 2001, the prolific author Marc Tardieu published in 2002 a novel joining sweethearts from Brittany and the Auvergne (*Le bal de la rue de Lappe*) and in the following year a history of Bretons in Paris to match that of the Auvergnats.[4] At the same time, Breton rural life was exoticized and celebrated in series of new books about the old days— books beautifully illustrated with postcards, photographs, and works of art, such as *Une Bretagne si étrange, 1900–1920*.[5] Celebration and commercialization have gone hand in hand with inclusion.

Bretons are now seen as provincials like any others who created a charming French past. When a story of past migrations was published for a broad public in 1997, Jean-Louis Beaucarnot used the title *Quand nos ancêtres partaient pour l'aventure* and gave the Bretons a chapter like any other group, albeit a chapter near the end of the book, with a title that described them as domestic servants, sellers of crêpes, and market gardeners ("bonnes à tout faire, crêperies, et oignons roses"). A review by the famed historian Emmanuel LeRoi Ladurie focused on "ces petits métiers qui poussaient à l'aventure," citing, as the last of the French, "the immortal Bécassine from the Montparnasse station and of the Marquise de Grandair." Perhaps the lesson lies in the final lines of this review: "We are all [toutes et tous] nurses of the Morvan, water carriers of the Auvergne, peddlers of Ubaye or Queyras."[6] That is, no longer do we have "our ancestors, the Gauls" as in the textbooks of the Third Republic, but rather "our ancestors the provincials." And from beyond France as well, to be fair, for Beaucarnot finishes with foreigners, Polish miners and Spanish maids, who arrived "when strangers took up the baton." One must also speak, LeRoi Ladurie writes, of those from outside France: Armenians, Gypsies, Jews, and Arabs.[7]

Exclusion and prejudice are now visited upon other quarters. The long history of postwar immigration—following substantial labor immigration in the 1920s and refugee immigration in the 1930s—has produced a most diverse French people.[8] Southern Europeans and North Africans— primarily Algerians—came to work in the immediate postwar years and continued to do so after Algerian independence in 1962. Since 1973, when immigration was at a maximum and a long economic downturn began, attention has been focused on foreign newcomers, and since the departure of the Ayatollah Khomeini in 1979 to head the new theocracy in Iran,

Muslim newcomers have been subject to particular attention, with a host of consequences for law and society.[9] France, along with the rest of the European Union, braced for a much greater wave of immigrants from post-communist central and eastern Europe than that which materialized. By the beginning of the twenty-first century Asians—whether Chinese or Southeast Asian—were second only to Portuguese and North Africans among immigrants. Although some newcomers are highly skilled and educated, many took unskilled work as a result of changes in the labor force that allowed French to take secure and white-collar work. As Chevalier wrote already in 1953, this change in the structure of the labor force, along with the arrival of less trained and ethnically distinct newcomers, created the rising tide that elevated Breton fortunes in Paris.[10]

Banlieues like Saint-Denis (where the last Breton Pardon was celebrated in 1996 and which lost its Breton-run crêperie about 2000) have been cursed by the economic restructuring of the past thirty years, which has wreaked havoc on their economic base and offered nearly insuperable challenges to mayors like Patrick Braouezec. The immigrant workers there—originally called "black Bretons" by some—who came for good jobs during the "trente glorieuses" of the postwar period, had children for whom no such jobs exist. Moreover, education and job training do not yet work equally for immigrants and their descendants, depending on origins.[11] Inclusion has worked for the French-born like the Bretons, and for most western European immigrant groups, but less so for newcomers from eastern Europe and Africa. Bretons may be the pariahs, but they are the pariahs of yesterday, and the current story of exclusion is a global one.

Bretons proved to be distinct in past years, and they are in some ways also distinct from current newcomers. Exceptionally, women made up a high proportion of Bretons in the city of Paris, setting them apart from many migrant groups in Paris such as the Auvergnats and the Creusois, who first came to work in the construction industry, and often as seasonal laborers. This also sets them apart from earlier immigrant groups like Italians and most immigrant groups that arrived since the Second World War, who were predominantly male. As a consequence, the large proportion of Bretonnes who began their urban lives as domestic servants operated in greater isolation from the Breton community than their male colleagues, who worked in a more collective and less isolated setting; this was the price paid for choosing work that afforded room and board. Yet it also meant that newcomers would meet and perhaps marry men from other areas. The choice of domestic service carried other consequences: primarily, it prolonged Bretons' place in an atavistic corner of the labor market that only gradually and partially improved. Also, a larger proportion of Bretons in Paris were women without any family support who could turn to prostitution in an economy that did not allow them to earn a living wage by other means. In any case, a larger proportion of Bretons were vulnerable to pregnancy than groups with a larger proportion of males, and for the poor this meant interaction with the social services of the city and with institutions like the maternity hospital for the indigent. Yet Bretonnes characteristically could, and did, also help their younger brothers and sisters, nephews, nieces, and cousins, since in many cases they were the first in their family to settle in Paris.[12]

Arriving in Paris in an age of proletarian labor, Breton men lacked any specific or picturesque niche for their efforts. No tradition as water carriers, masons, or chimneysweeps introduced Parisians to Breton newcomers, as it did for those from the Auvergne, the Creuse, and the Alps. Lacking apprenticeships and extensive education, Breton men were able to respond to the demand for unskilled labor on construction sites and in the Paris Métro and rail lines. Lacking the compliant reputation of Breton women, the mass of Breton men in many instances had trouble finding good or steady work. In this they resemble some groups of immigrants and their offspring in the twenty-first century, whose daughters are able to find work but whose sons are less likely to finish school, enter an apprenticeship, or find a good job.[13]

Breton culture was central to stereotypes held by Parisians. First and foremost, the religiosity of Bretons was held against them, particularly at the turn of the century when the battle to create a secular state and secular schools was at its most intense. Although much of this battle was waged far from Paris in the religious schools and convents of Brittany, the Bretons' reputation for faithful Catholicism and religious fervor put them in disfavor in many eyes. On the other hand, many employers found devout employees to be pliant and honest, hence desirable. Moreover, the church and a variety of voluntary organizations did their best to save the souls of Bretons in irreligious Paris and to keep them in the fold. Here in some ways Bretons resemble today's Muslim immigrants, who are by many lights seen as inassimilable because of their religious values, and who are increasingly identified by their common religion rather than according to their diverse origins in North and West Africa, Turkey, and elsewhere, as many scholars have noted.[14] One sign of this blinkered view has been the focus on Muslim women's attire and the legal ban on the headscarf in public secondary schools and on the burka in public, instituted in 2004 and 2010. For many of the Muslim and Breton faithful, faith and religious practice are perceived as rare effective shields against the visible corruptions and dangers of modern urban life. If devout Catholicism set Bretons apart, their Druids—to say nothing of the prehistoric dolmen and menhir rock formations—exoticized this group and rendered them more primitive, if not incomprehensible, in Parisian eyes.[15]

Like religion, language was a crucial and contested part of Breton culture. The Third Republic found the Celtic Breton language—much more so than the Gallo dialect of upper Brittany—to be anathema, associating it less with peasant practices than with the church, the lessons of religious schools, and the catechism. It expressed, in the words of one teachers' publication, "the worst ideas vomited from hell."[16] On the other hand, many Bretons cherished and sought to prolong the use of the Breton language, an effort that continues to this day not only in Breton schools but in the classrooms of Paris. Every prewar Breton newspaper published articles in Breton—even if some Bretons, like the federation leader René Le Fur, made it clear that doing so was not in the interest of, or interesting to, every Breton. More concretely, the lack of capacity to speak French with ease tied the tongue of many a newcomer, inhibiting the search for work and friendships in the city. This too provides a link between the Bretons of the past and newcomers of today: both have had to endure problems of language, religion in some cases, and gender relations in others, to say nothing of stigma by cartoon.[17]

The recent memoir of the noted historian Mona Ozouf, *Composition française: Retour sur une enfance bretonne*, thoughtfully articulates the range of forces at work in the life of a child wedded to speaking and identifying as a Breton, to the universalizing ideology of the schools of the Third Republic, and to the way of faith demonstrated by the church. These forces create a tension between the universal and particular that is characteristic, she contends, of French national life. Making the case for flexible and multiple identities, Ozouf recognizes the "plurality of ties" fostered by attachment to a home *pays*, the French nation, and religious faith, and recognizes these multiple ties in today's immigrants in France.[18] Bretons in the Paris of the Third Republic demonstrated flexible and multiple identities as they came to work and form new families in

Paris. Moreover, they showed how "diversity occurs and operates," as some married compatriots while others did not, and some joined regional organizations while others did not. In any case, Bretons combined their connections to home with life in greater Paris by a variety of means and to a variety of degrees.[19]

The Bretons in Paris connect the migrations of the past with the present. Suzanne Ascoët, a Bretonne who fought for the rights of servants to the end of her working life, recognizes this connection. At the age of seventy-two she observed: "My neighbors are maids of Filipino, Mauritian, Cape Verdean, Polish origins. I also get along well with my Portuguese concierge. We often party, and I dine with one or the other. I'm the only immigrant from the interior."[20] As pariahs of yesterday, Bretons make a demonstrable case for the integration of newcomers, but they also show that this integration is complex, involving different sending areas within a region and a variety of destinations in greater Paris. Although in the age of mass migrations Bretons were known to be uneducated bumpkins, they included an important educated elite that provided much of their leadership and whose experience was very distinct from that of rural workers who found themselves in Saint-Denis. Men and women at all levels of this group had distinct expectations and experiences. Moreover, they are revealed differently by the wide range of sources—bourgeois observations, marriage records, census data, literature, police records, and popular culture artifacts. Together the Bretons of Paris teach us the value of complexity and the long view of the history of migration.

Marriage Records

French demographic records offer a challenge to scholars of internal migrations. Unlike many nations in Europe, France did not develop population registers, and as a consequence migration (as well as immigration from abroad) must be inferred from other sources, such as censuses, civil status records, and legal and notarial documents. Despite these difficulties, two important and revelatory studies of internal migration in France have appeared in recent years. In *Les sentiers invisibles*, Paul-André Rosental employed the civil status and succession records of members of ninety-seven family lines from the enormous dataset of the "3,000 families" study; he was able to demonstrate that the French countryside was alive with movement and that the so-called rural exodus in response to crises and industrialization is a myth. The constellation of family ties, Rosental found, influenced whether and how far one moved. Although this study was able to trace a large number of family members, it could keep track of only a small proportion of women after marriage.[1]

Jean-Claude Farcy and Alain Faure used France's remarkably detailed conscript records to trace the movement of an entire cohort of men between the ages of twenty and forty-five. *La mobilité d'une génération de français* focused on those areas (départements) that sent men to Paris. Yet as the authors write of their revelatory study, "half the world is missing," because the movements of women and other family members are by necessity absent.[2] In both cases available sources prevent an evenhanded treatment of male and female migration, and thus unwillingly perpetuate the assumption that the migrations of men and women are essentially the same, when there is indeed much evidence to the contrary.[3] As is appropriate to their intent and design, neither of these large-scale, significant studies focuses on outsider or marginal groups in the French national context, such as the Flemish, Alsatians, Bretons, or Basques. Unfortunately the multicultural past is ignored, and the implication of such omissions is that national groups—in this case in France—were relatively homogeneous.

This book investigates the lives of one migrant group, the Bretons in Paris, using the records of their marriages in two destinations (the Fourteenth Arrondissement and the banlieue of Saint-Denis) during four years: 1875, 1890, 1910, and 1925. I chose the locations for the economic and social differences that they illustrate and the dates to provide an evolution across a significant span of time, most of the life of the Third Republic. Every marriage of a Breton-born man or woman residing in Saint-Denis or the Fourteenth Arrondissement in those four years was recorded.

Marriage records are a source at once problematic and rich. They are problematic because they are not representative of the entire group of migrants, and it is impossible to know exactly how they are not representative. Certainly they do not include those too ill to contemplate marriage, too lacking in resources to enforce a marriage promise or to marry, or most of those without interest in the opposite sex. Migration usually begins when people are unmarried, so migrants in urbanizing Europe were disproportionately single. Marriage records catch few if any seasonal workers, who are especially likely to marry elsewhere. And wide swathes of ages are excluded: few marriage partners are under the age of twenty in this period, and only those who marry for the second or third time are likely to be over the age of thirty-five. Fortunately for the migration scholar, throughout history the majority of people who have moved have done so between the ages of twenty and forty-five—in France at this time, usually after the age of twenty or twenty-three for men at this time (depending on military service) and earlier for women. Most people migrate in their marriageable years, and so marriage records are best at capturing settling people.

But do migrants marry at their destination—in this case greater Paris— or at home? Custom held that marriages occurred in the bride's home commune. Moreover, Bretons had the reputation for marrying at home— but this reputation is not justified by the findings of my research, which demonstrates that many Bretons did marry in Paris, even when they married a compatriot; this is doubtless partly because time and money did not allow a return home for working people, as explained by Jean

Chabot, the son of domestics, and Yvonne Yven in reference to the wedding in 1895 of Jean's parents.[4] The marriage records of some major sending areas in the Finistère and Côtes-d'Armor reveal virtually no mention of a Parisian residence for wedding partners.[5] This suggests that Bretons left their home town after marriage, with a spouse, rather than returning home for a wedding after years in Paris. Indeed this fits the narratives related in this book by interviewees who spoke with Françoise Cribier, Catherine Omnès, Catherine Rhein, and Didier Violain; many departed for Paris soon after their wedding and were included here although their marriages records were not available.[6]

The *actes de mariage* set themselves apart from most sources by the wealth of information that they contain about not only the wedding partners but also their friends and family.[7] Moreover, in many respects these records are unparalleled in accuracy, because the state insisted upon notarized documents to identify the bride and groom and to certify parental consent. Each acte includes the following information:

- The given name of the bride and groom;
- Precise dates and places of birth, assured by required copies of the birth certificates;
- The occupation of the bride and groom;
- The demographic status of the wedding partners, be they minors or *majeurs*, widowed or divorced; in the latter cases certification of divorce or death of the former spouse was required;
- Parents' consent (or grandparents' consent, in the absence of a parent), whatever the age or civil status of the wedding partners. Consent was communicated by the presence of those granting it or by a notarized statement of permission. If parents were deceased, a copy of the death certificate was in order or, in the alternative, testimony by the marriage partners, witnesses, or both to the lack of forebears. This rule, designed to assure the identity of the marriage partners, allowed three exceptions: Permission to marry for orphaned minors (under twenty-one) had to be sought from the *conseil de famille*, whose function it was to protect minors; the conseil met at the bidding of the cantonal court. Children born out of wedlock who were not recognized by their father or by both parents had only to produce their birth certificate. Finally, foreigners were not required to furnish this permission;

- Parents' domicile and sometimes occupation, if alive, and on occasion the place and age of death if deceased;

- Current domicile of bride and groom, and address of previous domicile if at the current address for less than six months. Minors were domiciled de jure with parents, even when they had a de facto address elsewhere;

- Addresses where banns announcing the marriage were published in the current arrondissement of residence and in the parents' commune, whether it was the commune of birth or not;

- The following information on four witnesses, who were required to be at least twenty-one, and until the twentieth century, male: name; age; domicile; usually occupation; and often the relationship between the witness and the wedding partner. The marriage records from 1910 are especially rich because after 1897 women as well as men served as witnesses. By 1925, however, only two witnesses presented themselves, and information on relationships was no longer noted;

- The existence of a marriage contract—or lack of a contract;

- The legitimization of children born before the marriage, although this was not noted by 1925;

- The signatures of the wedding partners, parents, witnesses, and municipal officers present.

Unfortunately, some of this information lent itself to imprecise recording. In marriage records used for this book, this was particularly true of occupational and relational specifics. Many men, for example, were listed as "employé," without an indication of whether they were clerks or employees of the railroad, and by the 1920s the term "sans profession" disguised many kinds of work for women—aside from the domestic service that women might have ceased to perform at marriage. When family relation was not specified for witnesses, as it was not in the 1920s, for example, it could sometimes be inferred from name, age, and occupation —but only inferred.

Moreover, it is impossible to know the quality of the relationship between a wedding witness and the bride or groom. Although name could imply a family relation and address a neighbor, beyond that the relationship is hard to tell. Repeated witnesses in the Fourteenth Arrondissement in 1890 suggest that there were a few men hanging around the *mairie* whose signature could be purchased for the price of a drink; Jean Chabot and Yvonne Yven paid a few sous for witnesses because their friends, like themselves, had little time to be away from work.[8] Even the presence of a less needy witness did not mean close friendship—one acute observer, Émile Zola, brought a cardboard box maker to witness Gervaise's and Coupeau's wedding in *L'assomoir*; this was arranged by the groom's sister although the witness had never met Gervaise. This witness was invited to lend the wedding a more distinguished tone, and it worked: he was the only member of the wedding party wearing "a real dress-suit with long tails, and passers-by stopped and stared at this elegant gentleman."[9] When kin, close neighbors, or workmates stood up for the bride and groom, we may be quite certain of acquaintance or even friendship, but more than that is difficult to know.

Marriage records, then, may be revelatory or opaque. At best, the acte de mariage can tell the history of two families and provide a rich story of migration and affective community at destination, but this was not always possible. Some records, on the other hand, reveal little, especially when occupational designations were vague or information about parents or witnesses was minimal. For this reason I have used the wedding records to demonstrate general patterns of occupational change, intermarriage, and the use of witnesses. In constructing emblematic cases to illustrate those patterns, I have employed pseudonyms in order to protect individual identities.

TABLE 1. BRETON MARRIAGES IN SAINT-DENIS, 1890–1925

	1890		1910		1925	
	No.	%	No.	%	No.	%
Marriages between Bretons	32	65	67	53	48	32
from same département	30		53		25	
from same arrondissement	18		33		14	
from same commune	4		5		0	
Breton groom, bride born elsewhere	9	18	27	21	43	28
Breton bride, groom born elsewhere	8	16	33	26	61	40
Total	49	100	127	100	152	100

Département of Origin for Breton Wedding Partners in Saint-Denis (Percent)

	1890	1910	1925
Côtes-d'Armor	83	68	45
Finistère	6	12	25
Morbihan	5	9	15
Ille-et-Vilaine	6	6	5
Loire Atlantique	0	5	11
Total	100	100	100
Total number	81	194	200

Note: Because of rounding, percentages may not sum to 100.

Source: Archives Départementales de Seine-Saint-Denis, 1 E 66, 48, Mariages de Saint-Denis, 1890; Archives de l'État civil de Saint-Denis, Mariages, 1910, 1925.

TABLE 2. BRETON MARRIAGES IN THE FOURTEENTH ARRONDISSEMENT, 1890–1925

	1890		1910		1925	
	No.	%	No.	%	No.	%
Marriages between Bretons	16	19	52	26	78	30
from same département	10		29		52	
from same arrondissement	7		17		40	
from same commune	2		8		16	
Breton groom, bride born elsewhere	24	28	37	19	55	21
Breton bride, groom born elsewhere	45	53	108	55	125	48
Total	85	100	197	100	258	100

*Département of Origin for Breton Wedding Partners
in the Fourteenth Arrondissement (Percent)*

	1890	1910	1925
Côtes-d'Armor	52	30	22
Finistère	9	16	34
Morbihan	13	25	21
Ille-et-Vilaine	16	19	13
Loire Atlantique	10	10	10
Total	100	100	100
Total number	99	253	343

Note: Because of rounding, percentages may not sum to 100.

*Source: Archives de Paris, E, Mariages, XIVᵉ Arrondissement, 1890; Archives de l'État
Civil du XIVᵉ Arrondissement de Paris, Mariages, 1910, 1925.*

TABLE 3.   WITNESSES TO BRETON WEDDINGS IN SAINT-DENIS
AND THE FOURTEENTH ARRONDISSEMENT, 1910

	Saint-Denis	14th Arrondissement
Weddings with a family member present (in percent)		
Breton bride	48	29
Breton groom	58	28
Breton couple	83	57
All Breton brides	60	31
All Breton grooms	51	32
Weddings with a bride's or groom's parent residing in Saint-Denis or Paris (in percent)		
Breton bride	21	12
Breton groom	4	17
Breton couple	19	12
Weddings with a female witness (in percent)		
Breton bride	64	67
Breton groom	4	17
Breton couple	19	12
Number of weddings		
Breton bride, non-Breton groom	33	101
Breton groom, non-Breton bride	26	36
Breton couple	68	58

Source: *Archives de l'État Civil de Saint-Denis, Mariages, 1910; Archives de l'État Civil du XIVᵉ Arrondissement de Paris, Mariages, 1910.*

INTRODUCING THE PARIAHS OF YESTERDAY

1 Gautier, *L'émigration bretonne*, 106, and Violain, *Bretons de Paris*, 29, quote the Father Rivalin, speaking at a congress of worker associations in Saint-Brieuc; François Cadic used the term in the July 1899 issue of the *Paroisse bretonne*, which was quoted by Chevalier, *La formation de la population parisienne au XIXᵉ siècle*, 210.

2 Simon-Barouh, "Assimilation and Ethnic Diversity in France," 15–39; Lucassen, *The Immigrant Threat*.

3 Noiriel, *Population, immigration et identité nationale en France*, 85; Weber, *Peasants into Frenchmen*.

4 Many scholars have addressed the exclusive nature of the citizenship philosophy forged in the Revolution and after, including Weil, *How to Be French*; Hufton, *Women and the Limits of Citizenship in the French Revolution*; Heuer, *The Family and Nation*; Silverman, *Deconstructing the Nation*; Surkis, *Sexing the Citizen*; Brubaker, *Citizenship and Nationhood in France and Germany*.

5 Blanc-Chaléard, *Les italiens dans l'est parisien*; Green, *Repenser les migrations*; Konig, *Deutsche Handwerker, Arbeiter une Dienstmädchen in Paris*; Lequin, *La mosaïque France*; Lewis, *The Boundaries of the Republic*; Milza, *Voyage en Ritalie*; Milza, Gervereau, Témime, and Berrou, *Toute la France*; Rygiel, *Destins immigrés*.

6 Teulières, "Immigration and National Identity," 69.

7 Harzig and Juteau, Introduction, 2; Hoerder et al. refer to the recasting of national histories to include the foreign-born and minority communities, but I also insist on this point for national histories and internal groups. Hoerder, Harzig, and Schubert, eds., *The Historical Practice of Diversity*; Hoerder, "Transcultural States, Nations, and People," 16.

8 Faure, "Urbanisation et exclusions dans le passé parisien," 68.

9 Eley and Suny, eds., *Becoming National*, 41; Renan, "What Is a Nation?," 46–52, quotation p. 49.

10 Ibid., 48.

11 Ibid., 49.

12 Noiriel, *Population, immigration et identité nationale en France*, 100–107; Weber, *Peasants into Frenchmen*, chaps. 16–18.

13 Weber, *Peasants into Frenchmen*; Lehning, *Peasant and French*.

14 Chanet, *L'école républicaine et les petites patries*.

15 Ford, *Creating the Nation in Provincial France*; Weber, *Peasants into Frenchmen*.

16 Châtelain, *Les migrants temporaires en France de 1800 à 1914*; Poitrineau, *Remues d'hommes*; Corbin, *Archaïsme et modernité en Limousin au XIXᵉ siècle*; Poussou, *Bordeaux et le sud-ouest au XVIIIᵉ siècle*; Raison-Jourde, *La colonie auvergnate de Paris au XIXᵉ siècle*; Blanc-Chaléard, *Les italiens dans l'est parisien*; Farcy and Faure, *La mobilité d'une génération de français*; Faure and Lévy-Vroelant, *Une chambre en ville*.

17 Teulières, "Immigration and National Identity," 69.

18 See for example Bade, *Migration in European History*, xii; Lucassen, *The Immigrant Threat*.

19 Ozouf, *Composition française*, 241.

20 Noiriel, *Population, immigration et identité nationale en France*; Weber, *Peasants into Frenchmen*.

21 Lucassen, *The Immigrant Threat*; Chin also notes the shift to a focus on immigrant culture, meaning Islam, as a way of naming immigrants as unassimilable. She also discusses gender relations, which I take up below, in *The Guestworker Question in Postwar Germany*.

22 Lucassen, *The Immigrant Threat*.

23 Hoerder, *Cultures in Contact*; Manning, *Migration in World History*.

24 Levine, ed., *Proletarianization and Family History*; Tilly, "Demographic Origins of the European Proletariat," 1–85; Winter, *Patterns of Migration and Adaptation in the Urban Transition*.

25 Châtelain, "Migrations et domesticité féminine urbaine en France"; Moch, *Paths to the City*; Moch, *Moving Europeans*.

26 As an entrée into this extensive literature see Anderson, *Doing the Dirty Work?*

27 Eley, "Historicizing the Global, Politicizing Capital," 167–68.

28 Chevalier, *La formation de la population parisienne au XIXᵉ siècle*; Chevalier, *Dangerous Classes and Laboring Classes in Paris during the First Half of the Nineteenth Century*.

29 These include most recently Faure, "Paris, 'Gouffre de l'espèce humaine'?," 49–86, and Raison-Jourde, *La colonie auvergnate de Paris au XIXᵉ siècle*, as well as Ratcliffe, "Classes laborieuses et classes dangereuses à Paris pendant la première moitié du XIXᵉ siècle?," 542–74.

30 Chevalier, *La formation de la population parisienne au XIXᵉ siècle*, x; Raison-Jourde, *La colonie auvergnate de Paris au XIXᵉ siècle*.

31 Faure, "Paris, 'Gouffre de l'espèce humaine'?"

32 Green, "Time and the Study of Assimilation," 239–58.

33 See especially Hochstadt, *Mobility and Modernity*; Jackson, *Migration and Urbanization in the Ruhr Valley*; Moch, *Moving Europeans*, 126–31.

34 Rosental, *Les sentiers invisibles*. The long history of migration in Europe also undercuts the assumption of modernization theory that mobility increases with time and that to move is to be modern. See the discussion in Hochstadt, *Mobility and Modernity*, chap. 1.

35 Chevalier, *La formation de la population parisienne au XIXᵉ siècle*, 205–13, 285.

36 Gautier, *L'émigration bretonne*, 65.

37 Dutertre, "Bretons de Versailles," 44.

38 Broudig, *A la recherche de la frontière*, 13.

39 The most compelling account of this experience may be Hélias, *Le cheval d'orgueil*, published in the United States as *The Horse of Pride*.

40 In contemporary literature and statistics, Brittany is composed of five departments; yet since 1941 the boundary of the region of Brittany excludes the Loire-Atlantique, which includes the city of St.-Nazaire and whose capital is the port of Nantes. I include the Loire-Atlantique as part of Haute-Bretagne in this study. McDonald, *"We Are Not French!,"* 15–16.

41 Broudig, *A la recherche de la frontière*, 8–15.

42 Rosental, "Between Macro and Micro," 476.

43 Chabot, *Jean et Yvonne, domestiques en 1900*; Cribier, *Une génération de parisiens arrive à la retraite*; Faure, "Camille et Jeanne, ouvrières à la raffinerie Say"; Girard, *Un parcours en noir et blanc dans la Bretagne de jadis*; Michel, *François et Marie de Bretagne*; Omnès, *Ouvrières parisiennes*; Prado and Barbichon, *Vivre sa ville*; Violain, *Bretons de Paris*. For use of life-writings see Hoerder, *Creating Societies*.

44 Bertaux-Wiame, "The Life History Approach to the Study of Internal Migration"; Rosental, "Between Macro and Micro," 473, 477.

45 Bourdieu and Wacquant, *An Invitation to Reflexive Sociology*, 119; Castles and Miller, *The Age of Migration*, 28–29; Granovetter, "The Strength of Weak Ties"; Kesztenbaum, "Cooperation and Coordination among Siblings"; Leseger, Lucassen, and Schrover, "Is There Life outside the Migrant Network?," 29–50; Moch, "Networks among Bretons?," 431–55; Moch and Fuchs, "Getting Along," 34–49; Tilly, "Migration in Modern European History," 48–72; Tilly, "Transplanted Networks," 79–95.

46 Rosental, "Between Macro and Micro."

CHAPTER ONE. CONTEXTS

1 Le Bouëdec, *Les bretons sur les mers*, 7, 134, 135, 217, 246; Fleuriot, *Les origines de la Bretagne*.

2 Choquette, *Frenchmen into Peasants*, 3, 201.

3 Weil, "French Migration to the Americas in the 19th and 20th Centuries as a Historical Problem," 443–60.

4 Centre de Recherches d'Histoire Nord-Américaine, Université de Paris I,

L'émigration française; Fouché, *Émigration alsacienne aux États-Unis*; Foucrier, *Le rêve californien*; Arrizabalaga, "Les basques dans l'ouest américain," 335–50; Moogk, "Manon's Fellow Exiles," 236–60.

5 Weil, "The French State and Transoceanic Emigration," 114–31, for exemplary discouragement of emigration to Argentina and Canada; see also administrative correspondence in the Archives Départementales d'Ille-et-Vilaine, series 6M 691, État nominative des émigrants partis pour l'étranger, and the Archives Départementales des Côtes-d'Armor, series 6M 808, Émigration intérieure et extérieure: circulaires, instructions, 1817–1936.

6 Quote from Pluchon, *Histoire des Antilles et de la Guyane*, 163; Moogk, "Manon's Fellow Exiles," 163, 165. This is not to say that France failed to develop penal colonies; see Toth, *Beyond Papillon*.

7 Choquette, *Frenchmen into Peasants* 247; Moogk, "Manon's Fellow Exiles," 255; personal communication from Sébastien DuBriel of the University of Notre Dame regarding connections between the Haitian language and the Breton language, particularly as spoken in the region of Nantes, 10 May 2005.

8 Debien, "Les engagés pour le Canada partis de Nantes," 583.

9 Forster and Forster, eds., *Sugar and Slavery, Family and Race*.

10 Choquette, *Frenchmen into Peasants*, 200–202.

11 Moogk, "Manon's Fellow Exiles," 253, 255.

12 Ibid., "Manon's Fellow Exiles," 240–43. See also Moch, *Moving Europeans*, chap. 2; those French who stayed on are threaded throughout Hoerder, *Creating Societies*.

13 Choquette, *Frenchmen into Peasants*, 29–33.

14 Ibid., 271–77; Landry, *Les filles du roi*; Moogk, "Manon's Fellow Exiles," 245.

15 The earlier mass emigration of some 200,000 Huguenots from France that followed the revocation of the Edict of Nantes in 1685 included few if any Bretons. Greer, *The Incidence of the Emigration during the French Revolution*, 118; Vidalenc, *Les émigrés français*, 111–14.

16 Daughton, *An Empire Divided*, 38–41.

17 Of the 255,000 copies of the *Annales* published in the mid-1880s, 165,000 were published in French and 6,000 more in Breton; the Breton issues peaked at 6,500 in 1893 and slumped to 5,225 by 1912. Daughton, *An Empire Divided*, 39, 278.

18 Lallemand, *Comme un long fleuve fertile de passion et d'action éducatives*, 6, 19–20.

19 Conklin, *A Mission to Civilize*, 77; Lallemand, *Comme un long fleuve fertile de passion et d'action éducatives*, 9, 19, 19–20; White, "Priests into Frenchmen?," 111–21.

20 Michel, *Missionnaires bretons d'outre-mer aux XIXᵉ et XXᵉ siècles*, 147.

21 Martin, "Celebrating the Ordinary," 289–317; Michel, *Missionnaires bretons d'outre-mer aux XIXᵉ et XXᵉ siècles*, 147, chaps. 7–11, back cover.

22 Katan, "Le voyage 'organisé' d'émigrants parisiens vers l'Algérie," 17, 40–42.

23 Lossouarn, *Les bretons dans le monde*, 156.

24 Annaba was then called Bone; Stora was then Philippeville. Lossouarn, *Les bretons dans le monde*, 157

25 Weil, "French Migration to the Americas in the 19th and 20th Centuries as a Historical Problem," 451–55. The history of the French in Argentina is yet to be written in depth; extant studies include Zago, *Los franceses en la Argentina / Les français en Argentine*; Andreu, Bennassar, and Gaignard, *Les aveyronnais dans la Pampa*. Recent case studies explore the histories of the French in the United States, such as Blaufarb, *Bonapartists in the Borderlands*; others explore the French-Canadians who moved to New England, such as Weil, *Les franco-américains*. The French invasion of Mexico, 1862–67, was not the first time the French appeared: Genin, *Les français au Mexique du XVIᵉ siècle jusqu'à nos jours*; Granet-Abisset, *La route réinventée*. According to Paul Gerbod, over 48,000 French decamped to Britain in 1846–60, and over 44,000 to Belgium and Holland, 33,000 to Germany and Austria, 19,000 to Switzerland, 28,000 to Italy, and over 6,000 to Iberia. Gerbod, "Parisiens et parisiennes hors de France au milieu du XIXᵉ siècle," 295.

26 Foucrier, *Le rêve californien*, 37–38.

27 Archives Départementales du Finistère, 4M379, Registre de passeports.

28 Bourset, "Une émigration insolite au XIXᵉ siècle," 129–88.

29 Ibid.; Foucrier, *Le rêve californien*, 23–28, 105–24; ADF, 4M379, Registre de passeports.

30 Le Clech, "Quelques figures de pionniers de l'émigration bretonne au Canada et aux États-Unis," 280; Le Clech, "Un épisode marquant l'émigration bretonne au Canada," 287–95.

31 Le Bail, *L'émigration rurale et les migrations temporaires dans le Finistère*, 45–46; Pénisson, "L'émigration française au Canada," 97; Weil, "French Migration to the Americas in the 19th and 20th Centuries as a Historical Problem," 454.

32 Berruer, *Les bretons migrateurs*, 50–69, tells the story of this group's initial trip and trials over the years.

33 Pénisson, "L'émigration française au Canada," 52–55.

34 Le Clech, "Quelques figures de pionniers de l'émigration bretonne au Canada et aux États-Unis," 294–95; Le Clech, "L'émigration bretonne au Canada au début du XXᵉ siecle," 219–37; for an account of the Saint-Brieux settlement see Berruer, *Les bretons migrateurs*, 50–69.

35 Mauras and Hamon, *Ces bretons du Canada*; figures are for 1911–31 from Lossouarn, *Les bretons dans le monde*, 2.

36 Déguignet, *Mémoires d'un paysan bas breton*.

37 Châtelain, *Les migrants temporaires en France de 1800 à 1914*, vol. 1, 178; Poitrineau, *Remues d'hommes*.

38 Châtelain, *Les migrants temporaires en France de 1800 à 1914*, vol. 1, 58; Désert is cited in Pelletier, *Histoire générale de la Bretagne et des bretons*, vol. 1, 418.

39 Châtelain, *Les migrants temporaires en France de 1800 à 1914*, vol. 1, 58

40 This concern expressed itself in a spate of publications all over France, most recently put to rest by Rosental, *Les sentiers invisibles*.

41 Vandervelde, *L'exode rural et le retour aux champs*.

42 I am the translator for all French passages in this volume. "Oh ! ne quittez jamais c'est moi qui vous le dis / De devant de la porte ou l'on jouait jadis. / Oh ! ne quittez jamais le devant de la porte; / Mourez dans la maison ou votre mère est morte." Le Bail, *L'émigration rurale et les migrations temporaires dans le Finistère*, ii; Birzeux lived from 1803 to 1858; his best-known creation is "Les bretons." Le Bail followed in his father's footsteps as mayor of Plozevet and went on to become a representative and then senator from the Finistère from 1902 until his death in 1937. There were other anti-urban law dissertations; see Jobert, "Les agglomérations urbaines et l'émigration rurale en France au XIXᵉ siècle." Jobert explicates the ruinous nature of city life.

43 Le Bail, *L'émigration rurale et les migrations temporaires dans le Finistère*, 3; Le Bail's 104-page dissertation listed only seven books; this is in marked contrast to the 360-page geography dissertation of Camille Vallaux, *La Basse-Bretagne* (1905), whose bibliography was extensive. See below.

44 "Qu'ils reviennent! Qu'ils prennent, un soir, à la gare Montparnasse l'un des trains qui partent vers la Bretagne, et quand la nuit sera passée, quand les grandes villes seront lointaines, lorsque la locomotive glissera, légère, sur ses rails, à travers la campagne bretonne, quand le petit jour poindra, ils verront soudain apparaître a leurs yeux émerveillés, la Terre Maternelle, enveloppée encore dans le brouillard bleu des aurores printanières, la Terre fertile, la Terre indulgente et oublieuse de leurs bandons qui tendra ses flancs féconds et riches vers l'effort de leurs bras." Le Bail, *L'émigration rurale et les migrations temporaires dans le Finistère*, 104.

45 Ibid., 13.

46 Ibid.

47 Farcy and Faure, *La mobilité d'une génération de français*, 67–68; Le Bail, *L'émigration rurale et les migrations temporaires dans le Finistère*, 13.

48 Le Bail, *L'émigration rurale et les migrations temporaires dans le Finistère*, 31–33.

49 Vallaux, *La Basse-Bretagne*, 188–90.

50 Ibid., 275.

51 Poussou, *Bordeaux et le sud-ouest au XVIIIᵉ siècle*.

52 Pelletier, *Histoire générale de la Bretagne et des bretons*, vol 1, 418.

53 Vallaux, *La Basse-Bretagne*, 279.

54 Ibid., 275.

55 Cornette, *Histoire de la Bretagne et des bretons*, vol. 2, 310, from *La Bretagne contemporaine*, vol. 1, Preface. Cited by Le Gallo, "Basse-Bretagne et bas-bretons," 171.

56 Jobert, "Les agglomérations urbaines et l'émigration rurale en France au XIXᵉ siècle," 102; Le Bail, *L'émigration rurale et les migrations temporaires dans le Finistère*, 18–19; Pelletier, *Histoire générale de la Bretagne et des bretons*, 418.

57 Vallaux, *La Basse-Bretagne*, 276.

58 Châtelain, *Les migrants temporaires en France de 1800 à 1914*, 214–18, quotation p. 218; Vallaux, *La Basse-Bretagne*, 276–77.

59 Le Bail, *L'émigration rurale et les migrations temporaires dans le Finistère*, 25; see also Vallaux, *La Basse-Bretagne*, 275.

60 Farcy and Faure, *La mobilité d'une génération de français*, 188, 208, 211. The conscript records on which their study is based served as an address book for men between the ages of twenty and forty-five, since conscripts were required to report each change of residence over a twenty-five-year period.

61 Farcy and Faure compare the movements of men from the Côtes-d'Armor with those from other départements that sent men to Paris: Cantal, Creuse, the Orne, Eure-et-Loir, Nièvre, Pas-de-Calais, Oise, Seine-et-Marne, and Seine-et-Oise. The Limousins have a rich history, beginning especially with Corbin, *Archaïsme et modernité en Limousin au XIXᵉ siècle*; Nadaud, *Mémoires de Léonard, ancien garçon maçon*, and most recently Harison, *The Stonemasons of Creuse in Nineteenth-Century Paris*. The signal work on Auvergnats in Paris is Raison-Jourde, *La colonie auvergnate de Paris au XIXᵉ siècle*. The history of provincial migrants and integration in Paris was evaluated in a special issue of *Ethnologie française* 10, no. 2 (1980), ed. Guy Barbichon, "Provinciaux et province à Paris."

62 Farcy and Faure, *La mobilité d'une génération de français*, 33, 37, 67–68.

63 Ibid., 203, 205, 208, 219, 305.

64 Ibid., 219. In this cohort 74 percent of men from the Côtes-du-Nord traveled to colonies, compared with a mean of 0.54 percent for all groups; 1.49 percent of Bretons went abroad, compared with a mean of 1.18 percent for all groups.

65 Farcy and Faure, *La mobilité d'une génération de français*, 219.

66 Ibid., *La mobilité d'une génération de français*, 60; see p. 231 for regional nuances within the Côtes-d'Armor.

67 Farcy and Faure, *La mobilité d'une génération de français*, 298–99, 304–5.

68 Ackerman, "Alternative to Rural Exodus," 131–35; Ackerman, *Village on the Seine*, chap. 4.

69 Farcy and Faure, *La mobilité d'une génération de français*, 306–8.

70 Harel, *L'île Saint-François*, 15–16; Meynier, "Les bretons au Havre," 387; Vallaux, *La Basse-Bretagne*, 278–79.

71 Farcy and Faure, *La mobilité d'une génération de français*, 26, 438. Statistique Générale, *Résultats statistiques du recensement général de la population effectué le 24 mars 1901*, vol. 4, 303–4.

72 Le Gallo, "Basse-Bretagne et bas-bretons," 143–44.

73 Gibson, *A Social History of French Catholicism*, 170–78; Le Gallo, "Basse-Bretagne et bas-bretons," 157–64; Pierre, *Les bretons et la république*, 227–40.

74 Le Gallo, "La Bretagne bretonnante," 24–27.

75 Pierre, *Les bretons et la république*, 46–49; Segalen, *Fifteen Generations of Bretons*.

76 Pierre, *Les bretons et la république*, 29.

77 Segalen, *Fifteen Generations of Bretons*, 3.

78 Ozouf, *Composition française*, 15.

79 Brittany's regionalist movements are summarized in Gildea, *The Past in French History*, 199–208, and in Cornette, *Histoire de la Bretagne et des bretons*, esp. chaps. 57, 62. For more recent regionalism see Loughlin and Mazey, eds., *The End of the French Unitary State?*

80 Déniel, *Le mouvement breton*, 26–27.

81 Wright, *The Regionalist Movement in France*, vii; see also Soltau, *French Parties and Politics*, and the longstanding observations of Fox, *History in Geographic Perspective*.

82 Ford, *Creating the Nation in Provincial France*.

83 Thiesse, *Écrire la France*; Thiesse, *Ils apprenaient la France*.

84 Prado and Barbichon, *Vivre sa ville*, 130.

CHAPTER TWO. A BRETON CROWD IN PARIS

1 Chabot, *Jean et Yvonne, domestiques en 1900*, 156. The term *bretonnant* indicates that Breton was spoken in that village; see Introduction.

2 Lemoine, "L'émigration bretonne à Paris," 41; the exact figures are 68,792 for Paris, 3,218 for Saint-Denis, and 3,648 for Versailles. The history of Bretons in Versailles has been written with great skill by Dutertre, "Bretons de Versailles."

3 Bertho, "L'invention de la Bretagne," 62.

4 Ibid., 57–62.

5 Gaillard, "Les migrants à Paris au XIXᵉ siècle," 132; Harison, *The Stonemasons of Creuse in Nineteenth-Century Paris*, chap. 7; Raison-Jourde, *La colonie auvergnate de Paris au XIXᵉ siècle*.

6 Barbichon, "Provinciaux et provinces à Paris," 123; Chevalier, *La formation de la population parisienne au XIXᵉ siècle*, 211; Gaillard, "Les migrants à Paris au XIXᵉ siècle," 134.

7 Violain, *Bretons de Paris*, 29, quotes Father Rivalin, speaking at a congress of worker associations in Saint-Brieuc; François Cadic used the term in the July 1899 issue of the *Paroisse bretonne*.

8 Chevalier, *La formation de la population parisienne au XIXᵉ siècle*, 211.

9 Lemoine, "L'émigration bretonne à Paris," 39–60, 165–84, 239–48, 362–73.

10 See Appendix: Marriage Records.

11 Herlihy, *Medieval and Renaissance Pistoia*; Herlihy and Klapish-Zuber, *Tuscans and Their Families*.

12 Châtelain, "Migrations et domesticité féminine urbaine en France," 506–28; see also the more general works on the eighteenth-century city, such as Poussou, *Bordeaux et le sud-ouest au XVIIIᵉ siècle*; and Moch, *Moving Europeans*, chaps. 2–3. More general works on the eighteenth-century French servant include Fairchilds, *Domestic Enemies*; Maza, *Servants and Masters in Eighteenth-Century France*.

13 The finest general studies of domestic servants are Martin-Fugier, *La place des bonnes*, and McBride, *The Domestic Revolution*.

14 The short story was published in the newspaper *Le Gaulois* in February 1884.

15 McBride points out the paradox of domestic service being the means by which women left the rural labor force and became "modernized;" McBride, *Domestic Revolution*, 117. For a discussion of these two kinds of work in history see Eley, "Historicizing the Global, Politicizing Capital," 153–88.

16 Chabot, *Jean et Yvonne, domestiques en 1900*, 156. This also recurs several times in Mirbeau, *The Diary of a Chambermaid*; Michel, ed., *Un moderne*; Michel, "Journal d'une femme de chambre," *Octave Mirbeau*, vol. 2, 547; see discussion in Martin-Fugier, *La place des bonnes*, 58.

17 For acute examples see the testimonies of both Yvonne Yven and her husband, Jean Chabot, in Chabot, *Jean et Yvonne, domestiques en 1900*, 132–34 and ff.

18 Theresa McBride, *Domestic Revolution*.

19 Statistique générale, *Résultats statistiques du recensement général de la population effectué le 24 mars 1901*, vol. 4, 305. See also McBride, *Domestic Revolution*, and Martin-Fugier, *La place des bonnes*.

20 For "la question du sixième" see Martin-Fugier, *La place des bonnes*, 125–45.

21 For scholarship on the domestic servants in the twentieth century see for example Andall, *Gender and Ethnicity in Contemporary Europe*; Anderson, *Doing the Dirty Work?*; Henkes, "Maids on the Move," 224–43; Moch, *Moving Europeans*; Parreñas, *Servants of Globalization*; Lutz, ed., *Migration and Domestic Work*.

22 Zola, *Pot-Bouille*, was later translated into English as *Restless House* (New York: Farrar, Straus and Young, 1953), 26. The tenth book in Rougon-Macquart series, *Pot-Bouille* was first serialized in the periodical *Le Gaulois* in 1882. Twenty years later the journalist Marcelle Tinayre recalled the novel in a plea for humanitarian treatment of domestic servants in "La question des domestiques," *L'Illustration*, no. 3126 (24 January 1903).

23 Zola, *Piping Hot*, 8, 44.

24 Ibid., 432.

25 Ibid., 432–38.

26 Lemoine, "L'émigration bretonne à Paris," 39–60, 165–84, 239–48, 362–73.

27 The historian Faure, for example, regards Lemoine's testimony as invaluable for understanding the housing in Saint-Denis. In their study he and Lévy-Vroelant cite Lemoine's careful observations of Breton housing, crowding, and the act of leaving the rooming-house upon marriage: *Une chambre en ville*, 155. Likewise, the historian of Saint-Denis Brunet repeatedly cites Lemoine as a "contemporary" in his descriptions of Bretons in Saint-Denis, their origins, and their dwellings. See, for example, Brunet, "L'immigration provinciale à la fin du XIXᵉ siècle," 75–76.

28 Lemoine, "L'émigration bretonne à Paris," 41.

29 Ibid., 173. For large farms in the Île-de-France see Ackerman, *Village on the Seine*.

30 Lemoine, "L'émigration bretonne à Paris," 56. Plougonver is a commune in inland Côtes-d'Armor.

31 Ibid., 174.

32 Ibid., 167–68. Lemoine wrote about agricultural workers in the large farms, Saint-Denis factory workers, market gardeners, railroad workers, and domestic servants.

33 Émile Souvestre lived from 1806 to 1854; *Les derniers bretons* had several editions beginning in 1835 and was last reprinted in 1995 by Terre de Brume publishers in Rennes.

34 Lemoine, "L'émigration bretonne à Paris," 177–82. "Le Breton, une fois séparé de son milieu primitif, a une tendance extraordinaire à se perdre dans le nouveau milieu où il se trouve transporté."

35 Lemoine, "L'émigration bretonne à Paris," 242–43, gives the figure of six thousand placements per year; this is most likely a misprint, since Lemoine's estimate is ten times that of others. The figure cited years later by the Abbé François Cadic is six hundred; see chap. 3.

36 Ibid., 245.

37 Ibid., 240, 239–42.

38 Ibid., 241–42.

39 Ibid., 172.

40 Ibid., 58.

41 Ibid., 60.

42 Ibid., 363–66.

43 I translate "*marchand de vin*" as café owner, as does Haine, understanding that this was the contemporary term for the café; *The World of the Paris Café*, 4.

44 This observation is corroborated by Garden, "Mariages parisiens à la fin du XIXᵉ siècle," 127, and Haine, *The World of the Paris Café*, 47–49, 134–35.

45 Weber, *Peasants into Frenchmen*.

46 Brunet, *Saint-Denis, la ville rouge*; Brunet, "Une banlieue ouvrière"; Brunet, "L'immigration provinciale à la fin du XIXᵉ siècle."

47 Brunet, "L'immigration provinciale à la fin du XIXᵉ siècle," 1995, 80.

48 Lombard-Jourdan, *La plaine Saint-Denis*, 154–56

49 Ibid., 160–61.

50 Archives de la Préfecture de Police, series B / A, Enquête industrielle, Saint-Denis, 1872.

51 Lombard-Jourdan, *La plaine Saint-Denis*, 7; Berlanstein, *Big Business and Industrial Conflict in Nineteenth-Century France*.

52 Lillo, *La petite Espagne de la Plaine-Saint-Denis*, 15.

53 Brunet, "Une banlieue ouvrière," 1575; Lombard-Jourdan, *La plaine Saint-Denis*, 159–61, 179.

54 Lillo, *La petite Espagne de la plaine-Saint-Denis*, 15–17.

55 Brunet, "Une banlieue ouvrière," 164.

56 Lombard-Jourdan, *La plaine Saint-Denis*, 177.

57 Jacquemet, *L'église de Saint-Denis*.

58 Duby, *La ville de l'âge industriel*, 609.

59 Perrot, *Les ouvriers en grève*, 574.

60 Faure, "Paris, le peuple, la banlieue," 88, 100. Faure also draws on the *Dictionnaire de la langue verte* (1868), whose entry for Cayenne reads, "Atelier éloigné de Paris; fabrique située dans la banlieue."

61 Perrot, *Les ouvriers en grève*, 220.

62 A. Goullé in the *Cri du people*, January 1885, quoted by Perrot, *Les ouvriers en grève*, 219.

63 Pottier, *Logements insalubres* (1887), 214, quoted by Perrot, *Les ouvriers en grève*, 219–20.

64 Lemoine, "L'émigration bretonne à Paris," 178–80.

65 Archives de Paris, series D2 M8 census lists, Saint-Denis, 1891, 28 (10, rue de la Charronnerie) and 29 (10, rue des Poissonniers).

66 They were only 10 Bretons in some 250 weddings in Saint-Denis in 1875. Archives Départementales de Seine-Saint Denis, 1E 66 32, Mariages, Saint-Denis, 1875.

67 Lemoine, "L'émigration bretonne à Paris," 175.

68 And after 1897 women also acted as witnesses. See Appendix: Marriage Records; Garden, "Mariages parisiens à la fin du XIXᵉ siècle"; Prost, "Mariage, jeunesse et société à Orléans en 1911," 672–701.

69 See Appendix: Marriage Records.

70 Garden, "Mariages parisiens à la fin du XIXᵉ siècle," 111–33.

71 Ibid., 121–27. Haine elaborates on the role of the café owner in weddings in *The World of the Paris Café*, 134–35.

72 Garden, "Mariages parisiens à la fin du XIXᵉ siècle," 116.

73 Gautier, *L'émigration bretonne*, 74.

74 The forty-nine marriages with a wedding partner from Brittany in Saint-Denis is the total number for that year, gleaned from all marriage records for 1890. See Appendix: Marriage Records. Of the forty-nine marriages 65 percent were between two Bretons and 49 percent between Bretons born in the same department; 67 percent were from the Côtes-d'Armor. Thirty-three of the grooms, or 67.3 percent, were unskilled workers. Archives Départementales de Seine-Saint-Denis, series 1E 66 48, Mariages, Saint-Denis, 1890.

75 And the mean age of first marriage was 23.51; the median age was 23. Sixteen of the forty-six Breton brides and grooms were living with at least one parent in Saint-Denis at the time of their marriage; 65 percent of the brides and 78 percent of the grooms could sign the wedding document.

76 Thirteen of forty-nine brides lived with (i.e., at the same address as) their husband before marriage; this is a much smaller proportion than in the Fourteenth Arrondissement. Only three of the forty-nine marriages included the legitimization of a child, two of whom were infants originally registered as the child of both mother and father.

77 Over 40 percent of the witnesses could be identified. The proportion of café owners is twice the proportion of marchands de vins serving as witnesses in Garden's study—about 40 percent rather than 20 percent.

78 Marriage 46, 1890, Saint-Denis. Pseudonyms have been assigned to all mar-

riage partners, witnesses, and family members mentioned in this manuscript. See Appendix: Marriage Records.

79 Chabot, *Jean et Yvonne, domestiques en 1900*, 172–74.

80 Marriages nos. 25, 72, 1890, Saint-Denis.

81 See Knibiehler, ed., *Cornettes et blouses blanches*; Gautier, *L'émigration bretonne*, 201–2.

82 Brunet's study of the electoral lists of 1891 reported in "L'immigration provinciale à la fin du XIXᵉ siècle."

83 Lemoine, "L'émigration bretonne à Paris," 56.

84 Marriage 239, Saint-Denis, 1890.

85 Brunet, "L'immigration provinciale à la fin du XIXᵉ siècle." 81.

86 Marriage 125, Saint-Denis, 1890. In this case the bride was "sans profession," so she probably was not planning to be employed, and may have worked with her parents before marriage.

87 "A la différence des autres groupes d'immigrés, qui semblent se fonder dans ce que l'on peut appeler le 'creuset dionysien' sans perdre de leur personnalité ni de leur force intrinsèque, le Breton de Saint-Denis apparait comme un déraciné, meurtri par la vie, ballotté au gré des circonstances." Brunet, "L'immigration provinciale à la fin du XIXᵉ siècle," 84; see also Brunet, *Saint-Denis, la ville rouge*, 26.

88 Gaillard, "Les migrants à Paris au XIXᵉ siècle," 131.

89 Cottard, *Vie et histoire du XIVᵉ arrondissement*, 12, 17–21.

90 Ibid., 30.

91 See, for example, Fuchs, *Poor and Pregnant in Paris*, chap. 5; Fuchs, *Abandoned Children*, chap. 1.

92 Cottard, *Vie et histoire du XIVᵉ arrondissement*, 46–49, 51–52.

93 Ibid., 58; Bindi and Lefeuvre, *Le Métro de Paris*, 12.

94 Nesbit, *Atget's Seven Albums*, 165–75, 390–410. So-called *apaches* did not become a danger until after 1900, although criminal youth were a concern; see Berlanstein, *The Working People of Paris*, 146–47; Rearick, *Pleasures of the Belle Époque*, 183. The *Petit Journal* on 20 October 1907 featured a cover portrait of a ferocious apache with the headline "L'apache est la plaie de Paris."

95 Nesbit, *Atget's Seven Albums*, 414–28; Brachev, "Mon père, horticulteur-guérisseur du Boulevard Brune"; Zola, "Promenade vers les fortifs, sorties champêtres . . . ," 31–36.

96 Zola, "Promenade vers les fortifs, sorties champêtres . . . ," 31.

97 Duhamel, "Sociologie d'un quartier disparu," 28–29.

98 Bonin and Costa, *Je me souviens du 14ᵉ arrondissement*, 52–53; Cottard, *Vie et histoire du XIVᵉ arrondissement*, 41, 67–68, 90; Rearick, *Pleasures of the Belle Époque*, 12–13, 96.

99 Cottard, *Vie et histoire du XIVᵉ arrondissement*, 63; see also Faure and Lévy-Vroelant, *Une chambre en ville*.

100 Cottard, *Vie et histoire du XIVᵉ arrondissement*, 63.

101 The Sceaux railroad line, instituted in 1846, ran to southern suburbs from the

Denfert station in the Fourteenth; it was extended to an underground station at Luxembourg Garden in 1890–95.

102 Archives de la Préfecture de Police, series B / A, Enquête industrielle, Fourteenth Arrondissement, 1872.

103 Cottard, *Vie et histoire du XIVe arrondissement*, 63.

104 Bonin and Costa, *Je me souviens du 14e arrondissement*, 74.

105 Faure, "Migrations intérieures et villes dans la France du XIXe siècle," 158.

106 Archives de Paris, series E, Marriages, XIVe arrondissement, 1875.

107 A terrassier and an homme de peine; Mariages, XIVe arrondissement, 1875.

108 Mariages, XIVe arrondissement, 1875, marriages nos. 580, 29.

109 Omnès, "Les provinciales dans la formation des populations ouvrières parisiennes," 174–91; Omnès, *Ouvrières parisiennes*, introduction, chaps. 9–10.

110 In other times and places women's work is less well recorded in marriage records—either because it was fashionable to say that one was "sans profession" or because women stopped working when they married.

111 Mariages, XIVe arrondissement, 1875, marriage 1.

112 Cottard, "L'évolution du 14e arrondissement de 1860 à nos jours," 63.

113 Archives de Paris, series D2 M8 28, *Recensement de 1891*, professions, Paris, XIVe arrondissement; Bindi and Lefeuvre, *Le Métro de Paris*, 6.

114 Duhamel, "Sociologie d'un quartier disparu," 26. "L'escalier monte, monte à travers des familles et des familles superposées comme des couches géologiques. On entend ici une mandoline, là un petit chien qui jappe, à droite le poitrinaire qui respire avec tant de peine. Et, déjà, c'est la grosse dame à l'éternelle chanson: 'Je t'aime, comprends-tu ce mot ?' Et le tap . . . tap . . . du monsieur qui travaille chez lui à des choses incompréhensibles. Et, partout, les machines à coudre et des piétinements d'enfants dans des couloirs, et des voix d'hommes et de femmes qui parlent et se querellent à propos des affaires de leur clan. Tout cela si clair à l'oreille fine et distraite du petit garçon."

115 Duhamel, "Sociologie d'un quartier disparu," 27, 30.

116 Ibid., 27.

117 Ibid., 30.

118 Cottard, *Vie et histoire du XIVe arrondissement*, 62; Zola, "Promenade vers les fortifs, sorties champêtres . . . ," 35. The *mairie* of the Fourteenth had formerly been that of the commune of Montrouge.

119 Garden, "Mariages parisiens à la fin du XIXe siècle," 123

120 In Garden's survey 18 percent of provincials married someone from their home Department; this was the case for only 11 percent of Bretons in the Fourteenth Arrondissement. Eight of the eleven Breton couples were from the Côtes-d'Armor. The mean age of first marriage for women was 27.87 years; the median was 27.

121 Forty-two of the eighty-five couples marrying in the Fourteenth Arrondissement were living at the same address at the time of the wedding; only five of the ninety-nine Bretons were living with a parent. The shared address could simply indicate that each marriage partner lived in the same building;

it could also indicate that cohabitation had begun shortly before the extensive paperwork required for marriage had been completed—it is impossible to know for certain whether a couple lived in a consensual union before marriage.

122 Battagliola, "Mariage, concubinage et relations entre les sexes," 76–84; Fuchs, *Poor and Pregnant in Paris*, 19–20.

123 Garden, "Mariages parisiens à la fin du XIXᵉ siècle," 120–21.

124 Alter, *Family and the Female Life Course*; Battagliola, "Mariage, concubinage et relations entre les sexes"; Frey, "Du mariage et du concubinage dans les classes populaires à Paris," 803–29; Fuchs, *Poor and Pregnant in Paris*; Tilly, Scott, and Cohen, "Women's Work and European Fertility Patterns," 447–76.

125 See Appendix: Marriage Records; Chabot, *Jean et Yvonne, domestiques en 1900*, 132.

126 Garden, "Mariages parisiens à la fin du XIXᵉ siècle," 120.

127 Only 25 percent of the witnesses to the weddings in 1890 could be identified as a neighbor, relative, or workmate of the bride or groom—fewer than in Saint-Denis. Marriages, Fourteenth Arrondissement, 1890.

128 Marriage 17, Fourteenth Arrondissement, 1890.

129 Marriage 250, Fourteenth Arrondissement, 1890.

130 On public dances see Berlanstein, *The Working People of Paris*; Coquiot, *Les bals publiques*; Rearick, *Pleasures of the Belle Époque*; Violain, *Bretons de Paris*, 122–39; For other public venues see Schwartz, *Spectacular Realities*.

131 Marriage 1036, Fourteenth Arrondissement, 1890.

132 Marriage 736, Fourteenth Arrondissement, 1890.

133 Gautier, *L'émigration bretonne*, 65.

134 Alter, *Family and the Female Life Course*; Fuchs, *Poor and Pregnant in Paris*.

135 Battagliola, "Mariage, concubinage et relations entre les sexes"; Frey, "Du mariage et du concubinage dans les classes populaires à Paris."

136 Fuchs, *Poor and Pregnant in Paris*, 32–33; Fuchs and Moch, "Pregnant, Single, and Far from Home," 1007–31; Mouillon, "Domestique de la belle époque à Paris," 1–9.

137 Fuchs, *Poor and Pregnant in Paris*, 21–34; Fuchs and Moch, "Pregnant, Single, and Far from Home," 1011.

138 Fuchs, *Poor and Pregnant in Paris*.

139 Fuchs and Moch, "Pregnant, Single, and Far from Home," 1018; Fuchs, *Poor and Pregnant in Paris*, 21–29.

140 Fuchs and Moch, "Pregnant, Single, and Far from Home," 1013–14.

141 Ibid., 1024. Although only 5 percent of the migrant women in Paris were from Brittany, 15 percent of the single mothers in La Maternité were from Brittany.

142 Fuchs, *Poor and Pregnant in Paris*, 28–29; Fuchs and Moch, "Pregnant, Single, and Far from Home," 1026.

143 Marriages, Fourteenth Arrondissement, 1890, 212.

144 Gautier, *L'émigration bretonne*, 59; Fuchs, *Poor and Pregnant in Paris*, 151–55; Fuchs, *Abandoned Children*; Fuchs and Moch, "Pregnant, Single, and Far from Home," 1027–30.

145 See Sussman, *The Wet-Nursing Business in France*.

146 Gautier, *L'émigration bretonne*, 57–58.

147 Châtelain, *Les migrations temporaries en France de 1800 à 1914*, vol. 2, 1069–70; Fuchs and Moch, "Pregnant, Single, and Far from Home," 1028; Sussman, *The Wet-Nursing Business in France*, 152–58.

148 Fuchs, *Abandoned Children*; Fuchs and Moch, "Pregnant, Single, and Far from Home," 1029.

149 Statistique Générale, *Résultats statistiques du recensement général de la population effectué le 24 mars 1901*, vol. 4, 303–4.

150 Archives de la Préfecture de Police; registers of commissariats, quartier 56, Plaisance, 1896. Police blotters detail each incident; each record includes each party's name, age, address, birthplace, and parents' names. For men the record includes particulars of their conscript class. The records were written in haste, and much is illegible.

151 Farcy and Faure, *La mobilité d'une génération de français*, 3, chap. 14, 477–519.

152 Harsin, *Policing Prostitution in Nineteenth-Century Paris*, 163.

153 Thirty-one of the fifty-six Bretons on the police blotters in 1896 were women; registers of commissariat, quartier 56, Plaisance, nos. 1561, 2058, 2362, 2647, 2652.

154 Registers of commissariat, quartier 56, Plaisance, nos. 2162, 1899, 2580, 2583, 2569, 3027.

155 Registers of commissariat, quartier 56, Plaisance, nos. 1709, 1787, 2402, 2903, 1529, 1555.

156 See chap. 1.

157 Chabot, *Jean et Yvonne, domestiques en 1900*, 132–34, 191; Martin-Fugier, *La place des bonnes*, 313.

158 Chabot, *Jean et Yvonne, domestiques en 1900*, 198–99, 204–5, 214–17.

159 Appadurai, *Modernity at Large*; Bryceson and Vuorela, eds., *The Transnational Family*; Parreñas, *Servants of Globalization*. Hodagneu-Sotelo, *Gendered Transitions*.

CHAPTER THREE. **THE TURN OF THE CENTURY**

1 Michel, *François et Marie de Bretagne*.

2 The exact figures for Bretons in Paris are 109,091 in 1911, 87,037 in 1901, and 68,792 in 1891; For the département of the Seine the figure for 1911 is 159,782; these census data are summarized in Gautier, *L'émigration bretonne*, 65, 67.

3 David Barnes uses the idea of the core narrative in *The Making of a Social Disease*, 78–81, drawing on Hunter, *Doctor Stories*.

4 Saint-Maurice, "La misère en Bretagne." This excellent source was signaled by Cornette, *Histoire de la Bretagne et des bretons*, vol. 2, chaps. 53, 54.

5 The exact figure is 12,427; 15,211 more Bretonnes worked as domestics in the area surrounding Paris (the département of the Seine); Statistique Générale, *Résultats statistiques du recensement général de la population effectué le 24 mars 1901*, vol. 4, 304–5.

6 Mirbeau, *The Diary of a Chambermaid*; this was not her first appearance, because most of the novel had been serialized in *L'écho de Paris*, 1891–92, and *La revue blanche*, early 1900. The novel sold 146,000 copies in the author's lifetime; Michel, *Octave Mirbeau*, 339.

7 Michel, "Journal d'une femme de chambre," *Octave Mirbeau*, vol. 2, 381.

8 Ibid., 571.

9 Ibid. 343–45.

10 Ibid., 346.

11 Buñuel's film, which starred Jeanne Moreau, changed the plot, however, and displaced the action to the 1930s, as did Jean Renoir's film of the same name from 1949, starring Paulette Goddard. See Lloyd, *Mirbeau's Fictions*, 62–63.

12 Mirbeau, *The Diary of a Chambermaid*, 74–76. Michel, "Journal d'une femme de chambre," *Octave Mirbeau*, vol. 2, 445–49. Martin-Fugier draws on Mirbeau extensively in *La place des bonnes*.

13 Michel, "Journal d'une femme de chambre," *Octave Mirbeau*, vol. 2, 652–67.

14 Ibid., 605.

15 Ibid., 609.

16 Ibid., 609, 605–14 (chap. 15).

17 Ibid., 599–604.

18 Specialists point out that Bécassine volumes are illustrated stories, not comic books, because there are no word balloons. On Bécassine's French character, in contrast to Astérix, for example, see Nye, "Death of a Gaulois"; Screech, *Masters of the Ninth Art*, 6.

19 Caumery and Pinchon, *Bécassine pendant la guerre*, 3; "Ridiculous, the character Bécassine who appeared in the pages of *La semaine de Suzette*," Bertho writes in "L'invention de la Bretagne," 62.

20 Lehembre, *Bécassine*, 12–13.

21 Groensteen, *Astérix, Barbarella & Cie*, 40.

22 Ibid., 38, 40; Lehembre, *Bécassine*, 13.

23 This toy won the Grand Prix du Concours Lepine in 1914; Bugat-Pujol, *Bécassine éternelle*, 4, 5, 12, 13. Dropping a pile of dishes echoes a scene from the previous year's volume; Caumery and Pinchon, *Bécassine en apprentissage*, 52.

24 Caumery and Pinchon, *L'enfance de Bécassine*, 2–4.

25 Ibid., 53.

26 Ibid., 61.

27 Dictionary definitions include, as a typical example, "n.f. (de bec). Oiseau échassier . . . 2. Fam. Femme, fille sotte." *Le Petit Larousse illustré* (1998), s.v. Bécasse.

28 Calvé, *Histoire des bretons à Paris*, 108, Violain, *Bretons de Paris*, 116.

29 Cadic, *Ça et là en Bretagne*; Cadic, *Contes et légendes de Bretagne*.

30 *La paroisse bretonne*, April 1899.

31 I focus on the opening issues of the journal because they are among the few available, and because it was here that Cadic best articulated the goals of the organization.

32 *La paroisse bretonne*, April 1899.

33 Charles Vincent, "Les bretons hors de la Bretagne," *La paroisse bretonne*, April 1899.

34 Botrel, "Les loups bretons," *La paroisse bretonne*, July 1899.

35 *La paroisse bretonne*, June 1899, August 1901.

36 This example is from June 1899. See Ford, "Religion and the Politics of Cultural Change in Provincial France," 1–33.

37 *La paroisse bretonne*, May 1899.

38 For pardons, the Breton religious processions, see Young, "Of Pardons, Loss, and Longing," 269–304.

39 *La paroisse bretonne*, May 1899: "Il semble que les maisons de religieuses elles-mêmes prennent à tâche de former leurs orphelines, comme une prime à l'exportation."

40 *La paroisse bretonne*, July 1899: "Comment ils laissent leurs pratiques religieuses. Quelle est leur misère."

41 Ibid.

42 Ibid.

43 Ibid., August 1899.

44 Renan, 1823–1892, born in Tréguier, professor at the Collège de France, well-known writer, philosopher, and historian, author of *Histoire des origines de christianisme* (1863–81), *La vie de Jésus* (1863), and *Qu'est-ce qu'une nation?* (1882). Cadic's announcement of the demise of this organization was premature, since it is still in existence.

45 *La paroisse bretonne*, August 1899.

46 Ibid., September 1899; this article was subtitled "Leur caractère social: Appel aux prêtres bretons: L'oeuvre de la paroisse bretonne."

47 *La paroisse bretonne*, September 1899.

48 Ibid.

49 Ibid., October 1899. McBride notes that French servants managed to accrue savings; see *The Domestic Revolution*, 92–94.

50 *La paroisse bretonne*, October 1899.

51 Ibid., September 1899.

52 Ibid., August 1899

53 Ibid., October 1899.

54 Ibid.

55 Ibid., September 1899.

56 "La tuberculose chez les bretons," *La paroisse bretonne*, September 1899, emphasis in original.

57 Barnes, *The Making of a Social Disease*, 6, 14; these publication figures are for 1902–6.

58 Ibid., 13.

59 Ibid., 16.

60 Ibid., 19.

61 Ibid., 143–44, 178. Renault, *La tuberculose chez les bretons*, was cited not only by Cadic but also by Bourgeois, "Exode rural et tuberculose."

62 Bourgeois, "Exode rural et tuberculose," 39, cited in Barnes, *The Making of a Social Disease*, 144.

63 Trégoat, *L'immigration bretonne à Paris*, 5.

64 Ibid., 5–6.

65 Ibid., 7, 10–15.

66 Ibid., 33–39.

67 Ibid., 30–35; for core narrative see Barnes, *The Making of a Social Disease*, 50 and chap. 5.

68 Trégoat, *L'immigration bretonne à Paris*, 44.

69 Ibid., 40–41.

70 Ibid., 41.

71 *Bretoned Paris: Bulletin mensuel de la Société La Bretagne*, January 1904; the Société, named the Association Catholique des Bretons à Paris in 1894, in 1895 became La Bretagne: Société de Secours aux Familles Indigentes des Bretons Résidant à Paris; Cornette, *Histoire de la Bretagne et des bretons*, 321.

72 *Bretoned Paris*, see for example April 1911.

73 *Bretoned Paris*, May–October 1906, "Pardon de Ste-Anne de la Maison-Blanche."

74 The church has been renamed Sainte-Anne de la Butte aux Cailles.

75 *Bretoned Paris*, special isssue, 1908.

76 Ibid., July 1909.

77 Ibid., October 1905.

78 Ibid.

79 Ibid., May–October 1906.

80 For an introduction to this concern see Fuchs, *Poor and Pregnant in Paris*, chap. 3.

81 *Bretoned Paris*, January–February 1909, December 1909; see also January 1911.

82 Ibid., August 1905, October 1905.

83 Ibid., October 1905, August 1913.

84 Ibid., November 1910.

85 Ibid., October 1909.

86 Ibid., December 1909.

87 Ibid., October 1909.

88 Ibid., May–October 1906.

89 Diximier and Diximier, *L'assiette au beurre*, 22, 45.

90 Ibid., 351–65. An issue is devoted to Alsace-Lorraine in May 1911, but this region was not then part of France; some issues were also devoted to colonies, England, Germany, etc.

91 Ibid., 371–72; Tailhade wrote nine issues of *L'assiette au beurre*, but this is the sole issue illustrated by the artist Torent.

92 Tailhade, "Le peuple noir, la Bretagne," 2202–3.

93 *L'assiette au beurre* 131 (3 October 1903), 2204–16.

94 These included the Ferry Laws of 1881–82, instituting secular education, and the Goblet Law of 1886, starting the process of secularizing the teaching personnel. The large bodies of historical work on the history of French public education and secularization include Curtis, *Educating the Faithful*; Clark and Kaiser, eds., *Culture Wars*; Reed-Danahay, *Education and Identity in Rural France*; Prost, *Histoire de l'enseignement en France*; Grew and Harrigan, *School, State, and Society*; Clark, *Schooling the Daughters of Marianne*; Mayeur, *L'enseignement secondaire des jeunes filles sous la Troisième République*.

95 This weekly was the first to introduce color photographs, in 1907.

96 This resistance is expertly delineated and analyzed in Ford, *Creating the Nation in Provincial France*, chap. 5; Ford, "Religion and the Politics of Cultural Change in Provincial France."

97 Saint-Maurice, "Les décrets Combes dans le Finistère."

98 Saint-Maurice, "L'exécution des décrets en Bretagne."

99 Saint-Maurice, "Les dernières expulsions des soeurs en Bretagne."

100 Saint-Maurice, "La messe à 2700 mètres d'altitude."

101 Le Roy, "Le cinéma avant 1914," 28.

102 Berlanstein, *The Working People of Paris*, 5–8.

103 Statistique Générale, *Résultats statistiques du recensement général de la population effectué le 24 mars 1901*, vol. 4, 292–99; as an entrée into scholarship on the Auvergnats and the Creusois see Corbin, *Archaïsme et modernité en Limousin au XIXᵉ siècle*; Corbin, "Les paysans de Paris," 169–76; Raison-Jourde, *La colonie auvergnate de Paris au XIXᵉ siècle*.

104 Harison, *The Stonemasons of Creuse in Nineteenth-Century Paris*. A fine multifaceted study of domestics in Belle Époque Paris is Martin-Fugier, *La place des bonnes*; McBride, *The Domestic Revolution*, compares domestic service in England and France.

105 Only about one in twelve male domestics was from Brittany in 1901; figures for occupations are calculated from Statistique Générale, *Résultats statistiques du recensement général de la population effectué le 24 mars 1901*, vol. 4, 292–305; Statistique Générale, *Résultats statistiques du recensement général de la population effectué le 5 mars 1911*, vol. 1, 110–11.

106 Statistique Générale, *Résultats statistiques du recensement général de la population effectué le 24 mars 1901*, vol. 4, 292–305; Statistique Générale, *Résultats statistiques du recensement général de la population effectué le 5 mars 1911*, vol. 1, 108–9. There were 3,372 Breton couturières in Paris in 1901 and 4,617 in 1911.

107 Knibiehler, ed., *Cornettes et blouses blanches*, chap. 1, 50.

108 Gautier, *L'émigration bretonne*, 201–2.

109 Statistique Générale, *Résultats statistiques du recensement général de la population effectué le 24 mars 1901*, vol. 4, 304–5; one male medical professional in ten

was a Breton, and women were 22.6 percent of those in the Seine and 23.5 percent of those in Paris. In 1911 about one male in nine in the medical profession was a Breton; the data on women are not published. Statistique Générale, *Résultats statistiques du recensement général de la population effectué le 5 mars 1911*, vol. 1, 106–7.

110 The Abbé Euzen wrote in the *Paroisse bretonne* (February 1908); he is cited in Gautier, *L'émigration bretonne*, 169.

111 Statistique Générale, *Résultats statistiques du recensement général de la population effectué le 5 mars 1911*, vol. 1, 104–5, 110–11; nearly 3,500 women were day laborers in the Seine, and just over 1,700 in the city.

112 Berlanstein, *The Working People of Paris*, 92.

113 Statistique Générale, *Résultats statistiques du recensement général de la population effectué le 24 mars 1901*, vol. 4, 300–301.

114 Euzon in *Paroisse bretonne* (February 1908), cited in Gautier, *L'émigration bretonne*, 169.

115 Statistique Générale, *Résultats statistiques du recensement général de la population effectué le 5 mars 1911*, vol. 1, 104–5.

116 Bindi and Lefeuvre, *Le Métro de Paris*, 6–7; Feller, "Vieillissement et société dans la France du premier XXᵉ siècle," 586; see also Feller, "Agents et retraités des transports parisiens," 121; Rigouard, *Le Métro de Paris*, 9–111.

117 Feller, "Vieillissement et société dans la France du premier XXᵉ siècle," 597, 602.

118 Ibid., 599.

119 Statistique Générale, *Résultats statistiques du recensement général de la population effectué le 24 mars 1901*, vol. 4, 300–301. Their numbers increased to nearly 4,000 in the Seine and over 2,800 in Paris in the subsequent decade. Statistique Générale, *Résultats statistiques du recensement général de la population effectué le 5 mars 1911*, vol. 1, 104–5.

120 Michel, *François et Marie de Bretagne*, 49–50, 54, 81–83.

121 Faure, "Urbanisation et exclusions dans le passé parisien," 67; Statistique Générale, *Résultats statistiques du recensement général de la population effectué le 5 mars 1911*, vol. 1, part 4, 116–17.

122 Archives de la Préfecture de Police, unnumbered registers, neighborhood 56, 1910, case 229, 734.

123 Police archives, unnumbered registers, quartier 53, 1910, case 70, 228.

124 Police archives, unnumbered registers, quartier 56, 1910, case 351; quartier 53, 1910, cases 535, 653. No other Bretons refused to name their parents.

125 Police archives, unnumbered registers, quartier 53, 1910, case 746.

126 Police archives, unnumbered registers, quartier 53, 1910, case 688.

127 Police archives, unnumbered registers, quartier 53, 1910, cases 68, 90, 129, 553.

128 Faure, "Comment devenait-on Parisien?," 45.

129 Ibid., 43; Garden, "Mariages parisiens à la fin du XIXᵉ siècle," 122. Garden's one thousand marriages occurred throughout the Paris basin, and Faure's marriages occurred only in the Eleventh Arrondissement; nonetheless, Faure

very effectively makes the case that every arrondissement had a broad mixture of Parisians, provincials, and foreigners, 45–51. Faure does not give figures for the Breton marriages in his study.

130 There were 52 Breton couples among the 197 Breton marriages in the Fourteenth Arrondissement in 1910. Of the 101 Breton women who married out, 30 married Parisians; of the 36 Breton men who did so, 11 married Parisians. Archives de l'État Civil du xive Arrondissement de Paris, 1910.

131 Well over half the Breton grooms in the Fourteenth Arrondissement married a Bretonne, but fewer than a third of the Breton brides married a Breton.

132 The mean age of marriage for the 142 first-time brides was 25.88 years, and only 43 percent married before the age of 25.

133 Fourteen of the 253 Bretons marrying in the Fourteenth Arrondissement (5.5 percent) lived with their mother or father; 49.2 percent of couples lived at the same address.

134 Marie is probably the sister, since the birthplaces and minimal information about the parents are identical, but it is possible that Marie is a cousin. Marriages, Fourteenth Arrondissement, 368, 679. Mécanicien can translate as mechanic or machine fitter.

135 Marriages, Fourteenth Arrondissement, 368, 679.

136 Of the Breton grooms twelve worked for the railroad and ten worked as carters, as horse grooms, or in like occupations; there were also mechanics, nurses, and excavators.

137 Marriages, Fourteenth Arrondissement, 682.

138 Marriages, Fourteenth Arrondissement, 1533.

139 Of the eighteen marriages that included a Breton nurse, siblings were witnesses at eleven, and at more than half of these the sibling was a nurse.

140 Marriages, Fourteenth Arrondissement, 383.

141 Brunet, "Une banlieue ouvrière," 781; Brunet, "L'immigration provinciale à la fin du xixe siècle," 85.

142 Archives of Paris, D2 M8 132, Recensement de 1911, Saint-Denis.

143 Faure, "Aspects de la 'la vie du quartier' dans le Paris populaire de la fin du 19e siècle," 283–97.

144 Archives de la Préfecture de Police, Registres de Commissariats, unnumbered registers, quartier 91, 1900, cases 1153, 1169, 1170.

145 Archives de la Préfecture de Police, unnumbered registers, quartier 92, 1905, cases 1126, 1129.

146 The police blotters of Saint-Denis South for 1905 show about 1,186 cases, 41 of which (3 percent) mention a perpetrator or victim born in Brittany; those of Saint-Denis north for 1900 only show about 674 cases, 43 of which (6 percent) mention a perpetrator or victim born in Brittany.

147 Police archives, unnumbered registers, Saint-Denis North, quartier 91, 1900, case 1189.

148 Police archives, unnumbered registers, Saint-Denis South, quartier 92, 1905, cases 575, 832, 857.

149 Police archives, unnumbered registers, Saint-Denis South, quartier 92, 1905, cases 603, 715.

150 Police archives, unnumbered registers, Saint-Denis North, quartier 91, 1900, case 1282.

151 Police archives, unnumbered registers, Saint-Denis North, quartier 91, 1900, case 120; police archives, unnumbered registers, Saint-Denis North, quartier 92, 1905, cases 270, 450, 521, 537, 590.

152 Police archives, unnumbered registers, Saint-Denis North, quartier 91, 1900, case 160.

153 Faure, "Banlieue, mon amour . . . ," 167.

154 Faure, "Migrations intérieures et villes dans la France du XIXᵉ siècle," 158–60.

155 Granovetter, "The Strength of Weak Ties."

156 There were 67 Breton couples among the 127 Breton marriages in Saint-Denis in 1910. Archives de l'État Civil de Saint Denis.

157 Of those who "married out" in Saint-Denis, six of the fifty-nine married a Parisian and eighteen of the fifty-nine married a native of Saint-Denis. Some of the Dyonisians were of Breton parentage, of course, but this is apparent in only very few cases.

158 Of the eighty-five first-time brides, the mean age of marriage was 23.8 years, and nearly two-thirds married before the age of 25.

159 Archives of Paris, D2 M8 132, Recensement de 1911, Saint-Denis; Brunet, "L'immigration provinciale à la fin du XIXᵉ siècle," 81–82.

160 Marriages, Saint-Denis, 1910. The remaining women included a few needle workers and white-collar workers.

161 Marriages, Saint-Denis, 1910, 55.

162 Marriages, Saint-Denis, 1910, 629. This couple was more fortunate, and had more support, than François Le Goff and Marguerite Guernalec, from inland villages in the Côtes-d'Armor; of their four parents only François's mother survived, at home. Marguerite had been orphaned at birth and her father had died when she was nine years old. Less than ten years later she had given birth to a baby girl in the Fourteenth Arrondissement—perhaps at La Maternité hospital. By the time she and her laborer partner married, the baby was four years old and Marguerite worked as a day laborer in Saint-Denis. A neighborhood marchand de vins and a gas worker stood up for François, along with Marguerite's brother-in-law, which suggests that her sister was also present, along with an illiterate uncle, both of whom also resided in Saint-Denis. Marriages, Saint-Denis, 1910, 122.

163 Marriages, Saint-Denis, 1910; 54 percent of the Breton men who wed another Breton were unskilled laborers and 19 percent were in transportation. The proportions for grooms who married a non-Breton women are 52 percent and 19 percent, and this group includes a few white-collar and commercial workers.

164 See Appendix: Marriage Records.

165 Gould, *Insurgent Identities*, 80–90.

166 Marriages, Saint-Denis, 1910, 44.

167 Prado, "Le va et vient," 192.

168 Marriages, Saint-Denis, 1910, 44, 122.

169 Statistique Générale, *Résultats statistiques du recensement général de la population effectué le 5 mars 1911*, vol. 1, part 4, 88–89. There were 109,091 Bretons living within the city limits and 50,691 in the banlieue.

170 Moya, "Immigrants and Associations," 839.

171 Schrover and Vermeulen, "Immigrant Organizations," 826–28.

172 Calvé, *Histoire des bretons à Paris*, 116, 166.

173 Ibid., 126, 136–37.

174 Ibid., 137–38; *Le breton de Paris*, 4 February 1912.

175 Calvé, *Histoire des Bretons à Paris*, 125–27; the author points out that Durocher is from a German family that settled in Brittany and changed its name from Duringer during the First Empire; Le Couédec, *Les architectes et l'idée bretonne*, 129–30.

176 Calvé, *Histoire des bretons à Paris*, 111; see for example Henkes, "Maids on the Move," 224–43. For the protection of young women—and train station greeters—by Protestant and Catholic organizations in Paris see Machen, "Traveling with Faith," and publications by such organizations as the Association Catholique Internationale des Oeuvres de Protection de la Jeune Fille. For the larger effort see Fuchs, *Poor and Pregnant in Paris*.

177 Calvé, *Histoire des bretons à Paris*, 98, 112; Ford, *Creating the Nation in Provincial France*, chap. 5.

178 Departmental archives of the Côtes-d'Armor, 6 M 808, letter of 22 May 1912 to prefect; poster: "Avis important."

179 *Le breton de Paris*, 4 June 1899.

180 Ibid., 29 June 1899.

181 These are available at the Bibliothèque Historique de la Ville de Paris. The most complete run of issues is that of 1912.

182 Calvé, *Histoire des bretons à Paris*, 112.

183 *Le breton de Paris*, 8 September 1912, 1 March 1914.

184 Ibid., 14 June 1908.

185 Ibid., 7 January 1912.

186 Ibid., 7 April 1912.

187 Ibid., 21 April 1912.

188 Ibid., 12 January 1912.

189 Ibid., 1 January 1912. This figure was also reported in *Le breton de Paris*, 13 October 1912, and in *Le petit parisien*, 29 July 1912.

190 *Le breton de Paris*, 1 June 1913.

191 Ibid., 7 April 1912, 14 April 1912. The alternate statue was never built, but the original continued to irritate Breton nationalists and was blown up by an underground Breton group in the summer of 1932. Calvé, *Histoire des bretons à Paris*, 130. The airplane project is reported in *Le breton de Paris* in March and April 1912.

192 *Le breton de Paris*, 10 November 1912 to 5 January 1913; the banner is pictured in Calvé, *Histoire des bretons à Paris*, 160–61.

193 For a broader history of the camps see Downs, *Childhood in the Promised Land*.

194 *Le breton de Paris*, 11 February 1912, 14 April 1912, 28 July 1912, 4 August 1912.

195 Ibid., 24 November 1912 to 29 December 1912.

196 Ibid., 26 May 1912 to 25 August 1912.

197 Ibid., 7 January 1912.

198 Ibid., 12 June 1912.

199 Ibid., 31 March 1912, 2 June 1912.

200 Ibid., 7 January 1912.

201 Ibid., 19 May 1912, 16 June 1912.

202 Ibid., 5 April 1914. See Prestwich, *Drink and the Politics of Social Reform*.

203 "Petit homme aux yeux doux, petit gars de ma race / Paris, le grand Paris est encore trop étroit / Pour que ton sang soit pur, pour que tu pousses droit." *Le breton de Paris*, 16 June 1912.

204 "Restez donc au pays, Bretonne insouciante; / La Ville de Lumières à chaque instant vous hante; / Vous soubissez l'attrait néfaste de Paris / Qui vous semble de loin fait de rosiers fleuris ! / Ils cachent à vox yeux une pente bien lisse / Où petit à petit de plus en plus l'on glisse." *Le breton de Paris*, 28 July 1912.

205 *Le breton de Paris*, 28 December 1913.

206 Calvé, *Histoire des bretons à Paris*, 111.

207 *Le breton de Paris*, 14 August 1914.

208 *La paroisse bretonne*, September 1914.

209 *Le petit parisien*, 29 July 1912.

210 Ogden and Winchester, "The Residential Segregation of Provincial Migrants in Paris in 1911," 36–37.

211 Faure, "Paris, 'Gouffre de l'espèce humaine'?," 74, 85.

212 Faure, "Urbanisation et exclusions dans le passé parisien," 68.

CHAPTER FOUR. BETWEEN THE WARS

1 Michel, *François et Marie de Bretagne*, 56–80; Cottard, *Vie et histoire du XIVe arrondissement*, 70.

2 Caumery and Pinchon, *Bécassine pendant la guerre*, 1.

3 In this respect Bécassine is like other figures in wartime children's literature; see Audoin-Rouzeau, *La guerre des enfants*.

4 "Tiens, sale Boche!," Caumery and Zier, *Bécassine chez les alliés*, 5.

5 Caumery and Pinchon, *Bécassine pendant la guerre*, 26.

6 Caumery and Zier, *Bécassine mobilisée*, 31; Bruggeman, Sellier, and Poete report that 1,570 women worked for the Métro in 1915, as did 3,037 in 1918, while in the same period the number of men declined from 3,602 to 2,656; women working for the tramways increased from 2,670 in 1915 to 5,001 in

1918, while the number of men increased from 8,412 to 10,552. *Paris pendant la guerre*, 45.

7 Caumery and Zier, *Bécassine chez les alliés*, 30–31.

8 Ibid., 14–21.

9 Caumery and Pinchon, *Bécassine pendant la guerre*, 60–61; Caumery and Zier, *Bécassine mobilisée*, 55.

10 Caumery and Zier, *Bécassine chez les alliés*, 61. "'Ça durera ce que ça durera; on souffrira ce qu'il faudra souffrir; les boches, on les aura!' Et tous les autres m'ont applaudi, en me disant que j'avais parlé en vrai Française." The phrase "on les aura," roughly translating as "we'll get them," comes from the famous words of encouragement of General Philippe Pétain to his troops at Verdun in April 1916; this watchword was popularized subsequently by a wartime propaganda poster featuring a picture of a beckoning soldier encouraging onlookers to enlist. http://images.library.uiuc.edu:8081/u?/wwposters,7.

11 Cornette, *Histoire de la Bretagne et des bretons*, vol. 2, 407–10.

12 Ibid., 415–18. These figures are based on the loss of about 150,000 men, the current figure used by historians, replacing the earlier Breton estimates of 240,000 dead.

13 In fact, Joffre is quoted in the Breton nationalist play of the 1930s discussed below, Calvez and Caouissin, *"Bécassine" vue par les bretons*, 51.

14 Cornette, *Histoire de la Bretagne et des bretons*, 422–23; for Foch see also Calvé, *Histoire des bretons à Paris*, 146–47.

15 Cornette, *Histoire de la Bretagne et des bretons*, 418.

16 Michel, *François et Marie de Bretagne*, 54–55, 81–85, 91–94.

17 Eley, "Historicizing the Global, Politicizing Capital," 153–88.

18 Chabot, *Jean et Yvonne, domestiques en 1900*, 191.

19 Michel, *François et Marie de Bretagne*, 88–103.

20 Ibid., 85, 98–99, 104–10.

21 Introductions to the vast and distinguished literature on this subject include such fundamental texts as Bruggeman, Sellier, and Poete, *Paris pendant la guerre*; Downs, *Manufacturing Inequality*; and Winter and Robert, *Capital Cities at War*.

22 Lawrence, "The Transition to War in 1914," 152–53.

23 Bonzon, "The Labor Market and Industrial Mobilization," 193–94.

24 Cole, "The Transition to Peace," 204.

25 See especially Brunet, *Saint-Denis, la ville rouge*, 174–88; Downs, *Manufacturing Inequality*.

26 Cole, "The Transition to Peace," 211.

27 Blévis, Lafont-Couturier, Jacomijn Snoep, and Zalc, *Les étrangers au temps de l'Exposition Coloniale*; Lewis, *The Boundaries of the Republic*.

28 This shift is best studied by Lewis, *Boundaries of the Republic*, but the rich literature includes Blévis, Lafont-Couturier, Jacomijn Snoep, and Zalc, *Les étrangers au temps de l'Exposition Coloniale*; Rygiel, *Destins immigrés*; Weber, *The Hollow Years*.

29 "Travailler en ville ?! Mon pauvre ami, il y a longtemps qu'on ne trouve plus de travail en ville: la crise y est encore plus aiguë qu'à la campagne et la misère plus grande." *La croix des Côtes-du-Nord*, 16 December 1934, cited in Cornette, *Histoire de la Bretagne et des bretons*, 443.

30 Gautier, *L'émigration bretonne*, 67.

31 Ibid., figure 11.

32 Feller, "Vieillissement et société dans la France du premier XXᶜ siècle, 1905–1953," 616–17; this idea is also expressed by Faure, "Banlieue, mon amour . . ."

33 Feller, "Vieillissement et société dans la France du premier XXᶜ siècle, 1905–1953," 609.

34 Ibid., 613–14.

35 About 10 percent of Métro employees were women, 1914–38. Deval, "Le personnel de la compagnie du chemin de fer métropolitain de Paris," 4, 11, 13, 18, 24, 25, 32, 40.

36 Cribier, *Une génération de parisiens arrive à la retraite*; Omnès, *Ouvrières parisiennes*; Violain, *Bretons de Paris*.

37 Omnès, *Ouvrières parisiennes*, 293, 298; the figure of 91 percent applies to women born in 1901, the majority of whom came to Paris between the wars, alone or with a husband.

38 *Bulletin*, January–March 1927, 39, cited in Omnès, *Ouvrières parisiennes*, 293. "Paris est le grand centre où viennent se réfugier, inconnues, toutes les jeunes femmes qu'un chagrin, un abandon, une malheur a chassées de leur ville natale."

39 Girard, *Un parcours en noir et blanc dans la Bretagne de jadis*, 7–40.

40 Moch, "Networks among Bretons?," 431–55.

41 Omnès, *Ouvrières parisiennes*, 271–88; 70 percent of the respondents to the mail questionnaire had friends or relatives waiting for them in Paris, 294.

42 Cribier and Rhein, "Migrations et structure sociale," 141–43.

43 Violain, *Bretons de Paris*, 26, 62–63.

44 Ibid., 18.

45 Ibid.

46 Ibid.

47 Rhein, *La vie dure qu'on a eu*, 107; to protect her anonymity, Germaine is the sole name given for this interviewee.

48 Violain, *Bretons de Paris*, 12.

49 Calvé, *Histoire des bretons à Paris*, 111.

50 Farcy and Faure, *La mobilité d'une génération de français*, 84.

51 See chaps. 2 and 5; 90 percent of the women studied by Omnès had their entire working lives in the Paris basin, *Ouvrières parisiennes*, 295.

52 Violain, *Bretons de Paris*, 26–27, 38–39.

53 Brunet, *Saint-Denis, la ville rouge*, 200; see also Cole, "The Transition to Peace."

54 Brunet, *Saint-Denis, la ville rouge*, 200–201.

55 Ibid., 201–4, 435.

56 Between the wars the proportion of provincials from the north of France stayed about the same, and those from other regions decreased. Many of the Alsatians went home when Alsace once again became part of France with the settlement of the war. Brunet, *Saint-Denis, la ville rouge*, 206–7.

57 Placard in exposition "Douce banlieue: mémoire retrouvée, identité partagée," Saint-Denis, 29 April to 23 July 2004, organized by the municipal archives in Saint-Denis under the direction of Frédérique Jacquet.

58 Brunet, *Saint-Denis, la ville rouge*, 207; in 1936, 9.1 percent of the population in Saint-Denis was foreign-born and 9.3 percent of the population was born in the five departments of Brittany; Lillo, *La petite Espagne de la plaine-Saint-Denis*, 44–45.

59 Brunet, *Saint-Denis, la ville rouge*, 319–20.

60 Violain, *Bretons de Paris*, 46, 62.

61 Gautier, *L'émigration bretonne*, 204–5.

62 Ibid., 207; Breton electors (adult males) made up 40.7 percent of the Breton population of Saint-Denis, yet only 19.4 percent of the Breton population of the Fourteenth Arrondissement.

63 Omnès, *Ouvrières parisiennes*, does not distinguish between Bretonnes and other provincials, but rather distinguishes between women of rural and urban origins, 271–84.

64 Ibid., 74.

65 Halévy, *Pays parisiens*, 161, cited in Brunet, "Une banlieue ouvrière," 94.

66 Faure and Lévy-Vroelant, *Une chambre en ville*, 163: "l'excellent connaisseur des milieux populaires de cette époque . . . qui a travaillé en usine et habité en garni un peu partout dans Paris."

67 Valdour, *Ateliers et taudis de la banlieue de Paris*, 3, 5.

68 "C'est vraiment un avenue royale. Entre ces gazomètres géants galopèrent à tombeau ouvert les quarante rois qui firent la France. . . . beauté absurde, perdue, insupportable, haïssable, cette beauté jaillie dans un siècle étranger." Drieu la Rochelle in *La Nouvelle Revue Française*, 1935, t. 45/XLV, 627–28, cited in Brunet, *Saint-Denis, la ville rouge*, 204.

69 Brunet, *Saint-Denis, la ville rouge*; see also Stovall, *The Rise of the Paris Red Belt*.

70 Brunet, *Saint-Denis, la ville rouge*, 151–52, 329; the pre-war figure was 46 percent for Saint-Denis but 71.5 percent for the suburb of Neuilly and 57.5 percent for Paris.

71 Violain, *Bretons de Paris*, 62–63; Young, "Of Pardons, Loss, and Longing."

72 Violain, *Bretons de Paris*, 62–63.

73 Lucas, "Vie quotidienne à Plaisance," 18–19, describes her mother's work across town, but these chores were hardly unique to the Fourteenth Arrondissement.

74 Archives de l'État Civil de Saint-Denis, Marriages, 1925, no. 95.

75 Marriages, Saint-Denis, 1925. The mean age of marriage for women was 23.77 and for men 25.84; medians were 23 and 25.

76 Marriages, Saint-Denis, 1925, 103.

77 Marriages, Saint-Denis, 1925, 308, 333.

78 For example, only 9 of the 110 brides of 1925 were from these cities.

79 Marriages, Saint-Denis, 1925, 897.

80 Marriages, Saint-Denis, 1925, 666.

81 See Blanc-Chaléard, *Les italiens dans l'est parisien*; Lillo, *La petite Espagne de la plaine-Saint-Denis*; Marriages, Saint-Denis, 1925, 996.

82 Marriages, Saint-Denis, 1925, 870, 871.

83 *La paroisse bretonne*, December 1914.

84 Omnès, *Ouvrières parisiennes*, 199–200.

85 Bruggeman, Sellier, and Poete, *Paris pendant la guerre*; Bonzon, "The Labor Market and Industrial Mobilization," 301; Cottard, *Vie et histoire du XIVᵉ arrondissement*, 70. Evenson, *Paris*, 206; http://www.demographia.com/db-paris-arr1999.htm, accessed 14 April 2008.

86 Cottard, *Vie et histoire du XIVᵉ arrondissement*, 72; Bonin and Costa, *Je me souviens du 14ᵉ arrondissement*, 108–10.

87 This area would be redeveloped in the 1970s; Evenson, *Paris*, 213, 288–89.

88 Bonin and Costa, *Je me souviens du 14ᵉ arrondissement*, 92–95.

89 Ibid., 52–63; Mousli, *Max Jacob*, 13–14, 29, 42–45.

90 Faure, "Comment devenait-on Parisien?," 47.

91 In 1896 Bretons had only been 4 percent of the population of this arrondissement. Bonin and Costa, *Je me souviens du 14ᵉ arrondissement*, 74–89; Gautier, *L'émigration bretonne*, figure 11 (no page number); http://www.demographia.com/db-paris-arr1999.htm, accessed 22 July 2009.

92 Faure, "Réflexions sur les ambiguïtés du quartier populaire," 449–50; Violain, *Bretons de Paris*, chap. 1.

93 Violain, *Bretons de Paris*, 50.

94 Ibid., 51; Hélias, *The Horse of Pride*, 219–20.

95 Bonin and Costa, *Je me souviens du 14ᵉ arrondissement*, 78–79; Cribier, "Jeunes provinciaux d'hier, vieux parisiens d'aujourd'hui," interviews by Françoise Cribier and Françoise Prouvoyeur; I thank Professor Cribier for permitting me to read transcripts of these interviews. Lucas, "Vie quotidienne à Plaisance," 18; Violain, *Bretons de Paris*, 40–41, 51, 124–25, 133, 136–37.

96 *La paroisse bretonne*, February 1922, cited in Gautier, *L'émigration bretonne*, 174–75.

97 Omnès, *Ouvrières parisiennes*, 271–76.

98 Faure, "Camille et Jeanne, ouvrières à la raffinerie Say," 49–59; Omnès, *Ouvrières parisiennes*, 296.

99 These figures from the Thirteenth Arrondissement are from Gautier, *L'émigration bretonne*, 204.

100 Archives de l'État Civil, Fourteenth Arrondissement, Marriages, 1925, 919.

101 Marriages, Fourteenth Arrondissement, 1925, 780.

102 Marriages, Fourteenth Arrondissement, 1925, 174.

103 In 1925 48 percent of Breton couples shared an address and 55 percent of all of

the couples married in the Fourteenth Arrondissement shared an address; the figures for 1910 were 43 percent and 49 percent.

104 In 1925 25 percent of brides and 38 percent of grooms were from *préfectures* and *chef-lieux d'arrondissement*.

105 Marriages, Fourteenth Arrondissement, 1925, 704, 708, 780.

106 Marriages, Fourteenth Arrondissement, 1925, 468, 301.

107 Of the 121 women who married to an outsider, 45 (37.2%) married a man born in Paris.

108 Marriages, Fourteenth Arrondissement, 1925, 342. Douet lists his profession as *toiler chaudronnier*.

109 Marriages, Fourteenth Arrondissement, 1925, 1272, 1298.

110 The proportion marrying foreigners is 5.8 percent, about one in seventeen of Breton women who married a non-Breton. Blanc-Chaléard, *Les italiens dans l'est parisien*; Blanc-Chaléard, *Les immigrés et la France*; Marriages, Fourteenth Arrondissement, 1925, 779.

111 Marriages, Fourteenth Arrondissement, 1925, 364.

112 Labé, "Bécassine débarque"; Lehembre, *Bécassine*, 32.

113 Bugat-Pujol, *Bécassine éternelle*, 26–39.

114 Caumery and Pinchon, *Les cent métiers de Bécassine*, 13.

115 Languereau (like the illustrator Pinchon) had married in 1918; his daughter, Louise-Charlotte, was called Loulotte. LeGuen, *La trépidante histoire de Bécassine*, 19; Vitruve, *Bécassine, oeuvre littéraire*, 32–33.

116 Caumery and Pinchon, *L'automobile de Bécassine*, 36.

117 Ibid., 57; Caumery and Pinchon, *Bécassine à Clocher-les-Bécasses*, 36.

118 Frenz, *Nobel Lectures, Literature*.

119 Schalk, *Roger Martin du Gard*, 1–2; Becker, *Everyman His Own Historian*, 252–253.

120 Martin du Gard, *Les Thibaults*, 32.

121 Ibid., 289–90, 463.

122 Ibid., 290, 472.

123 Ibid., 584, 703.

124 Violain, *Bretons de Paris*, 18, 26–27, 136.

125 Violain, *Bretons de Paris*, 92, 95, 96: "Elles sont jolies les filles de nos campagnes / que Paris voit venir si tôt matin / elles ne pleurent pas encore / leur lointaine Bretagne / elles ont le rire d'enfant / Paris les fait putains."

126 Violain, *Bretons de Paris*, 91–93.

127 Ibid., 116.

128 L'Ermite, *La femme aux yeux ouverts*, 328–46.

129 Calvé, *Histoire des bretons à Paris*, 102–3.

130 Gautier, *L'émigration bretonne*, 6.

131 Violain, *Bretons de Paris*, 29.

132 Calvé, *Histoire des bretons à Paris*, 142–44, 166–67, 171–72; Beaufrère would run the paper until his death in 1940. Public dances are mentioned throughout works on the third Republic, including Violain, *Bretons de Paris*, cover,

133–35; Bonin and Costa, *Je me souviens du 14ᵉ arrondissement*, 20–21; for the fundamental role of associative life see Jose Moya, "Immigrants and Associations," 839.

133 Violain, *Bretons de Paris*, 62–63; see also Young, "Of Pardons, Loss, and Longing," 269–304.

134 This institution would last fifty years, interrupted only in 1939–45; Calvé, *Histoire des bretons à Paris*, 146–48, 169.

135 Bonin and Costa, *Je me souviens du 14ᵉ arrondissement*, 85–86; Violain, *Bretons de Paris*, 102–5.

136 Cornette, *Histoire de la Bretagne et des bretons*, 453–73. Breton nationalists ranged from the socialist Yann Sohier (1901–35) to François Debauvais (1902–44), who in 1937 traveled to Nazi Germany and received assurances that an autonomous Brittany would be in the "realm of the possible" in the Third Reich; the history of the Breton movement is also analyzed in Nicolas, *Le séparatisme en Bretagne*; Nicolas, *Histoire du movement breton*; Déniel, *Le mouvement breton*.

137 The society Gwenn ha Du (White and black) was named after the colors of the Breton flag. Hélias wrote, "La destruction par explosifs du monument de l'union de la Bretagne à la France nous était apparue, à mes camarades et à moi, comme un attentat symbolique, commis par quelques exaltés, mais sans grand rapport avec la situation actuelle de la Bretagne. Trop vieille affaire. Nous avions d'autres chats à fouetter." Cornette, *Histoire de la Bretagne et des bretons*, 463–64.

138 Thiesse, *Écrire la France*; Violain, *Bretons de Paris*, 11.

139 Violain, *Bretons de Paris*, 78, 80, 82, 84; Violain draws on the work of the postwar psychiatrist Louis Leguillant, 84.

140 Louis Beaufrère, "Une nouvelle offensive de Bécassine," *La Bretagne à Paris*, 23 December 1938; Violain, *Bretons de Paris*, 81.

141 Thiesse, *Écrire la France*.

142 Violain, *Bretons de Paris*, 82.

143 Calvez and Caouissin, *Bécassine vue par les bretons*.

144 Lehembre, *Bécassine*, 124–125.

145 Calvez and Caouissin, *Bécassine vue par les bretons*, 51.

146 Louis Beaufrère, "Les bretons réagissent vigoureusement contre leurs insulteurs," *La Bretagne à Paris*, 16 January 1937.

147 Louis Beaufrère, "Le film indésirable est désormais largement expurgé." *La Bretagne à Paris*, 16 January 1937.

148 Lebovics, *Bringing the Empire Back Home*, 153.

149 Peer, *France on Display*, 3.

150 Le Couédic, *Les architectes et l'idee bretonne*, 686–704; Peer, *France on Display*, 59, 95–96; *La Bretagne à Paris*, 8 May 1937, 17 July 1937, 7 August 1937. For the part of the Seiz Breur in the International Exposition of 1937 see Le Couédic, "Les seiz Breur," 58–73.

151 *La Bretagne à Paris*, 24 December 1938.

152 Déniel, *Le mouvement breton*, cover.

153 For example, the poster for a meeting at Ploumanac'h on 3 June referred to "l'insulte permanent à la Bretagne: La Bécassine sotte et ridicule," Violain, *Bretons de Paris*, 83; *La Bretagne à Paris*, 10 June 1939, 24 June 1939.

154 Violain, *Bretons de Paris*, 81–83.

155 *La Bretagne à Paris*, 24 June 1939; "un mannequin de cire avec un air idiot." For the Musée Grevin see Schwartz, *Spectacular Realities*.

156 "En tout cas la Bretagne bouge—elle haït Bécassine." Le Guen, *La trépidante histoire de Bécassine*, 65.

157 *La Bretagne à Paris*, 24 June 1939.

158 Le Guen, *La trépidante histoire de Bécassine*, 55.

159 *La Bretagne à Paris*, 8 July 1939.

160 Le Guen, *La trépidante histoire de Bécassine*, 66.

161 "Bécassine provoque le rire, par les bévues où sa naïveté l'entraîne, par les aventures et mésaventures qui en résultent. Mais tout en riant, les enfants murmurent: 'Cette bonne Bécassine !' Et ils prononcent ces mots avec un accent d'affection profonde. La bonté est bien, en effet, le fond de Bécassine. Constamment, elle néglige son intérêt et son plaisir." Langereau is quoted in Le Guen, *La trépidante histoire de Bécassine*, 75.

162 One of the three recounted the plan and failed to get away years later, recalling that the police contacted the prime minister's office and that Édouard Daladier said he wanted no trouble with the Bretons, so the police told the young men to get out. After all, war would break out in less than three months, and France would need its loyal soldiers. Interview with Patrick Guérin in Violain, *Bretons de Paris*, 82.

163 Bécassine fans speculate that the patriotic nature of Great War albums may have caused this interdiction; vintage *bande dessinée* specialists speculate that it was more likely that these albums easily concealed correspondence and illicit papers. Langereau died during the war at seventy-four; Vitruve, *Bécassine, oeuvre littéraire*, 54.

164 Blanc-Chaléard, *Les immigrés et la France*; Lewis, *The Boundaries of the Republic*; Rygiel, *Destins immigrés*; Noiriel, *Population, immigration et identité nationale en France*, 70 (lists, in descending order of numerical importance, Italians, Poles, Spaniards, Belgians, Algerians, and Portuguese); Ponty, *Les polonais méconnus*, 319; Rosenberg, *Policing Paris*.

165 Weil, *How to Be French*, chap. 4. French-born Jews were also targeted, including the Breton artist Max Jacob, who died in the Drancy camp in 1944, despite his conversion to Catholicism thirty years earlier, in despair at the persecution and deaths of family members; Mousli, *Max Jacob*, 422–39.

CHAPTER FIVE. A LONG RESOLUTION IN POSTWAR PARIS

1 Beginning in 1949 André Yhuellou, from the same town, opened a hotel in the same neighborhood that "sheltered a modest, but homogeneous, clien-

tele." Calvé, *Histoire des bretons à Paris*, 156, 281–82; Violain, *Bretons de Paris*, 38–39, 56–57.

2 Michel, *François et Marie de Bretagne*, 108–11. This wartime account is echoed by retired interviewees studied by Françoise Cribier; I am grateful to Mme. Cribier for allowing me to read her notes on interviews with Bretons.

3 These figures are from the survey by Gautier, *L'émigration bretonne*, 210–11.

4 The "trente glorieuses" refers to the thirty years of economic prosperity following the Second World War. These figures for Bretons (15 percent of new arrivals) actually undercount, because they only include the four departments of the Finistère, Côtes-d'Armor, Morbihan, and Ille-et-Vilaine; the Loire-Atlantique had been assigned out of the region of Brittany in 1941. Gildea, *The Past in French History*, 205; Pourcher, *Le peuplement de Paris*, 86–87. Pourcher's inquiry of newcomers arriving after the war is based on a survey of 2,534 provincial residents in greater Paris, 270.

5 Gravier, *Paris et le désert français*, 254.

6 Pourcher, *Le peuplement de Paris*, 122.

7 Ibid., 166–68.

8 Ibid., 147.

9 Ibid., 279.

10 Noiriel, *Population, immigration et identité nationale en France*, 70; Noiriel, *The French Melting Pot*, was published in France in 1988 as *Le creuset français*. Indeed the only article in the INED journal *Population* in the year of Pourcher's publication (1964) was concerned with the number of blacks in France, whether from the Antilles, sub-Saharan Africa, or the United States: Robert Delem, "La population noire en France," *Population* 19, no. 3 (1964), 515–28. Scholars from other immigrant nations wrote about immigrants in France, as Noiriel notes; the first was Dignan, "Europe's Melting Pot."

11 Gautier, *L'émigration bretonne*, 222; Pourcher, *Le peuplement de Paris*, 276–77.

12 Gautier, *L'émigration bretonne*, 222, 209. Women accounted for 299 of the employees; the Bretons came from (in order) the Côtes-d'Armor, the Finistère, the Morbihan, Ille-et-Vilaine, and the Loire-Atlantique.

13 Gautier, *L'émigration bretonne*, 224–25

14 Personal communication, Suzanne Ascoët, 5 May 1998; Lemieux, "Bonne et méchante," 36–38; for postwar domestics see also Violain, *Bretons de Paris*, 30–31, 112–13, 32–33.

15 Lemieux, "Bonne et méchante," 38.

16 Ibid. Ascöet worked through the Fédération des Employés Chrétiens de la CFTC though its mutation into the CFDT.

17 Gautier, *La dure existence des paysans et paysannes*; Gautier, *Un siècle d'indigence*. Note the review of Gautier's work by Maurice Le Lannou in *Annales E.S.C.* 7, no. 1 (1952), 95–97.

18 Chevalier, *La formation de la population parisienne au XIXᵉ siècle*, 206, 210. Gautier's quotation was from the Frère Rivalin in 1898; see Introduction.

19 Chevalier, *La formation de la population parisienne au XIXᵉ siècle*, 209–11; Gautier, *L'émigration bretonne*, 3–4.

20 Calvé, *Histoire des bretons à Paris*, 148; Violain, *Bretons de Paris*, 118.

21 Violain, *Bretons de Paris*, 118.

22 I am grateful to Pierre Guillard for the gift of this poster; a black-and-white reproduction of which appears in Violain, *Bretons de Paris*, 21.

23 Le Bras, *Études de sociologie religieuse*, 480–81: "Quant à moi, je puis dire qu'un expérience qui porte sur 25 bonnes bretonnes me donne un résultat impressionnant: sur les 25, il n'y en avait pas une qui n'allât à la messe dans son village et nous en avons même connu qui étaient secrétaires des Enfants de Marie; aucune n'a continué de pratiquer, une fois arrivée à Paris, et même l'une d'entre elles est maintenant danseuse a Pigalle. Voilà le résultat du transfert."

24 Calvé, *Histoire des bretons à Paris*, 148; Violain, *Bretons de Paris*, 118.

25 http://bretonsdeparis.gwalarn.org/baparis.html#titre2, accessed 15 June 2009.

26 Calvé, *Histoire des bretons à Paris*, 152; Violain, *Bretons de Paris*, 65, 106–7.

27 Gravier, *Paris et le désert français*, 248–49.

28 *L'Express* was founded by Jean-Jacques Servan Schreiber, future president of the Radical Party, and Françoise Giroud, who went on to become France's first minister of women's affairs in 1974 and minister of culture in 1976. The magazine had a left-of-center orientation revealed partly by its opposition to the war in Algeria and to the use of torture. After the magazine changed its editorial policy in the mid-1960s and began to emulate *Time*, circulation rose dramatically.

29 Cau's report is excerpted in Violain, *Bretons de Paris*, 89.

30 This report by the morbihannais mayor was published in the Paris weekly *La Bretagne à Paris* and is excerpted in Violain, *Bretons de Paris*, 90.

31 The commune of Plozévet included the *bourg*, a center, four villages of over a hundred people, and nearly eighty hamlets of three or more houses in 1954. Robert Gessain, Preface, Burguière, *Bretons de Plozévet*, 7–8, 28.

32 Burguière, *Bretons de Plozévet*, 2.

33 Morin, *Commune en France*; Morin, *The Red and the White*.

34 Morin, *The Red and the White*, 37, 89, chap. 8.

35 In this way Morin (as well as Burguière) went beyond the village study by Wylie that was produced at the same time, *Village in the Vaucluse*.

36 Burguière, *Bretons de Plozévet*, 317.

37 Hélias, *Le cheval d'orgueil*, was translated as *The Horse of Pride* (New Haven: Yale University Press, 1978). Over two million copies were sold in France. Joël Cornette, *Histoire de la Bretagne et des bretons*, 587.

38 Laurence Wylie, Foreword, *The Horse of Pride*, xi; Wylie is author of *Village in the Vaucluse*. Not everyone shared this enthusiasm: an ethnologist of the Bigouden family observed that Hélias was the "self-appointed poet of a sublimated culture"; Segalen, *Fifteen Generations of Bretons*, 2. Other ethnologists like Prado and Barbichon recognize the profound appeal of the book, ibid., 130–31. Claude Chabrol made a film of *The Horse of Pride* in 1985.

39 Prado and Barbichon, *Vivre sa ville*; this work is based on conversations with

forty-two women and twenty-eight men who left Brittany for Paris in the 1940s, 1950s, and 1960s, including those from agricultural families, non-agricultural rural families, and small-town families. In the same study Prado and Barbichon also interviewed Bretons who had moved to Le Mans.

40 Prado and Barbichon, *Vivre sa ville*, 130. "Les Bretons de Paris aiment leur pays, mais je ne crois pas qu'ils ont la nostalgie, je crois qu'ils sont implantés à Paris. Notre sort, à ceux qui sont partis est préférable à celui de ceux qui sont restés."

41 Michel, *François et Marie de Bretagne*; Feller, "Agents et retraités de transports parisiens," 127.

42 Prado and Barbichon, *Vivre sa ville*, 62–66.

43 Ibid., 93, 202, and *passim*. The Pari Mutuel Urbain, PMU, founded in 1930, is France's off-track betting institution.

44 Prado and Barbichon, *Vivre sa ville*, 152–54.

45 Caerléon, *La révolution bretonne permanente*; Violain, *Bretons de Paris*, 78–85.

46 Prado and Barbichon, *Vivre sa ville*, 93, 204.

47 Ibid., 82.

48 Ibid., 41–44, 118.

49 Ibid., 119.

50 Ibid., 44, 64.

51 Michel, *François et Marie de Bretagne*, 104; Cribier, "La constitution de la population parisienne," 82–83.

52 Cribier, "Jeunes provinciaux d'hier, vieux parisiens d'aujourd'hui"; Cribier, "Les migrations de retraite des Parisiens," 250–51.

53 Prado and Barbichon, *Vivre sa ville*, 39, 164–65.

54 Michel, *Francois et Marie de Bretagne*, 95–108; chap. 3, above.

55 Prado and Barbichon, *Vivre sa ville*, 40, 64, 170–72.

56 Ibid., 195–99.

57 Ibid., 78.

58 Ibid., 75, 79, 184.

59 Ibid., 199.

60 Violain, *Bretons de Paris*, 102–7, 118–19.

61 Ibid., 102–7.

62 The Breton nationalist Ronen Caerléon put it like this: "It took a quarter-century of active and passive resistance and a worldwide cultural revolution for the old structures to collapse in a record time that one would not have imagined ten years earlier." *La révolution bretonne permanente*, 16. Changing conditions in postwar Brittany and the many political, linguistic, and educational organizations and impulses that made up the Breton movement are beyond the scope of this work; scholarship on this topic includes Cornette, *Histoire de la Bretagne et des bretons*, 587–92; Reece, *The Bretons against France*, 191–231; McDonald, *"We Are Not French!,"* 73–96. It is important to note, however, that the tradition of violent protest established between the wars by Breton activists (who exploded the statues in Rennes in 1932, for example

—see chap. 4) returned with farmers' protests and attacks against tax bureaus by the Breton Liberation Front. Reece, *The Bretons against France*, chaps. 8–9.

63 Cornette, *Histoire de la Bretagne et des bretons*, 587–89; Violain, *Bretons de Paris*, 96, 100–101, 121, 126.

64 Cornette, *Histoire de la Bretagne et des bretons*, 589

65 Violain, *Bretons de Paris*, 100–101, 120–21; Prado and Barbichon, *Vivre sa ville*, 131, 158–59.

66 Calvé, *Histoire des bretons à Paris*, 160–161; Violain, *Bretons de Paris*, 80–81, 83; Caerléon, *La révolution bretonne permanente*. Caerléon is the pseudonym of Ronan Caouissin, who died in 1986; Herri Caouissin died in 2003; Charles Le Quintrec died in 2008.

67 Prado and Barbichon, *Vivre sa ville*, 156–58.

68 Ibid., 200.

69 For these see especially Chevalier, *La formation de la population parisienne au XIXe siècle*, and Raison-Jourde, *La colonie auvergnate de Paris au XIXe siecle*.

70 Le Guen, *La trépidante histoire de Bécassine* (Port Louis: A. Le Guen, 1994), 69, 82; Trubert, *Bécassine revient*.

71 Prado and Barbichon, *Vivre sa ville*, 147; Lebesque, *Comment peut-on être Breton?*, 112–13. I thank Annie Couëdel for this image, which has been reprinted with fewer frames than the original in Violain, *Bretons de Paris*, 81.

72 Bécassine was listed as "type humoristique de servante bretonne (XXe s.) créé par Pinchon et Caumery," *Petit Larousse illustré* (Paris: Larousse, 1979); "type humoristique de servante bretonne, héroïne d'une des premières bandes dessinées (1905), créée par Pinchon et Caumery," *Petit Larousse illustré* (Paris: Larousse, 1983).

73 Le Guen, *La trépidante histoire de Bécassine*, 72.

74 The fifteenth film festival in Douarnenez projected the film. LeGuen, *La trépidante histoire de Bécassine*, 77; Bugat-Pujol, *Bécassine éternelle*.

75 Le Guen, *La trépidante histoire de Bécassine*, 74.

76 Bécassine: "personnage de bande dessinée créé en 1905 par le scénariste Caumery et le dessinateur Pinchon dans l'hebdomadaire français *La Semaine de Suzette*. Bretonne naïve et dévouée, elle campe le type de la servante au grand coeur." *Le petit Larousse illustré* (Paris: Larousse, 1998, 2003). This entry is illustrated by the cover of *Bécassine en apprentissage*.

77 For one informative account of postwar change see Morin, *Commune en France*.

78 First editions of *L'enfance de Bécassine* and *Bécassine chez les alliés*, for example, are listed at the price of 220€. Béra, Denni, and Mellot, *Trésors de la bande dessinée*, 93–94.

79 Puyuelo, Rémy. *Héros de l'enfance, figures de la survie*. The fourth hero, Poil de Carotte, is a redhead suffering through an unhappy childhood. The novel in which he appears, Jules Renard, *Poil de carotte* (Paris: Calmann-Lévy, 1907), has inspired films and cartoons.

80 Le Guen, *La trépidante histoire de Bécassine*; Hélène Bugat-Pujol, *Bécassine éternelle*.

81 Couderc, *Bécassine inconnue*.

82 Labé, "Bécassine débarque." The opening line refers to the extremely negative feelings toward this character on the part of Bretons: "Bécassine was born from a sneeze, but it was the Bretons that caught the cold. Not all, of course. But the militant nationalists and many other inhabitants of the West without nationalist sentiments, wounded by the image of Bécassine in which they see a nasty mistake and enormous ignorance, wanted to see her pilloried."

83 Gratitude for this welcome is well expressed in Segalen, *Fifteen Generations of Bretons*, 3.

84 Groensteen, *Astérix, Barbarella & Cie*, 42; Nye, "Death of a Gaulois."

CONCLUSION

1 Noiriel, *Population, immigration et identité nationale en France*, 85; see also Alba and Nee, *Remaking the American Mainstream*.

2 Violain, *Bretons de Paris*, 64.

3 Calvé, *Histoire des bretons à Paris*; Violain, *Bretons de Paris*.

4 Tardieu, *Les auvergnats de Paris*; Tardieu, *Le bal de la rue de Lappe*; Tardieu, *Les bretons de Paris de 1900 à nos jours*.

5 Eveillard and Huchet, *Une Bretagne si étrange*; similarly, see Frélaut, *La Bretagne, il y a un siècle*.

6 Beaucarnot, *Quand nos ancêtres partaient pour l'aventure*, 341; LeRoi Ladurie, "Ces petits métiers qui poussaient à l'aventure," *Le Figaro*, 19 June 1997.

7 Beaucarnot, *Quand nos ancêtres partaient pour l'aventure*; Ladurie, "Ces petits métiers qui poussaient à l'aventure."

8 The substantial and multifaceted history of postwar immigration into France has produced enormous and outstanding scholarly analyses; here I can only mention a few introductions to this literature: Blanc-Chaléard, *Les immigrés et la France*; Rygiel, ed., *Le bon grain et l'ivraie*. See also Blanc-Chaléard, *Les italiens dans l'est parisien*; Green, *Repenser les migrations*; Konig, *Deutsche Handwerker, Arbeiter une Dienstmädchen in Paris*; Lequin, *La mosaïque France*; Lewis, *The Boundaries of the Republic*; Milza, *Voyage en Ritalie*; Milza, Gervereau, Témime, and Berrou, *Toute la France*; Rygiel, *Destins immigrés*.

9 Two areas of controversy and concern are anti-Semitic and anti-Muslim violence and the 2004 law banning headscarves in secondary schools; for two English-language studies of the headscarf law see Killian, "The Other Side of the Veil"; Scott, "Symptomatic Politics."

10 Chevalier, Preface to Gautier, *L'émigration bretonne*, 5.

11 Tribalat, *Faire France*.

12 On female migrants in Paris see Fuchs and Moch, "Pregnant, Single, and Far from Home"; Fuchs and Moch, "Invisible Cultures"; for women helping

family members see Prado and Barbichon, *Vivre sa ville*, 98, 204; Rosental finds hints of this in "La migration des femmes (et des hommes) en France au XIXᵉ siècle," 109.

13 Lucassen, *The Immigrant Threat*, 188–91; Meurs, Pailhé, and Simon, "Persistance des inégalités entre générations liées à l'immigration"; Simon, "France and the Unknown Second Generation"; Tribalat, *Faire France*, 147.

14 See for example Lucassen, *The Immigrant Threat*, chap. 7.

15 Bertho, "L'invention de la Bretagne," 45–62.

16 *Revue de l'enseignement primaire*, cited by Chanet, *L'école républicaine et les petites patries*, 211.

17 Dantec, "Bécassine–Banania, destins croisés," 21–28.

18 Ozouf, *Composition française*, 16, 240, 242–43.

19 Rosental, "Between Macro and Micro," 476.

20 Lemieux, "Bonne et méchante," 38.

APPENDIX. MARRIAGE RECORDS

1 Rosental, *Les sentiers invisibles*; Rosental, "La migration des femmes (et des hommes) en France au XIXᵉ siècle."

2 Farcy and Faure, *La mobilité d'une génération de français*.

3 A rather vast literature is being published on this point, including Rosental's discussion of information from his work "La migration des femmes (et des hommes) en France au XIXᵉ siècle." For an overview of this literature see Schrover and Yeo, *Gender and Migration in Global, Historical and Theoretical Perspective*.

4 Chabot, *Jean et Yvonne, domestiques en 1900*, 131–35.

5 Archives Départementales des Côtes-d'Armor, series 7E, Mariages, Guingamp, 1792–1890; 8 E 5/3 Publications de mariages, Belle-Isle-en-Terre, 1891–1900 and 1905; 8 E 47/5 Publications de mariages, Corlay, 1891–1905; 8 E 47/6 Publications de mariages, Corlay, 1906–1926; 8 E 70/7 Publications de mariages, Guingamp, 1905. Archives Départementales du Finistère, 3 E 73, Mariages, Fouesnant, 1890; 3 E 285 Mariages, Quimper, 1890.

6 Cribier, *Une génération de parisiens arrive à la retraite*; Omnès, *Ouvrières parisiennes*; Rhein, *La vie dure qu'on a eu*; Violain, *Bretons de Paris*.

7 A fine description of the utility of marriage records for historians is Garden, "Mariages parisiens à la fin du XIXᵉ siècle."

8 Chabot, *Jean et Yvonne, domestiques en 1900*, 131–35.

9 Zola, *L'assomoir*, 67, 72, 77–79.

ARCHIVES
Archives de Paris

E Mariages, XIVe arrondissement, 1875
  Mariages, XIVe arrondissement, 1890

DIM2 Listes éléctorales, XIVe arrondissement, 1893.

DIM8 Recensement de 1886, professions, Paris
  Recensement de 1886, professions, Saint-Denis

D2 M8 28 Recensement de 1891, professions, Paris
  Recensement de 1891, professions, Saint-Denis

D2 M8 132 Recensement de 1911, Saint-Denis

Archives Départementales des Côtes-d'Armor

7 E Mariages, Guingamp, 1792–1890

8 E 5/3 Mariages, Belle-Isle-en-Terre, 1891–1900 and 1905

8 E 47/5 Mariages, Corlay, 1891–1905

8 E 47/6 Mariages, Corlay, 1906–1926

8 E 70/7 Mariages, Guingamp, 1905

4 M 244 Passeports, enregistrement, 1817–1952

6 M 808 Emigration intérieure et extérieure: circulaires, instructions, 1817–1936

Archives Départementales du Finistère

3 E 73 Mariages, Fouesnant, 1890

3 E 285 Mariages, Quimper, 1890

4M 379 Passeports, enregistrement, 1854–1912

Archives Départementales d'Ille-et-Vilaine

6M 691 État nominatif des émigrants partis pour l'étranger

Archives Départementales de Seine–Saint Denis

I E 66 32 Mariages, Saint Denis, 1875

48 Mariages, Saint Denis, 1890

Archives de l'État Civil du XIVᵉ Arrondissement de Paris

Mariages 1910, 1925

Archives de l'État Civil de Saint Denis

Mariages 1910, 1925

Archives de la Préfecture de Police

B/A 400   Enquête industrielle, 1872
          XIVᵉ arrondissement   Saint-Denis
Non-numbered registers of *commissariats*
          53rd quartier, Montparnasse, 1910
          56th quartier, Plaisance, 1896 and 1910
          91st quartier, Saint Denis north, 1900
          92nd quartier, Saint Denis south, 1905

PERIODICALS

L'assiette au beurre
La Bretagne à Paris
Le breton de Paris
Bretoned Paris: Bulletin mensuel de la Société La Bretagne
L'Illustration
Le Matin
La paroisse bretonne
Le petit parisien
War Sao: Organe central des bretons émancipés de la région parisienne

BOOKS AND ARTICLES

Ackerman, Evelyn. "Alternative to Rural Exodus: The Development of the Commune of Bonnières-sur-Seine in the Nineteenth Century." *French Historical Studies*, spring 1977, 126–48.

——. *Village on the Seine: Tradition and Change in Bonnières, 1815–1914*. Ithaca: Cornell University Press, 1978.

Alba, Richard D., and Victor Nee. *Remaking the American Mainstream: Assimilation and Contemporary Immigration*. Cambridge: Harvard University Press, 2005.

Alexandropoulos, Jacques, and Patrick Cabanel, eds. *La Tunisie mosaïque*. Toulouse: Presses Universitaires du Mirail, 2000.

Alter, George. *Family and the Female Life Course: The Women of Verviers, Belgium, 1849–1880*. Madison: University of Wisconsin Press, 1988.

Andall, Jacqueline. *Gender and Ethnicity in Contemporary Europe*. New York: Berg, 2003.

Anderson, Bridget. *Doing the Dirty Work? The Global Politics of Domestic Labour*. London: Zed, 2000.

Andreu, Jean, Bartolomé Bennassar, and Romain Gaignard. *Les aveyronnais dans la Pampa*. Toulouse: Privat, 1977.

Appadurai, Arjun. *Modernity at Large: Cultural Dimensions of Globalization*. Minneapolis: University of Minnesota Press, 1996.

Applegate, Celia. "A Europe of Regions: Reflections on the Historiography of Sub-national Places in Modern Times." *American Historical Review* 104 (1999), 1157–82.

ArMen staff. "La population bretonne de 1800 à 1990." *ArMen* 43 (1992), 2–15.

Arrizabalaga, Marie-Pierre. "Les Basques dans l'ouest américain (1900–1910)." *Lapurdum* 5 (2000), 335–50.

Arzur, Marie-Aude. "Le Havre, colonie bretonne." *ArMen* 75 (1996), 2–14.

Audoin-Rouzeau, Stéphane. *La guerre des enfants, 1914–1918: Essai d'histoire culturelle*. Paris: Armand Colin, 1993.

Bade, Klaus. *Migration in European History*. Oxford: Blackwell, 2003.

Barbichon, Guy. "Provinciaux et provinces à Paris: Propositions pour l'analyse." *Ethnologie française* 10 (1980), 119–27.

Barnes, David S. *The Making of a Social Disease: Tuberculosis in Nineteenth-Century France*. Berkeley: University of California Press, 1995.

Bastien, Bernard. "Sociabilités populaires dans l'espace de la banlieue parisienne." *Un siècle de banlieue parisienne*, ed. Fourcaut, 211–23.

Battagliola, Françoise. "Mariage, concubinage et relations entre les sexes: Paris, 1880–1890." *Genèses* 18 (1995), 68–96.

Beaucaire, Francis. "Les transports collectifs devant l'extension des banlieues et l'essor de la mobilité citadine." *Un siècle de banlieue parisienne*, ed. Fourcaut, 81–99.

Beaucarnot, Jean-Louis. *Quand nos ancêtres partaient pour l'aventure*. Paris: Lattès, 1997.

Becker, Carl. *Everyman His Own Historian*. New York: Crofts, 1935.

Benoit-Guilbot, Odile, ed. *Changer de région, changer de métier, changer de quartier*. Nanterre: Université de Nanterre, 1982.

Béra, Michel, Michel Denni, and Philippe Mellot. *Trésors de la bande dessinée: catalogue encyclopédique de la B.D.* Paris: Éditions de l'Amateur, 2006.

Berlanstein, Lenard R. *Big Business and Industrial Conflict in Nineteenth-Century France*. Berkeley: University of California Press, 1991.

——. *The Working People of Paris, 1871–1914*. Baltimore: Johns Hopkins University Press, 1984.

Berruer, Pierre. *Les bretons migrateurs*. Paris: Presses de la Cité, 1977.

Bertaux-Wiame, Isabelle. "The Life History Approach to the Study of Internal Migration." *Oral History* 7 (1979), 26–32.

Bertho, Catherine. "L'invention de la Bretagne: Genèse social d'un stéréotype." *Actes de la recherche en sciences sociales* 35 (November 1980), 45–62.

Bertillon, Jacques. *Origine des habitants de Paris*. Paris: Chaix, 1895.

Bindi, Armand, and Daniel Lefeuvre. *Le Métro de Paris: Histoire d'hier à demain*. Rennes: Ouest-France, 1990.

Blanc-Chaléard, Marie-Claude. *Les immigrés et la France, XIXᵉ–XXᵉ siècle*. Paris: La Documentation Française, 2003.

——. *Les italiens dans l'est parisien: Une histoire d'intégration (1880–1960)*. Rome: École Française de Rome, 2000.

Blaufarb, Rafe. *Bonapartists in the Borderlands: French Exiles and Refugees on the Gulf Coast, 1815–1835*. Tuscaloosa: University of Alabama Press, 2005.

Blévis, Laure, Hélène Lafont-Couturier, Nanette Jacomijn Snoep, and Claire Zalc. *1931: Les étrangers au temps de l'Exposition Coloniale*. Paris: Gallimard, 2008.

Bonin, Sylvie, and Bernadette Costa. *Je me souviens du 14ᵉ arrondissement*. Paris: Parigramme, 1993.

Bonzon, Thierry. "The Labor Market and Industrial Mobilization, 1915–1917." *Capital Cities at War*, ed. Winter and Robert, 164–96.

Botrel, Théodor. "Les loups bretons." *La paroisse bretonne*, July 1899.

Bourdieu, Pierre, and Loïc Wacquant. *An Invitation to Reflexive Sociology*. Chicago: University of Chicago Press, 1992.

Bourgeois, Georges. "Exode rural et tuberculose." Thesis, Faculté de Médecine, Paris. Paris: Félix Alcan, 1904.

Bourset, Madeleine. "Une émigration insolite au XIXᵉ siècle: Les soldats des barricades en Californie, 1848–1853." *L'émigration française*, by Centre de Recherches d'Histoire Nord-Américain, Université de Paris I, 129–88.

Brachev, Léon. "Mon père, horticulteur-guérisseur du Boulevard Brune (1824–1904)." *Revue historique du quatorzième arrondissement* 26 (1981), 37–44.

"Les bretons de Paris." Fédération des sociétés bretonnes de la région parisienne, http://bretonsdeparis.gwalarn.org/baparis.html#titre2, consulted 15 June 2009.

Broudig, Fañch. *A la recherche de la frontière: La limite linguistique entre Haute et Basse-Bretagne aux XIXᵉ et XXᵉ siècles*. Brest: Ar Skol Vrezoneg, 1995.

Brubaker, Rogers. *Citizenship and Nationhood in France and Germany*. Cambridge: Harvard University Press, 1992.

Bruggeman, Auguste, Henri Sellier, and Marcel Poete. *Paris pendant la guerre*. Paris: Presses Universitaires de France, 1926.

Brunet, Jean-Paul. "Une banlieue ouvrière: Saint-Denis (1890–1939): Problèmes d'implantation du socialisme et du communisme." Thesis, Paris IV, 1978; Lille: University of Lille, 1982. BN-T & R 8-LL36–436 (1–3).

——. "L'immigration provinciale à la fin du XIXᵉ siècle: L'exemple de Saint-Denis." *Immigration, vie politique et populisme en banlieue parisienne (fin XIXᵉ–XXᵉ siècles)*, 69–92.

——. *Immigration, vie politique et populisme en banlieue parisienne (fin XIXᵉ–XXᵉ siècles)*. Paris: L'Harmattan, 1995.

——. *Saint-Denis, la ville rouge: Socialisme et communisme en banlieue ouvrière, 1890–1939*. Paris: Hachette, 1980.

Bryceson, Deborah, and Ulla Vuorela, eds. *The Transnational Family: New European Frontiers and Global Networks*. New York: Oxford University Press, 2002.

Bugat-Pujol, Hélène. *Bécassine éternelle*. Paris: H. Bugat-Pujol, 2004.

Burguière, André. *Bretons de Plozévet*. Paris: Flammarion, 1975.

Cadic, François. *Ça et là en Bretagne*. Paris: Terre de Brume, 2002.

———. *Contes et légendes de Bretagne*. Paris: Terre de Brume, 1997–2002.

Cadic, M. F. *L'oeuvre de la paroisse bretonne*. Paris: L'Oeuvre des Pauvres du Sacre-Coeur, 1899.

Caerléon, Ronan. *La révolution bretonne permanente*. Paris: La Table Ronde, 1969.

Calvé, Armel. *Histoire des bretons à Paris*. Kerangwenn: Coop Breizh, 1994.

Calvez, Léone, and Herri Caouissin. *"Bécassine" vue par les bretons: Comédie dramatique en 4 actes*. Pleyer-Christ: Ronan, 1937.

Castles, Stephen, and Mark Miller. *The Age of Migration: International Population Movements in the Modern World*. 4th edition. New York: Guilford, 2009.

Caumery [Maurice Languereau] and Joseph Porphyre Pinchon. *L'automobile de Bécassine*. Paris: Gautier-Langureau, 1927.

———. *Bécassine à Clocher-les-Bécasses*. Paris: Gautier-Languereau, 1935.

———. *Bécassine en apprentissage*. Paris: Gautier-Languereau, 1913.

———. *Bécassine pendant la guerre*. Paris: Gautier-Languereau, 1915.

———. *Les cent métiers de Bécassine*. Paris: Gautier-Languereau, 1920.

———. *L'enfance de Bécassine*. Paris: Gautier-Languereau, 1913.

Caumery [Maurice Languereau] and Édouard Zier. *Bécassine chez les alliés*. Paris: Gautier-Languereau, 1917.

———. *Bécassine mobilisée*. Paris: Gautier-Languereau, 1918.

Céline, Louis-Ferdinand. *Voyage au bout de la nuit*. Paris: Gallimard, 1952.

Centre de Recherches d'Histoire Nord-Américain, Université de Paris I. *L'émigration française: Études de cas: Algérie, Canada, États-Unis*. Paris: La Sorbonne, 1985.

Chabot, Paul. *Jean et Yvonne, domestiques en 1900: Souvenirs recueillis par Michel Chabot*. Paris: Terma, 1977.

Chanet, Jean-François. *L'école républicaine et les petites patries*. Paris: Aubier, 1996.

Châtelain, Abel. *Les migrants temporaires en France de 1800 à 1914*. Lille: Université de Lille, 1976.

———. "Migrations et domesticité féminine urbaine en France, XVIIIe siècle–XXe siècle." *Revue d'histoire économique et sociale* 47 (1969), 506–28.

Chevalier, Louis. *Dangerous Classes and Laboring Classes in Paris during the First Half of the Nineteenth Century*. New York: Fertig, 1973.

———. *La formation de la population parisienne au XIXe siècle*. Paris: Presses Universitaires Françaises, 1950.

Chin, Rita. *The Guestworker Question in Postwar Germany*. Cambridge: Cambridge University Press, 2007.

Choleau, Jean. *L'expansion bretonne au XXe siècle*. Paris: Champion, 1922.

Choquette, Leslie. *Frenchmen into Peasants: Modernity and Tradition in the Peopling of French Canada*. Cambridge: Harvard University Press, 1997.

Clark, Christopher and Wolfram Kaiser, eds. *Culture Wars: Secular Catholic Con-

flict in Nineteenth-Century Europe. Cambridge: Cambridge University Press, 2003.

Clark, Linda L. *Schooling the Daughters of Marianne: Textbooks and the Socialization of Girls in Modern French Primary Schools*. Albany: State University of New York Press, 1984.

Cole, Joshua. "The Transition to Peace, 1918–1919." *Capital Cities at War*, ed. Winter and Robert, 196–226.

Collet, Daniel. "L'émigration sud-finistérienne à la veille de la première guerre mondiale." *Mélanges offerts au chanoine Jean-Louis Le Floc'h: Chrétientés de Basse-Bretagne et d'ailleurs*. Quimper: Société Archéologique du Finistère, 1998.

Conklin, Alice L. *A Mission to Civilize: The Republican Idea of Empire in France and West Africa, 1895–1930*. Stanford: Stanford University Press, 1997.

Coquiot, Gustave. *Les bals publiques*. Paris: Noizette, 1896.

Corbin, Alain. *Archaïsme et modernité en Limousin au XIXe siècle*. Paris: Marcel Rivière, 1975.

——. "Les paysans de Paris: Histoire des limousins du bâtiment au XIXe siecle." *Ethnologie française* 10, no. 2 (1980), 169–76.

Cornette, Joël. *Histoire de la Bretagne et des bretons*. Paris: Le Seuil, 2005.

Cottard, René-Léon. "L'évolution du 14e arrondissement de 1860 à nos jours: Territoire, peuplement et habitat." *Revue historique du quatorzième arrondissement* 29 (1984–85), 9–48.

——. *Vie et histoire du XIVe arrondissement*. Paris: Hervas, 1995.

Couderc, Marie-Anne. *Bécassine inconnue*. Paris: CNRS, 2000.

Cribier, Françoise. "La constitution de la population parisienne: Contribution à l'étude des parisiens venus des provinces entre les deux guerres." *Cahiers d'analyse de l'espace*, 1986, 68–86.

——. *Une génération de parisiens arrive à la retraite*. Paris: Cordes-CNRS, 1978.

——. "Jeunes provinciaux d'hier, vieux parisiens d'aujourd'hui." Enquête sous la direction de Françoise Cribier, Équipe de géographie sociale et gérontologie, Centre National de la Recherche Scientifique, Université de Paris VII.

——. "Les migrations de retraite des Parisiens." *Cahiers de l'institut d'aménagement et d'urbanisme de la Région d'Île-de-France (L'IAURIF)* 122 (1996), 249–60.

Cribier, Françoise, and Catherine Rhein. "Migrations et structure sociale: Une génération de provinciaux venus à Paris entre les deux guerres." *Ethnologie française* 10 (1980), 137–45.

Croix, Alain, and Jean-Yves Veillard, *Dictionnaire du patrimoine breton*. Rennes: Apogée, 2000.

Curtis, Sarah. *Educating the Faithful: Religion, Schooling, and Society in Nineteenth-Century France*. DeKalb: Northern Illinois University Press, 2000.

Dantec, Ronan. "Bécassine–Banania, destins croisés." *Hommes et migrations* 1260 (2006), 21–28.

Daru, Napoléon. "Associations et sociétés des provinciaux à Paris." *Le Correspondant*, 10 February 1910, 561–84; 26 February 1910, 691–706.

Daughton, James P. *An Empire Divided: Religion, Republicanism, and the Making of French Colonialism, 1880–1914*. New York: Oxford University Press, 2006.

Debien, Gabriel. "Les engagés pour le Canada partis de Nantes (1725–1732)." *Revue d'histoire de l'Amérique française* 33, no. 4 (1980), 583–86.

Déguignet, Jean-Marie. *Contes et légendes de Basse-Cournouaille*. Le Relecq-Kerhoun: An Here, 1998.

———. *Mémoires d'un paysan bas breton*. Releg-Kerhoun: An Here, 1998.

Déniel, Alain. *Le mouvement breton: 1919–1945*. Paris: François Maspero, 1976.

Deval, Pierre. "Le personnel de la compagnie du chemin de fer métropolitain de Paris." Thesis, Université de Paris, 1939.

Dignan, Don. "Europe's Melting Pot: A Century of Large-Scale Immigration into France." *Ethnic and Racial Studies* 4, no. 2 (1981), 137–52.

Diximier, Elisabeth, and Michael Diximier. *L'assiette au beurre*. Paris: Maspero, 1974.

Downs, Laura Lee. *Childhood in the Promised Land: Working-Class Movements and the Colonies de Vacances in France, 1880–1960*. Durham: Duke University Press, 2002.

———. *Manufacturing Inequality: Gender Division in the French and British Metalworking Industries, 1914–1939*. Ithaca: Cornell University Press, 1995.

Duby, Georges, ed. *Histoire de la France urbaine*, vol. 4, *La ville de l'âge industriel: Le cycle haussmannien*. Paris: Le Seuil, 1983.

Duhamel, Georges. "Sociologie d'un quartier disparu: Rue Vandamme (14ᵉ) de 1889 à 1894." *Revue historique du quatorzième arrondissement* 25 (1980–1981), 25–42.

Dutertre, Marc. "Bretons de Versailles: L'intégration des migrants au début du xxᵉ siècle." Thesis, Université de Versailles Saint-Quentin-en-Yvelines, 2008.

Eley, Geoff. "Historicizing the Global, Politicizing Capital: Giving the Present a Name." *History Workshop Journal* 63 (2007), 153–88.

Eley, Geoff, and Ronald Suny, eds. *Becoming National*. New York: Oxford University Press, 1996.

Eveillard, James, and Patrick Huchet. *Une Bretagne si étrange, 1900–1920*. Rennes: Ouest-France, 1999.

Evenson, Norma. *Paris: A Century of Change, 1878–1978*. New Haven: Yale University Press, 1979.

Fairchilds, Cissie. *Domestic Enemies: Servants and Masters in Old-Regime France*. Baltimore: Johns Hopkins University Press, 1984.

Faivre, Jules Abel. "On les aura!" Poster, University of Illinois, Urbana-Champaign, Library, http://images.library.uiuc.edu:8081/u?/wwposters,7, consulted 21 July 2009.

Farcy, Jean-Claude, and Alain Faure. *La mobilité d'une génération de français: Recherche sur les migrations et les déménagements vers et dans Paris à la fin du XIXᵉ Siècle*. Paris: INED, 2003.

Faure, Alain. "Aspects de la 'vie du quartier' dans le Paris populaire de la fin du 19ᵉ siècle." *Recherches contemporaines* 6 (2000–2001), 283–97.

——. "Banlieue, mon amour . . . " *Les premiers banlieusards*, 167–83.

——. "Camille et Jeanne, ouvrières à la raffinerie Say." *Bulletin du Centre d'Histoire de la France Contemporaine* 11 (1990), 49–59.

——. "Comment devenait-on parisien? La question de l'intégration dans le Paris de la fin du XIXᵉ siècle." *Paris le peuple*, ed. Robert and Tartakowsky, 37–57.

——. "Migrations intérieures et villes dans la France du XIXᵉ siècle." *Historiens et géographes* 338 (1992), 151–60.

——. "Paris, 'Gouffre de l'espèce humaine'?" *French Historical Studies* 27, no. 1 (winter 2004), 49–86.

——. "Paris, le peuple, la banlieue." *Les premiers banlieusards*, 73–119.

——, ed. *Les Premiers Banlieusards: Aux origines des banlieues de Paris (1860–1914)*. Paris: Créaphis, 1991.

——. "Réflexions sur les ambiguïtés du quartier populaire (Paris, 1880–1914)." *Histoire, économie et société* 13 (1994), 449–55.

——. "Urbanisation et exclusions dans le passé parisien (1850–1950)." *Vingtième siècle: Revue d'histoire* 47 (1995), 58–69.

Faure, Alain, and Claire Lévy-Voelant. *Une chambre en ville: Hotels meublés et garnis à Paris, 1860–1990*. Paris: Créaphis, 2007.

Feller, Elise. "Agents et retraités des transports parisiens: Trajectoires individuelles et changement social au début du XXᵉ siècle." *Métro, dépôts, réseaux*, ed. Gérôme and Margairaz, 117–28. Paris: La Sorbonne, 2002.

——. "Vieillissement et société dans la France du premier XXᵉ siècle, 1905–1953." Thesis, Université Paul Diderot–Paris VII, 1997.

Fleuriot, Léon. *Les origines de la Bretagne: L'émigration*. Paris: Payot, 1980.

Ford, Caroline. *Creating the Nation in Provincial France: Religion and Political Identity in Brittany*. Princeton: Princeton University Press, 1993.

——. "Religion and the Politics of Cultural Change in Provincial France: The Resistance of 1902 in Lower Brittany." *Journal of Modern History* 62 (1990), 1–33.

Forster, Elborg, and Robert Forster, eds. *Sugar and Slavery, Family and Race: The Letters and Diary of Pierre Dessalles, Planter in Martinique, 1808–1856*. Baltimore: Johns Hopkins University Press, 1996.

Fouché, Nicole. *Émigration alsacienne aux États-Unis, 1815–1870*. Paris: La Sorbonne, 1985.

Foucrier, Annick. *Le rêve californien: Migrants français sur la côte pacifique (XVIIIᵉ–XXᵉ siècles)*. Paris: Belin, 1999.

Fourcaut, Annie. *Femmes à l'usine en France dans l'entre deux guerres*. Paris: Mastero, 1982.

——. *Un siècle de banlieue parisienne (1859–1964): Guide de recherche*. Paris: L'Harmattan, 1988.

Fouquier, Henri. "La Province à Paris." *Le Matin*, 2 July 1901.

Fox, Edward Whiting. *History in Geographic Perspective: The Other France*. New York: W. W. Norton, 1971.

Frélaut, Bertrand. *La Bretagne, il y a un siècle: La vie quotidienne des bretons*. Rennes: Ouest-France, 2003.

Frenz, Horst, ed. *Nobel Lectures, Literature, 1901–1967*. Amsterdam: Elsevier, 1969.

Frey, Michel. "Du mariage et du concubinage dans les classes populaires à Paris (1846–1847)." *Annales: Économies, sociétés, civilisations* 33 (1978), 803–29.

Fuchs, Rachel G. *Abandoned Children: Foundlings and Welfare in Nineteenth-Century France*. Albany: State University of New York Press, 1984.

———. *Poor and Pregnant in Paris: Strategies for Survival in the Nineteenth Century*. New Brunswick: Rutgers University Press, 1992.

Fuchs, Rachel, and Leslie Page Moch. "Invisible Cultures: Poor Women's Networks and Reproduction Strategies in Nineteenth-Century Paris." *Situating Fertility: Anthropology and Demographic Inquiry*, ed. Susan Greenhalgh, 86–107. Cambridge: Cambridge University Press, 1995.

———. "Pregnant, Single, and Far from Home: Migrant Women in Nineteenth-Century Paris." *American Historical Review* 95 (1990), 1007–31.

Gaillard, Jeanne. "Les migrants à Paris au XIXᵉ siècle: Insertion et marginalité." *Ethnologie française* 10 (1980), 128–36.

———. *Paris, La Ville (1852–1870)*. Lille: Université de Lille III, 1976.

Garden, Maurice. "Mariages parisiens à la fin du XIXᵉ siècle: Une micro-analyse quantitative." *Annales de démographie historique* (1998), 111–33.

Gasnault, François. *Guinguettes et lorettes: Bals publics et danse sociale à Paris entre 1830 et 1870*. Paris: Aubier, 1986.

Gautier, l'Abbé Elie. *La dure existence des paysans et paysannes: Pourquoi les bretons s'en vont*. Paris: Éditions Ouvrières, 1950.

———. *L'émigration bretonne: Où vont les bretons émigrants: Leurs conditions de vie*. Paris: Bulletin de l'Entraide Bretonne dans la Région Parisienne, 1953.

———. "L'émigration bretonne étudiée à travers l'évolution démographique, économique et sociale des Côtes-du-Nord au cours des XIXᵉ et XXᵉ siècles: La dispersion géographique des bretons émigrés, leur situation sociale, morale et religieuse." Doctoral thesis, Faculté des Lettres de Paris, 1950.

———. *Un siècle d'indigence: Pourquoi les bretons s'en vont*. Paris: Éditions Ouvrières, 1950.

Genève, Paul. "Les bretons de Paris." *L'Opinion*, 17 December 1910, 781–82.

Genin, Auguste. *Les français au Mexique du XVIᵉ siècle jusqu'à nos jours*. Paris: Argo, 1933.

Gerbod, Paul. "Parisiens et parisiennes hors de France au milieu du XIXᵉ siècle (1946–1860)." *Revue historique* 604 (1997), 287–95.

Gérôme, Noëlle, and Michel Margairaz. *Métro, dépôts, réseaux: Territoires et personnels des transports parisiens au XXᵉ siècle*. Paris: La Sorbonne, 2002.

Gibson, Ralph. *A Social History of French Catholicism, 1789–1914*. London: Routledge, 1989.

Gildea, Robert. *The Past in French History*. New Haven: Yale University Press, 1994.

Girard, Emma. *Un parcours en noir et blanc dans la Bretagne de jadis*. Paris: Pensée Universelle, 1995.

Gould, Roger. *Insurgent Identities: Class, Community, and Protest in Paris from 1848 to the Commune*. Chicago: University of Chicago Press, 1995.

Granet-Abisset, Anne-Marie. *La route réinventée: Les migrations des Queyrassins au XIXᵉ et XXᵉ siècles*. Grenoble: Presses Universitaires de Grenoble, 1994.

Granovetter, Mark. "The Strength of Weak Ties." *American Journal of Sociology* 73 (1978), 1360–80.

Gravier, Jean-François. *Paris et le désert français*. Paris: Flammarion, 1947.

Green, Nancy. *Repenser les migrations*. Paris: Presses Universitaires Françaises, 2002.

——. "Time and the Study of Assimilation." *Rethinking History* 10, no. 2 (2006), 239–58.

Greer, Donald. *The Incidence of the Emigration during the French Revolution*. Cambridge: Harvard University Press, 1951.

Grew, Raymond, and Patrick Harrigan. *School, State, and Society: The Growth of Elementary Schooling in Nineteenth-Century France*. Ann Arbor: University of Michigan Press, 1991.

Groensteen, Thierry. *Astérix, Barbarella & Cie: Histoire de la bande dessinée*. Paris: Somogy, 2000.

Haine, W. Scott. *The World of the Paris Café: Sociability among the French Working Class, 1789–1914*. Baltimore: Johns Hopkins University Press, 1996.

Halévy, Daniel. *Pays parisiens*. Paris: Emile-Paul Frères, 1929.

Harel, Jean-Michel. *L'île Saint-François: Le Havre*. Le Havre: J-M Harel, 1996.

Harison, Casey. *The Stonemasons of Creuse in Nineteenth-Century Paris*. Newark: University of Delaware Press, 2008.

Harsin, Jill. *Policing Prostitution in Nineteenth-Century Paris*. Princeton: Princeton University Press, 1985.

Harzig, Christiane, and Danielle Juteau. Introduction. *The Social Construction of Diversity: Recasting the Master Narrative of Industrial Nations*, ed. Harzig and Juteau, 1–12.

——, eds. *The Social Construction of Diversity: Recasting the Master Narrative of Industrial Nations*. New York: Berghahn, 2003.

Hélias, Pierre-Jakez. *The Horse of Pride: Life in a Breton Village*. New Haven: Yale University Press, 1978.

Henkes, Barbara. "Maids on the Move: Images of Femininity and European Women's Labour Migration during the Interwar Years." *Women, Gender and Labour Migration: Historical and Global Perspectives*, ed. Pamela Sharpe, 224–43. New York: Routledge, 2001.

Herlihy, David. *Medieval and Renaissance Pistoia: The Social History of an Italian Town, 1200–1430*. New Haven: Yale University Press, 1967.

Herlihy, David, and Christiane Klapish-Zuber. *Tuscans and Their Families: A Study of the Florentine Catasto of 1427*. New Haven: Yale University Press, 1985.

Heuer, Jennifer. *The Family and Nation: Gender and Citizenship in Revolutionary France, 1789–1830*. Ithaca: Cornell University Press, 2005.

Hochstadt, Steve. *Mobility and Modernity: Migration in Germany, 1820–1989*. Ann Arbor: University of Michigan Press, 1999.

Hodagneu-Sotelo, Pierrette. *Gendered Transitions: Mexican Experiences of Immigration*. Berkeley: University of California Press, 1994.

Hoerder, Dirk. *Creating Societies: Immigrant Lives in Canada*. Montreal: McGill-Queen's University Press, 1990.

——. *Cultures in Contact: World Migrations in the Second Millennium*. Durham: Duke University Press, 2002.

——. "Negotiating Nations: Exclusions, Networks, Inclusions: An Introduction." *Histoire Sociale / Social History* 66 (2000), 221–29.

——. "Transcultural States, Nations, and People." *The Historical Practice of Diversity*, ed. Hoerder, Harzig, and Schubert, 13–32.

Hoerder, Dick, Christiane Harzig, and Adrian Schubert, eds. *The Historical Practice of Diversity*. New York: Berghahn, 2003.

Hufton, Olwen. *Women and the Limits of Citizenship in the French Revolution*. Toronto: University of Toronto Press, 1992.

Hunter, Karen Montgomery. *Doctor Stories: The Narrative Structure of Medical Knowledge*. Princeton: Princeton University Press, 1991.

Jackson, James, Jr. *Migration and Urbanization in the Ruhr Valley, 1821–1914*. Atlantic Highlands, N.J.: Humanities Press, 1997.

Jacquemet, Jules. *L'église de Saint-Denis: Sa crypte, ses tombeaux, ses chapelles, son trésor*. Paris: Putois-Cretté, 1867.

Jobert, René. "Les agglomérations urbaines et l'émigration rurale en France au XIXᵉ siècle." Doctoral thesis, Faculty of Law, University of Rennes, 1905.

Katan, Yvette. "Le voyage 'organisé' d'émigrants parisiens vers l'Algérie, 1848–1849." *L'émigration française*, by Centre de Recherches d'Histoire Nord-Américain, Université de Paris I, 17–50.

Kesztenbaum, Lionel. "Cooperation and Coordination among Siblings: Brothers' Migration in France, 1870–1940." *History of the Family* 13 (2008), 85–104.

Killian, Caitlin. "The Other Side of the Veil: North African Women in France Respond to the Headscarf Affair." *Gender and Society* 17, no. 4 (2003), 567–90.

Knibiehler, Yvonne, ed. *Cornettes et blouses blanches: Les infirmières dans la société française, 1880–1980*. Paris: Hachette, 1984.

König, Mareike. *Deutsche Handwerker, Arbeiter und Dienstmädchen in Paris: Eine vergessene Migration im 19. Jahrhundert*. Munich: Oldenbourg, 2003.

Labé, Yves-Marie. "Bécassine débarque." *Le Monde*, 27 August 2005.

Lallemand, Maurice. *Comme un long fleuve fertile de passion et d'action éducatives: 150 années de présence à l'enseignement en Afrique des Frères de Ploërmel*. Ploërmel: Frères d'Instruction Chrétienne de Ploërmel, 1992.

Landry, Yves. *Les filles du roi: Orphelines en France, pionnières au Canada*. Montreal: Lemeac, 1992.

Lawrence, Jon. "Material Pressures on the Middle Classes." *Capital Cities at War*, ed. Winter and Robert, 229–54.

——. "The Transition to War in 1914." *Capital Cities at War: Paris, London, Berlin, 1914–1919*, ed. Jay Winter and Jean-Louis Robert, 135–63. Cambridge: Cambridge University Press, 1997.

Le Bail, Georges. *L'émigration rurale et les migrations temporaires dans le Finistère.* Paris: Giard et Brière, 1913.

Lebesque, Morvan. *Comment peut-on être breton? Essai sur la démocratie française.* Paris: Le Seuil, 1970.

Le Bouëdec, Gérard. *Les bretons sur les mers.* Rennes: Ouest-France, 1999.

Lebovics, Herman. *Bringing the Empire Back Home.* Durham: Duke University Press, 2004.

Le Bras, Gabriel. *Études de sociologie religieuse.* Paris: Presses Universitaires de France, 1956.

Le Clech, Grégoire. "L'émigration bretonne au Canada au début du xxe siècle: Le témoignage du pionnier Joseph Béléguic, de Douarnenez." *Bulletin de la Société Archéologique du Finistère* 106 (1978), 219–37.

——. "Un épisode marquant l'émigration bretonne au Canada: La fondation en 1904 de la paroisse de Saint-Brieux, au Saskatchewan." *Bulletin de la Société Archéologique du Finistère* 93 (1967), 287–329.

——. "Quelques figures de pionniers de l'émigration bretonne au Canada et aux États-Unis." *Bulletin de la Société Archéologique du Finistère* 95 (1969), 277–304.

Le Couédic, Daniel, *Les architectes et l'idée bretonne, 1904–1945: D'un renouveau des arts à la renaissance d'une identité.* Rennes: Société d'Histoire et d'Archéologie de Bretagne, 1995.

——. "Les seiz Breur." *ArMen* 55 (1993), 58–73.

Le Gall, Michael. "Bécassine." *Dictionnaire du patrimoine breton*, by Croix and Veillard.

Le Gallo, Yves. "Basse-Bretagne et bas-bretons." *Histoire littéraire et culturelle de la Bretagne*, vol. 2, ed. Louis Le Guillou and Donatien Laurent, 143–74. Paris: Champion, 1987.

——. "La Bretagne bretonnante." *Histoire littéraire et culturelle de la Bretagne*, vol. 3, ed. Jean Balcou and Yves Le Gallo, 5–39. Paris: Champion, 1987.

Le Guen, Annik. *La trépidante histoire de Bécassine.* Port Louis: A. Le Guen, 1994.

Lehembre, Barnard. *Bécassine: Une légende du siècle.* Paris: Hachette / Gautier-Langereau, 2005.

Lehning, James. *Peasant and French: Cultural Contact in Rural France during the Nineteenth Century.* New York: Cambridge University Press, 1995.

Le Lannou, Maurice. Review of Gautier, "L'émigration bretonne." *Annales: économies, sociétés, civilisations* 7, no. 1 (1952), 95–97.

Lemieux, Emmanuel. "Bonne et méchante." *Les Inrockuptibles* 148 (22 April 1998), 36–38.

Lemoine, Jean. "L'émigration bretonne à Paris." *Science sociale*, 7e année, t. 14, 1ère livraison, 1892, 39–60, 165–84, 239–48, 362–73.

"Le Peuple Noir: La Bretagne." *L'assiette au beurre*, 3 October 1903.

Lequin, Yves. *La mosaïque France: Histoire des étrangers et de l'immigration.* Paris: Larousse, 1988.

L'Ermite, Pierre. *La femme aux yeux ouverts.* Paris: La Bonne Presse, 1927.

Le Roi Ladurie, Emmanuel. "Ces petits métiers qui poussaient à l'aventure" [review of *Quand nos ancêtres partaient pour l'aventure*, by Jean-Louis Beaucarnot]. *Le Figaro Littéraire*, 19 June 1997.

Le Roy, Eric. "Le cinéma avant 1914: La Bretagne vue de Paris." *ArMen* 50 (1993), 26–33.

Lesger, Clé, Leo Lucassen, and Marlou Schrover. "Is There Life outside the Migrant Network?: German Immigrants in the xixth Century Netherlands and the Need for a More Balanced Migration Typology." *Annales de démographie historique*, 2002, no. 2, 29–50.

Levine, David, ed. *Proletarianization and Family History*. Orlando: Academic, 1984.

Lewis, Mary Dewhurst. *The Boundaries of the Republic: Migrant Rights and the Limits of Universalism in France*. Stanford: Stanford University Press, 2007.

Lillo, Natacha. *La petite Espagne de la plaine-Saint-Denis, 1900–1980*. Paris: Autrement, 2004.

Lloyd, Christopher. *Mirbeau's Fictions*. Durham: University of Durham, 1996.

Lombard-Jourdan, Anne. *La plaine Saint-Denis: Deux mille ans d'histoire*. Paris: Centre National de Recherches Scientifiques, 1994.

Lossouarn, Olivier Vincent. *Les bretons dans le monde*. Paris: John Didier, 1969.

Loughlin, John and Sonia Mazey, eds. *The End of the French Unitary State? Ten Years of Regionalization in France (1982–1992)*. London: Frank Cass, 1995.

Lucas, Andrée. "Vie quotidienne à Plaisance (1914–1925)." *Revue Historique du Quatorzième Arrondissement* 28 (1983), 18–20.

Lucassen, Leo. *The Immigrant Threat: The Integration of Old and New Migrants in Western Europe since 1850*. Urbana: University of Illinois Press, 2005.

Lutz, Helma, ed. *Migration and Domestic Work: A European Perspective on a Global Theme*. Aldershot: Ashgate, 2008.

Machen, Emily. "Traveling with Faith: The Creation of Women's Immigrant Aid Associations in Nineteenth and Twentieth-Century France." *Journal of Women's History* 23, no. 3 (2011).

Manning, Patrick. *Migration in World History*. New York: Routledge, 2005.

Martin, Phyllis M. "Celebrating the Ordinary: Church, Empire and Gender in the Life of Mère Marie-Michel Dédié (Senegal, Congo, 1882–1931)." *Gender and History* 16, no. 2 (2004), 289–317.

Martin du Gard, Roger. *Les Thibault*. Trans. Stuart Gilbert. New York: Viking, 1946.

Martin-Fugier, Anne. *La place des bonnes: La domesticité féminine en 1900*. Paris: Grasset, 1979.

Mauras, Véronique, and Olivier Hamon. *Ces bretons du Canada*. Saint-Thonan: Cloître, 1997.

Mayeur, Françoise. *L'Enseignement secondaire des jeunes filles sous la Troisième République*. Paris: Fondation Nationale des Sciences Politiques, 1977.

Maza, Sarah. *Servants and Masters in Eighteenth-Century France: The Uses of Loyalty*. Princeton: Princeton University Press, 1983.

McBride, Theresa. *The Domestic Revolution: The Modernization of Household Service in England and France, 1820–1920*. London: Croom Helm, 1976.

McDonald, Maryon. *"We Are Not French!": Language, Culture and Identity in Brittany*. London: Routledge, 1989.

Merriman, John. *The Margins of City Life: Explorations on the French Urban Frontier, 1815–1851*. Oxford: Oxford University Press, 1991.

Meurs, Dominique, Ariane Pailhé, and Patrick Simon. "Persistance des inégalités entre générations liées à l'immigration: L'accès à l'emploi des immigrés et de leurs descendants en France." *Population* 61, nos. 5–6 (2006), 763–802.

Meynier, André. "Les bretons au Havre." *Annales de Bretagne* 48 (1941), 387.

Michel, Jacques. *François et Marie de Bretagne*. Brest: Le Télégramme, 2002.

Michel, Joseph. *Missionnaires bretons d'outre-mer aux XIXᵉ et XXᵉ siècles*. Rennes: Presses Universitaires de Rennes, 1997.

Michel, Pierre. *Octave Mirbeau: Oeuvre romanesque*. Paris: Buchet/Chastel, 2001.

——, ed. *Un moderne: Octave Mirbeau*. Paris: Euroedit, 2004.

Milza, Pierre. *Voyage en Ritalie*. Paris: Plon, 1993.

Milza, Pierre, Laurent Gervereau, Emile Témime, and Jean-Hugues Berrou. *Toute la France: Histoire de l'immigration en France au XXᵉ siècle*. Paris: Somogy, 1998.

Mirbeau, Octave. *The Diary of a Chambermaid*. London: Paul Elek, 1966.

Moch, Leslie Page. *Moving Europeans: Migration in Western Europe since 1650*. 2nd edition. Bloomington: Indiana University Press, 2003.

——. "Networks among Bretons? The Evidence for Paris, 1875–1925." *Continuity and Change* 18 (2003), 431–55.

——. *Paths to the City: Regional Migration in Nineteenth-Century France*. Beverly Hills: Sage, 1983.

Moch, Leslie Page, and Rachel Fuchs. "Getting Along: Poor Women's Networks in Nineteenth-Century Paris." *French Historical Studies* 18 (1993), 34–49.

Moogk, Peter. "Manon's Fellow Exiles: Emigration from France to North America before 1763." *Europeans on the Move: Studies on European Migration, 1500–1800*, ed. Nicholas Canny, 236–60. Oxford: Clarendon, 1994.

Morin, Edgar. *Commune en France: La métamorphose de Plodémet*. Paris: Arthème Fayard, 1967.

——. *The Red and the White: Report from a French Village*. Trans. A. M. Sheridan-Smith. New York: Random House, 1970.

Mouillon, Juliette. "Domestique de la belle époque à Paris (1904–1912)." *Études de la région parisienne* 44 (1970), 1–9.

Mousli, Béatrice. *Max Jacob*. Paris: Flammarion, 2005.

Mouthon, F.-I. "La province à Paris." *Le Matin*, 2 July 1901.

——. "Les provinces à Paris: La Bretagne." *Le Matin*, 13 July 1901.

Moya, José. "Immigrants and Associations: A Global and Historical Perspective." *Journal of Ethnic and Migration Studies* 31, no. 5 (2005), 833–64.

Nadaud, Martin. *Mémoires de Léonard, ancien garçon maçon*. Paris: Hachette, 1976.

Nesbit, Molly. *Atget's Seven Albums*. New Haven: Yale University Press, 1992.

Nicolas, Michel. *Histoire du mouvement breton*. Paris: Syros, 1982.

——. *Le séparatisme en Bretagne*. Brasparts: Beltan, 1986.

Noiriel, Gérard. *The French Melting Pot: Immigration, Citizenship, and National Identity*. Minneapolis: University of Minnesota Press, 1996.

——. *Population, immigration et identité nationale en France, XIXᵉ–XXᵉ siècle*. Paris: Hachette, 1992.

Nye, Russel B. "Death of a Gaulois: Renée Goscinny and Astérix." *Journal of Popular Culture* 14 (1980), 181–83.

Ogden, Philip E., and S. W. C. Winchester. "The Residential Segregation of Provincial Migrants in Paris in 1911." *Transactions* 65 (July 1975), 29–44.

Omnès, Catherine. *Ouvrières parisiennes: Marchés du travail et trajectoires professionnelles au 20ᵉ siècle*. Paris: École des Hautes Études en Sciences Sociales, 1997.

——. "Les provinciales dans la formation des populations ouvrières parisiennes." *Villes en parallèle* 15–16 (1990), 174–91.

Ozouf, Mona. *Composition française: Retour sur une enfance bretonne*. Paris: Gallimard, 2009.

"Paris Arrondissements: Post 1860 Population and Population Density." Demographia, http://www.demographia.com/db-paris-arr1999.htm, updated 24 March 2001, consulted 14 April 2008.

Parreñas, Rhacel. *Servants of Globalization: Women, Migration and Domestic Work*. Stanford: Stanford University Press, 2001.

Peer, Shanny. *France on Display: Peasants, Provincials, and Folklore in the 1937 Paris World's Fair*. Albany: State University of New York Press, 1998.

Pelletier, Yannick. *Histoire générale de la Bretagne et des bretons*. Paris: Nouvelle Librairie de la France, 1990.

Pénisson, Bernard. "L'émigration française au Canada (1882–1929)." *L'émigration française*, by Centre de Recherches d'Histoire Nord-Américain, Université de Paris I, 51–106.

Perrot, Michelle. *Les ouvriers en grève (France, 1871–1890)*. Paris: Mouton, 1974.

Perroy, Gilbert, "L'urbanisation en deux siècles d'un coin de Montparnasse." *Revue Historique du Quatorzième Arrondissement* 24 (1979–80), 26–32.

Persancier, Auguste. *Souvenirs de Saint-Denis, 1907–1986*. Sassenage: Imprimeurs Réunis, 1985.

Pierre, Patrick. *Les bretons et la république: La construction de l'identité bretonne sous la Troisième République*. Rennes: Presses Universitaires de Rennes, 2001.

Pinède, Christiane. "L'immigration bretonne en aquitaine." *Revue géographique des Pyrénées et du sud-ouest* 31 (1960), 5–43, 181–96.

Pluchon, Pierre. *Histoire des Antilles et de la Guyane*. Toulouse: Privat, 1982.

Poitrineau, Abel. *Remues d'hommes: Essai sur les migrations montagnardes en France au XVIIᵉ et XVIIIᵉ siècles*. Paris: Aubier Montagne, 1983.

Ponty, Janine. *Les polonais méconnus: Histoire des travailleurs immigrés en France dans l'entre-deux-guerres*. Paris: La Sorbonne, 1988.

Pourcher, Guy. *Le peuplement de Paris*. Paris: Presses Universitaires de France, 1964.

Poussou, Jean-Pierre. *Bordeaux et le sud-ouest au XVIIIe siècle: Croissance économique et attraction urbaine*. Paris: École des Hautes Études en Sciences Sociales, 1983.

Prado, Patrick. "Le va et vient: Migrations bretons à Paris." *Ethnologie française* 10 (1980), 161–96.

Prado, Patrick, and Guy Barbichon. *Vivre sa ville: Migrants bretons et champ urbain*. Paris: Centre d'Ethnologie Française, 1978.

Prestwich, Patricia. *Drink and the Politics of Social Reform: Antialcoholism in France since 1870*. Palo Alto: Society for the Promotion of Science and Scholarship, 1988.

Prost, Antoine. *Histoire de l'enseignement en France, 1800–1967*. Paris: Colin, 1968.

——. "Mariage, jeunesse et société à Orléans en 1911."*Annales: économies, sociétés, civilisations* 36, no. 4 (1981), 672–701.

Puyuelo, Rémy. *Héros de l'enfance, figures de la survie: De Bécassine à Pinocchio, de Robinson Crusoé à Poil de Carotte*. Paris: ESF, 1998.

Raison-Jourde, Françoise. *La colonie auvergnate de Paris au XIXe siècle*. Paris: Ville de Paris, 1976.

Ratcliffe, Barrie. "Classes laborieuses et classes dangereuses à Paris pendant la première moitié du XIXe siècle? The Chevalier Thesis Reexamined." *French Historical Studies* 17 (1991), 542–74.

Rearick, Charles. *Pleasures of the Belle Époque: Entertainment and Festivity in Turn-of-the-Century France*. New Haven: Yale University Press, 1985.

Reece, Jack. *The Bretons against France: Ethnic Minority Nationalism in Twentieth-Century Brittany*. Chapel Hill: University of North Carolina Press, 1977.

Reed-Danahay, Deborah. *Education and Identity in Rural France: The Politics of Schooling*. Cambridge: Cambridge University Press, 1996.

Renan, Ernst. "What Is a Nation?" *Becoming National*, ed. Eley and Suny, 42–55.

Renard, Jules. *Poil de carotte*. Paris: Calmann-Lévy, 1907.

Renault, Léon. *La tuberculose chez les bretons*. Paris: Faculté de Médecine, 1899.

Reybaud, Louis. *Le coton: Son régime, ses problèmes, son influence en Europe*. Paris: Michel Levy, 1873.

Rhein, Catherine. *La vie dure qu'on a eu*. Paris: CORDES, 1980.

Rigouard, Jean-Pierre. *Le Métro de Paris*. St-Cyr-sur-Loire: Alan Sutton, 2002.

Robert, Jean-Louis, and Danielle Tartakowsky, eds. *Paris le peuple, XVIIIe–XXe siècle*. Paris: La Sorbonne, 1999.

Rosenberg, Clifford. *Policing Paris: The Origins of Modern Immigration Control between the Wars*. Ithaca: Cornell University Press, 2006.

Rosental, Paul-André. "Between Macro and Micro: Theorizing Agency in Nineteenth-Century French Migrations." *French Historical Studies* 20, no. 3 (2006), 457–81.

——. "Maintien/Rupture: Un nouveau couple pour l'analyse des migrations." *Annales: économies, sociétés, civilisations*, 1990, no. 6 (November–December), 1403–31.

——. "La migration des femmes (et des hommes) en France au XIXe siècle." *Annales de démographie historique* (2004), 107–35.

——. *Les sentiers invisibles: Espace, familles et migrations dans la France du 19ᵉ siècle*. Paris: École des Hautes Études en Sciences Sociales, 1999.

Rygiel, Philippe, ed. *Le bon grain et l'ivraie: La sélection des migrants en occident, 1880–1939*. La Corneuve: Au Lieu de l'Être, 2006.

——. *Destins immigrés: Cher, 1920–1980: Trajectoires d'immigrés d'Europe*. Besançon: Presses Universitaires Franc-comtoises, 2001.

——. "Dissolution d'une groupe ethnique: Origines des témoins et des conjoints des enfants des familles polonaises implantées dans le Cher, 1940–1975." *Mouvement Social* 191 (April 2000), 69–89.

Saint-Maurice, Rémy. "Les décrets Combes dans le Finistère." *L'Illustration*, no. 3102 (9 August 1902).

——. "Les dernières expulsions des soeurs en Bretagne." *L'Illustration*, no. 3104 (23 August 1902).

——. "L'exécution des décrets en Bretagne." *L'Illustration*, no. 3103 (16 August 1902).

——. "La messe à 2700 mètres d'altitude." *L'Illustration*, no. 3105 (30 August 1902).

——. "La misère en Bretagne." *L'Illustration*, no. 3125 (17 January 1903).

Schalk, David L. *Roger Martin du Gard: The Novelist and History*. Ithaca: Cornell University Press, 1967.

Schrover, Marlou, and Floris Vermeulen. "Immigrant Organizations." *Journal of Ethnic and Migration Studies* 31, no. 5 (2005), 823–33.

Schrover, Marlou, and Eileen Yeo. *Gender and Migration in Global, Historical and Theoretical Perspective*. New York: Routledge, 2010.

Schwartz, Vanessa. *Spectacular Realities: Early Mass Culture in Fin-de-Siècle Paris*. Berkeley: University of California Press, 1998.

Scott, Joan. "Gender: A Useful Category of Historical Analysis." *Gender and the Politics of History*, ed. J. Scott, 28–52. New York: Columbia University Press, 1988.

——. "Symptomatic Politics: Banning Islamic Headscarves and French Public Schools." *French Politics, Culture and Society* 23, no. 3 (2005), 106–27.

Screech, Matthew. *Masters of the Ninth Art: Bandes dessinées and Franco-Belgian Identity*. Liverpool: Liverpool University Press, 2005.

Segalen, Martine. *Fifteen Generations of Bretons: Kinship and Society in Lower Brittany, 1720–1980*. Trans. J. A. Underwood. Cambridge: Cambridge University Press, 1991.

Service de la Statistique Municipale, Préfecture de la Seine. *Annuaire statistique de la Ville de Paris, années 1925 et 1926*. Paris: Société Anonyme de Publications Périodiques, 1930.

——. *Annuaire statistique de la Ville de Paris, XXIᵉ année: 1901*. Paris: Masson, 1903.

Silverman, Maxim. *Deconstructing the Nation: Immigration, Racism and Citizenship in Modern France*. London: Routledge, 1992.

Simon, Patrick. "France and the Unknown Second Generation: Preliminary Results on Social Mobility." *International Migration Review* 37, no. 4 (2003), 1091–1119.

Simon-Barouh, Ida. "Assimilation and Ethnic Diversity in France." *The Social Construction of Diversity: Recasting the Master Narrative Industrial Nations*, ed. Harzig and Juteau, 15–39.

Soltau, Roger. *French Parties and Politics*. New York: Russel and Russel, 1965.

Statistique Générale. *Résultats statistiques du recensement général de la population effectué le 24 mars 1901*. Paris: Imprimerie Nationale, 1904–7.

——. *Résultats statistiques du recensement général de la population effectué le 5 mars 1911*. Paris: Imprimerie Nationale, 1915–17.

——. *Résultats statistiques du recensement général de la population effectué le 6 mars 1921*. Paris: Imprimerie Nationale, 1923–26.

——. *Résultats statistiques du recensement général de la population effectué le 7 mars 1926*. Paris: Imprimerie Nationale, 1928–30.

——. *Résultats statistiques du recensement général de la population effectué le 8 mars 1931*. Paris: Imprimerie Nationale, 1933–39.

——. *Résultats statistiques du recensement général de la population effectué le 8 mars 1936*. Paris: Imprimerie Nationale, 1938–44.

Stovall, Tyler. *The Rise of the Paris Red Belt*. Berkeley: University of California Press, 1990.

Surkis, Judith. *Sexing the Citizen: Morality and Masculinity in France, 1870–1914*. Ithaca: Cornell University Press, 2006.

Sussman, George. *The Wet-Nursing Business in France, 1715–1914*. Urbana: University of Illinois Press: 1982.

Tailhade, Laurent. "Le peuple noir, la Bretagne." *L'Assiette au Beurre* 131 (3 October 1903).

Tardieu, Marc. *Les auvergnats de Paris*. Monaco: Éditions du Rocher, 2001.

——. *Le bal de la rue de Lappe*. Monaco: Éditions du Rocher, 2003.

——. *Les bretons de Paris de 1900 à nos jours*. Monaco: Éditions du Rocher, 2003.

Teulières, Laure. "Immigration and National Identity: Historiographical Perspectives in France." *Imagining Frontiers, Contesting Identities*, ed. Klusáková and Ellis, 43–58. Pisa: Pisa University Press, 2007.

Thiesse, Anne-Marie. *Écrire la France: Le mouvement littéraire régionaliste de langue française entre la Belle Époque et la Libération*. Paris: Presses Universitaires de France, 1991.

——. *Ils apprenaient la France: L'exaltation des régions dans le discours patriotique*. Paris: Maison des Sciences de l'Homme, 1991.

Tilly, Charles. "Demographic Origins of the European Proletariat." *Proletarianization and Family History*, ed. Levine, 1–85.

——. "Migration in Modern European History." *Human Migration: Patterns and Policies*, ed. W. H. McNeill and Ruth Adams, 48–72. Bloomington: Indiana University Press, 1978.

——. "Transplanted Networks." *Immigration Reconsidered*, ed. Virginia Yans-McLaughlin, 79–95. New York: Oxford University Press, 1990.

Tilly, Louise. "People's History and Social Science History." *Social Science History* 7, no. 4 (1983), 457–84.

Tilly, Louise, Joan Scott, and Miriam Cohen. "Women's Work and European Fertility Patterns." *Journal of Interdisciplinary History* 6 (1976), 447–76.

Tinayre, Marcelle. "La question des domestiques." *L'Illustration*, no. 3126 (24 January 1903).

Toth, Stephen. *Beyond Papillon: The French Overseas Penal Colonies, 1854–1952*. Lincoln: University of Nebraska Press, 2006.

Trégoat, Arsène Guillaume. *L'immigration bretonne à Paris: Son importance, ses causes, ses conséquences intéressantes au point de vue médical, de quelques moyennes propres à la diminuer*. Thesis, Faculté de Médecine, Paris; Paris: A. Maloine, 1900.

Tribalat, Michèle. *Faire France: Une grande enquête sur les immigrés et leurs enfants*. Paris: La Découverte, 1995.

Trubert, Jean. *Bécassine revient*. Paris: Gautier-Langereau, 1959.

Turquan, Victor. "Rapport sur les migrations internes a Paris." *Journal de la Société de Statistique de Paris* 37 (1896), 18.

Valdour, Jacques. *Ateliers et taudis de la banlieue de Paris: Observation vécues*. Paris: Spes, 1923.

Vallaux, Camille. *La Basse-Bretagne: Étude de géographie humaine*. Geneva: Slatkine, 1905.

Vandervelde, Émile. *L'exode rural et le retour aux champs*. Paris: Alcan, 1903.

Van Ruymbeke, Bertrand. *From New Babylon to Eden: The Huguenots and Their Migration to Colonial South Carolina*. Columbia: University of South Carolina Press, 2006.

Vidalenc, Jean. *Les émigrés français, 1789–1925*. Caen: Association des Publications de la Faculté des Lettres et Sciences Humaines, Université de Caen, 1963.

Violain, Didier. *Bretons de Paris: Des exilés en capitale*. Paris: Parigramme, 1997.

Vitruve, Raymond. *Bécassine, oeuvre littéraire*. Paris: Pensée Universelle, 1991.

Weber, Eugen. *The Hollow Years: France in the 1930s*. New York: W. W. Norton, 1994.

——. *Peasants into Frenchmen: The Modernization of Rural France, 1870–1914*. Stanford: Stanford University Press, 1976.

Weil, François. *Les franco-américains: 1860–1980*. Paris: Belin, 1989.

——. "French Migration to the Americas in the 19th and 20th Centuries as a Historical Problem." *Studi Emigrazione / Études Migrations* 33, no. 123 (1996), 443–60.

——. "The French State and Transoceanic Emigration." *Citizenship and Those Who Leave: The Politics of Emigration and Expatriation*, ed. Nancy Green and François Weil, 114–31. Urbana: University of Illinois Press, 2007.

Weil, Patrick. *How to Be French: Nationality in the Making since 1789*. Trans. Catherine Porter. Durham: Duke University Press, 2008.

White, Owen. "Priests into Frenchmen? Breton Missionnaires in Côte d'Ivoire, 1896–1918." *French Colonial History* 8 (2007), 111–21.

Winter, Anne. *Patterns of Migration and Adaptation in the Urban Transition: Newcomers to Antwerp, c. 1760–1860*. Brussels: Vrije Universiteit Brussel, 2007.

Winter, Jay, and Jean-Louis Robert, eds. *Capital Cities at War: Paris, London, Berlin 1914–1919*. Cambridge: Cambridge University Press, 1997.

Wright, Julian. *The Regionalist Movement in France, 1890–1914*. Oxford: Clarendon, 2003.

Wylie, Laurence. *Village in the Vaucluse*. Cambridge: Harvard University Press, 1957.

Young, Patrick. "Of Pardons, Loss, and Longing: The Tourist's Pursuit of Originality in Brittany, 1890–1935." *French Historical Studies* 30, no. 2 (spring 2007), 269–304.

Zago, Manrique. *Los Franceses en la Argentina / Les français en Argentine*. Buenos Aires: M. Zago, 1986.

Zola, Émile. *L'assomoir*. Harmondsworth: Penguin, 1970.

——. *Piping Hot*. New York: Boni and Liveright, 1924.

——. "Promenade vers les fortifs, sorties champêtres . . ." *Revue Historique du Quatorzième Arrondissement* 26 (1981), 31–36.

LESLIE PAGE MOCH is a professor of history
at Michigan State University.

Library of Congress Cataloging-in-Publication Data

Moch, Leslie Page.
The pariahs of yesterday : Breton migrants in Paris / Leslie Page Moch.
p. cm.
Includes bibliographical references and index.
ISBN 978-0-8223-5169-6 (cloth : alk. paper)
ISBN 978-0-8223-5183-2 (pbk. : alk. paper)
1. Bretons—France—Paris—History.
2. Migration, Internal—France—History.
3. Rural-urban migration—France—History.
4. Immigrants—France—Paris—History. I. Title.
DC718.B72M63 2012
305.891′68044361—dc23
2011030979

www.ingramcontent.com/pod-product-compliance
Lightning Source LLC
Chambersburg PA
CBHW050345270326
41926CB00016B/3610